Heathen Soul Lore

A Personal Approach

Winifred Hodge Rose

Heathen Soul Lore Series Book II

Wordfruma Press

2022

©2022 Winifred Hodge Rose. Dale Wood artwork ©2022 Dale Wood. All rights reserved for all original material in this book. Brief quotations with full citation are allowed, for the purposes of news reporting, criticism, comment, scholarship, research, or teaching.

Wordfruma Press
Urbana Illinois USA

WordfrumaPress.com

ISBN 978-1-7379327-9-6 (Hardcover)
ISBN 978-1-7379327-1-0 (Paperback)
ISBN 979-8-9855536-0-4 (EPUB)
ISBN 979-8-9855536-1-1 (Kindle ebook)
ISBN 979-8-9855536-2-8 (PDF)

Library of Congress Control Number: 2022900462

Cover painting by Dale Wood.
Cover design by Winifred Hodge Rose.

Epigraph and Dedication

We consider 'understanding' to be a 'deep' thing, and it is. It reaches profoundly into our self, into the selves of others, and the world around us. The roots of 'understanding' are sunk deeply into Time itself.

We know more than we realize we know, and we discover this by digging deeply into what we think is unknown, using 'understanding' as our digging-tool.

After all the digging, we discover something that we knew all along, on some level of our being, but did not realize that we knew it. Thus it is, with Heathen soul lore.

To the pursuit of Understanding,
to all who seek its treasures,
and to our shared experiences along the way,
this book is most respectfully dedicated.

Time to dig in!
'Understanding' is down there somewhere….

Table of Contents

Introduction 1
    How to approach this study 5
    The layout of the book 6

1. Review: Definition and Overview of Heathen Souls 9
    Defining a soul 9
    A brief summary of each soul 11
        Ferah 11
        Ahma 12
        Ghost 13
        Hama 14
        Aldr 15
        Saiwalo 16
        Hugr 17
        Mod 18
        Sefa 19
        Associated spirits 21
    Soul-Footholds 21

2. Foundations of Experiential Exploration 25
    Methods for learning 25
    The most essential ability: Imagination 27
    Critical thinking and critical knowing 29
    "We really don't / can't know anything about the soul…." 30
    Knowledge as skilled experience 32

Basic premises of Soul-Craft 35
Your Daybook 36
Preliminary exercise: Where are you starting from? 39
Focused awareness 40
Exercise 2-1. Thinking about soul-ideas. 41
Exercise 2-2. Feeling and reacting to soul-ideas. 42
The role of our sensory-organ analogs 49
   Exercise 2-3. Your sensation-strengths. 50
Your Soul-Habitat 50
Consolidation 50
….And more Daybook! 52
The Eihwaz Rune Poem 54

3. Exploring your Ferah Soul 55
Join your Ferah in its habitat 56
Exercise 3-1: Ancient roots.. 57
Exercise 3-2: Ancient Deities 60
Exercise 3-3: Your Ferah-habitat....................................... 62
Ferah's sensory awareness 63
Exercise 3-4: Nourishing Ferah 69
Ferah and Law... 70
   Exercise 3-5: The path of priesthood 71
   Exercise 3-6: Ferah and sacrifice 72
Exercise 3-7: Afterlife of Ferah 73
Exercise 3-8: Ferah during your childhood.................... 74
Summary of Ferah, with further meditations................ 75

Focusing your awareness on Ferah 78
Extra: On trees, hierarchy and natural law. 79
Extra: A discussion on Ferah and Magic 82

4. Exploring your Ahma and Ghost Souls 91
The Natures of Ahma, Ghost, and Deities 91
Exercise 4-1: Becoming aware of Ahma's habitat 95
Awareness 98
Our Soul-Spindle 100
Exercise 4-2: Tuning Ghost, Ahma and Lichama to the same wavelength. 101
Exercise 4-3: Combine tuning with rune-galdor and with forms of art. 105
Exercise 4-4: Your Ghost-habitat. 107
Ghost-Mind, Intellect 111
   What Ghost loves to do 112
Disembodiment 115
Nurturing your Ghost 116
   Exercise 4-5: Expressing your Ghost 117
   Exercise 4-6: Choosing words for Ghost-practice 118
   Exercise 4-7: Fostering the Ghost of children 118

5. Ghost and Wode 121
Dysfunctions and imbalances of Ghost 122
A note on creative Wode and substance abuse 125
Controlled development and use of Wode 126
Exercise 5-1: Evaluating wode in your life 133

6. Exploring your Hama, Lich-Hama and Ellor-Hama ... 135
   Hama as a covering ... 137
      Exercise 6-1: Sensing your Hama ... 139
      Exercise 6-2: Sensing Hama-shifts ... 141
   Exercise 6-3: Shaping your Hama ... 143
   The Ellor-Hama ... 145
   Evaluating Hama's communication ... 147
      Exercise 6-4: Are you sending mixed messages? ... 148
   A word about Hamingja ... 150
   Summary ... 151
7. Exploring your Aldr, Ørlög, Werold ... 155
   Aldr-Wita ... 155
      Exercise 7-1: Aldr-flow ... 156
      Exercise 7-2: Healing Aldr-flow ... 159
   Aldr, Ørlög, and the Ordeal ... 160
      Exercise 7-3: Being shaped by ørlög ... 162
   Weaving a Werold ... 165
      Exercise 7-4: Your Werold as a work of art ... 166
   Nourishment as ørlög ... 168
      Exercise 7-5: Understanding nourishment ... 169
   Exercise 7-6: Exploring your Aldr's time-body ... 170
   In closing ... 171
8. Mod and Hugr: Motivating Forces ... 173
   First, the context ... 174
   Exercise 8-1: Observing your motivating forces ... 176

Observing Hugr and Mod 179
   Exercise 8-2: Observing Mod and Hugr in action 180
   Exercise 8-3: Wiliness and frustration 181
The effects of honest observation 184
9. Exploring your Mod Soul 187
The nature and strengths of Mod and mægen 187
   Exercise 9-1: Sensing your Mod 188
Mod and Wode as states of being 192
   Exercise 9-2: Do you squash your Mod-force? 194
The Thorlings 199
   Exercise 9-3: Your Mod-magnets 201
Mod's nature 204
Building character 206
Mod as Will 207
   Exercise 9-4: Shaping character and will 209
Roots, trunk, and branches 210
….And then the seeds 211
How does this work? 212
Exercise 9-5: The power of the gut 213
Exercise 9-6: Where is courage? 215
Exercise 9-7: Partnering with Mod 218
Exercise 9-8: Who or what do you admire? 223
Help from the Holy Ones 223
The Battle of Maldon 226
10. Exploring your Hugr 227

- A framework of thought ... 227
- *Hlutro Hugiu:* Clarifying the Hugr ... 231
  - Emotions as fuel for Hugr ... 232
  - The role of awareness ... 232
  - Courage and clarity ... 233
  - The value of clarity ... 235
- The role of desire or wish ... 236
- Exercise 10-1: Your deepest longings ... 239
- Exercise 10-2: Attuning actions with longings ... 241
- Exercise 10-3: Making friends with Hugr ... 242
  - Friendship Song ... 246

11. Will and Wish: The Dynamism of Mod and Hugr ... 247
- Will ... 248
- Wish ... 250
- Love as Wish fulfilled ... 251
- Dynamic Tension of Will and Wish ... 252
- Exercise 11-1: Finding Will within you ... 252
- Exercise 11-2: Working with Wish ... 257
- Dealing with the unachievable Wish ... 259
  - Exercise 11-3: Examining your difficult wishes ... 262
- In closing ... 262

12. Sefa, Hugr and Modsefa ... 265
- Sefa ... 265
  - The selfish, grim, or savage Sefa ... 267
- Hugr as Sefa's warder ... 269

Invitations to Goddesses 272

Exercise 12-1: Pursuing Sefa-awareness 274

Attuning Sefa and Hugr 276

    Exercise 12-2: Awareness of Hugr as warder 276

    Exercise 12-3: Tuning in to your warding Hugr 280

Modsefa and ethical action 281

    Exercise 12-4: Tuning in to your Modsefa 282

Gender stereotypes 283

Building trust between Sefa, Hugr and Mod 284

    Souls working together 286

13. Sefa: The Channel of Compassion 287

Sefa's role 290

Exercise 13-1: Sensing compassion-energy 291

The nature of compassion-energy 293

The mystery of compassion 295

Keeping compassion flowing 298

    Exercise 13-2: Fine-tuning your flow of compassion
    301

In closing 302

14. Saiwalo-Dwimor and the Sea of Images 303

Summary of Saiwalo 303

The impacts of cultural beliefs 306

Dwimor grips image-energy 307

Exercise 14-1: Growing your awareness of images 309

Saiwalo and Sowilo 311

Exercise 14-2: Navigating the sea of images	311
Feeding the images	314
Image-winnowing	315
Exercise 14-3: Clarifying Dwimor's hoard	316
Images as prayers and magical intentions	320
Exercise 14-4: Practicing prayer and magical intent	323
15. Fields of Awareness	325
Ferah's Awareness	326
Ahma's Awareness	329
Ghost's Awareness	330
Hama's Awareness	332
Aldr's Awareness	335
Mod's Awareness	338
Hugr's Awareness	340
Sefa's Awareness	342
Saiwalo-Dwimor's Awareness	345
Eormensoul	347
Exercise 15-1: Experiments with your soul-council	348
About Frigg and her spinning	351
16. Finding the Time: A Guide for Daily Soul-Work	355
Fitting practices into your day	356
Awareness	359
Soulful communication	362
Daily experiences	366
17. Walking a Soul-Path	369

The Path of Relationships among your souls 370
The Path of Vocation 371
Paths of Relationship with others 372
The Path of Healing 373
The Path of Creativity 374
Heathen Esoteric Paths 375
The Challenge of the Heathen Soul-Path 376
Acknowledgements 379
Word-Hoard / Glossary 381
Art and Photograph Credits 399
Book-Hoard / Bibliography 403
About the Author 407
A Word about Wordfruma Press 409

May the Holy Ones speak wisdom to us as we explore the mysteries of our souls.

Heimdal

(Artist: Willy Pogany)

Introduction

As we move from soul lore concepts to Heathen practice, we bridge the soul-distance between the past and today.

This is Book II of my Heathen Soul Lore series, which follows after Book I, entitled *Heathen Soul Lore Foundations: Ancient and Modern Germanic Pagan Concepts of the Souls*. To understand and work with the book you now hold, you will need to be familiar with the material in Book I, or else refer to the relevant articles on my website, *HeathenSoulLore.net*. Each chapter about individual souls in this book is preceded by the recommended background reading for that chapter, from Book I or from my website.

Book I offers both intellectual and inspirational perspectives for exploring concepts of the souls rooted in ancient Germanic languages and cultures. Much of it is scholarly, analytical and detailed. In this book, we move on

Introduction

from the conceptual and theoretical levels, to the personal and practical levels of soul exploration.

In doing so, we bridge the distance from the experiences and viewpoints of the ancient past, to life in the present day. Though the outer shape of daily human experiences may have changed a good deal during this span of time, the inner meanings of these experiences are not so different. As people did in the past, we face challenges and dangers, stresses and strains. We pursue achievement and recognition, even though they might take different forms than in the past. We love, we grieve, we desire, we dream. We are born, we grow, we enact the deeds of our lives, we face death and the unknown, as every human does. In all of these experiences, our souls are the participants, the actors, the foundation and the generators of who we are and what we achieve in this life.

Each of us is unique: our path of life, our life experiences, our soul development, our dreams and aspirations. We are unique because our souls are unique, our own household of soul-beings who together sing our unique Self into existence during this life in Midgard. At the same time, our individual souls possess some commonalities with other souls of the same kind: our Mod has similarities with other Mod-souls, our Ahma with other Ahma-souls. These similarities extend into the past, giving us points of contact with folk of ancient times. Humans in the past, the present and the future are shaped by the nature of our souls, and they provide us with human links through time.

Ancient Heathens had understandings and perceptions about the natures of our souls that were shaped by Heathen cultures and beliefs. In many ways, these were

Introduction

quite different from the soul-perceptions of the cultures that gave rise to the Mediterranean and Middle Eastern religions and philosophies that have so greatly influenced our Western cultures.

Certainly, all of these interweaving strands of culture have enriched our world over many centuries. But they have also almost erased some other strands, ancient Heathen understandings of soul, life and world. Many of us who follow Heathen ways seek to unearth these buried strands and bring them into expression in our own lives and world-view. We cannot know all the details for sure, except that we can take for granted that there was a great deal of variation over the expanses of place and time when old Heathen cultures flourished.

But these uncertainties are of less importance than the realities that underlie them. We still have souls, we modern people. They still create who we are. Our perceptions of our souls are taught to us by our culture, and to an extent, our experiences of our souls shape themselves to conform to what we are taught. Ambivalence or denial about the existence and nature of souls can lead to our souls' 'failure to thrive'; to soul-weaknesses and soul-illnesses because our souls are not nurtured and developed as they should be. Our character, our motivations, our deeds, our hopes and fears, our ethical principles, our ability to love and relate, to grow spiritually, and to face the challenges of the world with spiritual strength, are all affected by our beliefs about what the soul really is, 'who is in charge of it' and what their rules are, and whether it even exists at all.

When we become Heathen, we gradually become aware of a whole different world-view, one that includes

Introduction

views of what our souls are, and how they interact with all other beings and other Worlds of the cosmos. We have the basis for pursuing new and different understandings of the souls, and of all the aspects of our lives that are shaped by those understandings. By trying to understand the Heathen past as well as we can, we discover cues and clues that call to our own souls, that offer experiences of enlightenment, validation, and inspiration to us in the present day.

The test of the validity of our findings is not ironclad academic-historical 'proof of truth', which is not fully achievable in any case, though the effort itself is very worthwhile. The real test of validity is *what this means to us*, to the conduct of our lives and our life-experiences, to the development of ourselves as spiritual beings rooted in a Heathen world-view.

Factual, scholarly work is very useful for uncovering clues, directions where we can seek knowledge and inspiration. It gives us a place to start, and guideposts to shape our path. But this scholarly endeavor must eventually provide links to spiritual realities; otherwise it is an empty exercise for our purposes here. It is this soulful connection, this "aha!" moment of enlightenment when we touch on those realities, that validates both the scholarly enterprise and the pursuit of Heathen spirituality in today's world. This is what I strive for in my soul lore work: the moment of enlightenment when intellect meets inspiration in a flash of spiritual power that opens great new vistas of understanding.

Book I lays the foundations for this enterprise, gathers the clues, shapes the concepts, and strives to communicate them intellectually and through the imagination. Here, in Book II, is where we explore what all

Introduction

of this means to you, personally. Who are each of your souls? They are complex beings, and getting to know each of them is like getting to know another person, but a person who is yourself, expanded in directions you may not have known were there. Are you ready for this great spiritual adventure? Here is a map offered for your use, however you see fit to use it.

How to approach this study

There is a lot of work outlined here; keep in mind that you don't need to follow any particular order, nor complete one chapter before going on to the next. You can choose which souls and which exercises are most relevant to you now, and work on those. I do suggest, however, working through Chapter 2 first, which provides the foundation for your methods of study and experience here.

The purpose of the work in this book is to become familiar with your souls as they are envisioned in the approach to Heathen soul lore that I describe in Book I: to expand your awareness of them and how they shape your life and your self, and to begin partnering with them consciously so that the shaping of your life is a matter of awareness, will, and intent.

If any of the suggestions throughout this course of study feel uncomfortable, wrong, or unsafe for you, then obviously, don't pursue them. You may be able to figure out alternative ways of reaching the same goal, if you wish, or you may prefer just to leave those particular exercises alone for now.

If you proceed with learning Heathen soul lore simply on an intellectual level rather than through actual experience, you may find that after a time of study, when

Introduction

you come back and try these exercises and approaches again, they will feel more comfortable and familiar to you. Our mind needs to process and adjust to new ideas, before we can feel comfortable with pursuing an intense personal experience of these ideas, and each of us goes at our own pace.

So, study and digest the ideas in this book first, work through Chapter 2, then when you feel ready, choose a place to begin from the following chapters about each of the souls, and proceed at your own pace and in your own way. Always keep your well-being and sense of what is right for you foremost in your mind, and adapt your approach to soul lore accordingly.

The layout of the book

Each chapter in this book is preceded with the recommended background reading for that chapter, either from Book I or from my website, *HeathenSoulLore.net*.

Chapter 1, for your convenience, begins with a review of the basic definition and descriptions of the souls, condensed from the same chapter in Book I. It also includes a review of soul-footholds: places or functions of our body where each of our souls interface most strongly with our body or Lich. Chapter 2 discusses the conceptual tools and approaches needed for your soul-work here. Chapters 3 through 14 offer discussions, exercises, guidelines and suggestions for exploring each of your individual souls. Most of these chapters include brief sections written by study participants about their experiences, to enrich our study with different people's perspectives and insights.

Chapter 15 summarizes aspects of each soul's awareness and nature, and offers a beginning exercise in

Introduction

working with the souls as a group. Chapter 16 provides suggestions for how you can integrate soul work into your busy life, enhancing both your studies and other aspects of your daily life as well. The final chapter goes over some suggestions for areas of life where you might want to apply what you have learned in this course of study. I've also included a Word-Hoard / Glossary toward the end of the book, for your convenience.

At the beginning of each of the following chapters about specific souls, I've offered a bind-rune for meditation on the subject of that chapter. A bind-rune is made of several runes combined into an artistic shape that is meant to provide meditative insights. (This book does not offer any teachings about the runes, though some rune resources are suggested in the Book-Hoard / Bibliography.)

I identify the primary runes of each bind-rune, but there are many more that appear in the designs. If you practice rune-craft, I encourage you to design bind-runes of your own as you proceed with your soul lore practice, to deepen and personalize your experience of your souls. Additionally, artwork, poetry or stories, music, or movement arts are encouraged as expressions of what you are learning about your souls.

Let's move ahead now, with a review of the material from Book I, to provide the foundation for your work here. I wish you all success in this great endeavor of soul-exploration!

Introduction

*Constantin Kouznetzoff
"Caveman playing the flute."*

*The caveman in this painting seems to call to us,
breathing through his flute,
reaching soul to soul across the ages.
The eerie notes echo through great spaces of time.
'We are all children of the Earth,' he sings,
but perhaps his souls know this
more deeply than ours do.*

(Note: The original is a small, dark-shaded, full-color painting. I wanted to use it, but it didn't show well in black and white, so I converted it to grayscale.)

Chapter 1

Our souls extend outward from the earthly plane of Midgard life, into planes of Being that are distant from our everyday awareness.

1. Review: Definition and Overview of Heathen Souls

This is a condensed version of Chapter 1, Book I, as a review and a place to begin our personal approach, along with a review of soul-footholds from Book I.

Defining a soul

Here are the criteria I use to define what a soul is.

Definition and Overview

1) It confers life by its presence with the body, and its departure is synonymous with physical death. The souls which fit this definition I call the Life-Souls.

Or, conversely,

2) It is capable of leaving and returning to the living body as an active metaphysical entity, either intentionally or inadvertently (for example during sleep and dreaming, or as the result of shock or trauma). It may also be removed from the body, or prevented from returning to it, by hostile supernatural or magical acts, which have deleterious but not immediately fatal results for the body. I call these the Daemon souls or Wander-Souls.

In addition:

3) Some souls are considered to have an independent afterlife and perhaps a before-life existence, and may reincarnate. Having an independent afterlife indicates that this is an existential soul-being, not simply a psychological part of a person. Some, but not all, of the Heathen souls I've identified have this characteristic.

There is a partial exception: the *Sefa,* which has many soul-like characteristics but does not fit into any of these criteria. I think that Sefa, and the sense of 'self' that is rooted there, comes into being through the interaction and synergy of all our other souls together.

Definition and Overview

A brief summary of each soul

I. The Life-Souls

Ferah

(*Feorh, Ferhth, Fjör, Fairhw, Ferh, Ferch, Verch.* 'Ferah' is the Old Saxon word. Pronounced 'FAIR-ah.')

This is a very ancient word, going back to the Proto-Indo-European (PIE) word **perku,* meaning 'life-soul' or animating principle. It is connected with PIE words for 'chest / breast', for oak, pine, fir, and other trees, for earth and mountains, and is related to the name of the PIE Thunder-God *Perkwunos and with the verb 'to strike'. The Norse Deity-names Fjǫrgyn and Fjǫrgynn, and a plural Norse word for 'Gods', *fjarg,* are all descendants of these words.

Ferah is a vitalizing Life-soul not only in humans, but in animals, trees, and other living entities as well. A lovely Anglo-Saxon word is *feorh-cynn,* 'the kindred of the living, of those who share the Ferah soul'. As I understand it, Ferah was the soul enclosed within the Trees that were transformed into the mythical first humans, Ask and Embla. The Tree-Ferahs were first released from the trees by Thor's mighty Hammer-strike, then given the gifts of breath, spirit, wode, the human body-shape and its abilities, by Odin and his brothers as they shaped the mythical first humans.

Ferah is a vitalizing, life-giving substance that fills us during life, and mysteriously leaves at death. Ferah has personal characteristics such as wisdom, piety, emotions and thoughts, and connects us with the great Powers of

Definition and Overview

Nature, Earth and Sky. It is perceptive, aware and responsive to everything in our environment, and is the locus of our bodily sensations and reactions to events around us.

In my understanding, our individual Ferah comes into being during conception as egg and sperm unite in a lightning-flash of power and set the forces of life into action, followed in due time by the thunder of the heartbeat and the lightning-energy of all our body's bioelectrical functions.

Ahma

(*Ǫnd, And, Æðm, Athom, Ethma, Atum, Atem, Adem.* 'Ahma' is the Gothic word. Pronounced 'AH-ma.')

All of these words go back to Proto-Indo-European words for both 'breath' and 'spirit,' and are linguistically related to the Hindu Atman, the highest, most refined soul in Hindu belief. In the Germanic languages, these words applied to the indwelling human spirit. In Old Norse and Gothic they also applied to otherworldly beings like ghosts, devils, dwarves, and other wights. The Christian Holy Spirit was called by variations of this word in the different languages, such as *Ahmeins Weihis* in Gothic and *Hellige Ånd* in modern Norwegian.

Ahma is our 'spirit' and is the channel for divine gifts of inspiration and the highest mental abilities such as abstract thought and inspired creativity. This soul, in human form, is more connected with the divine realms and cosmic powers, and less concerned with earthly, mundane matters than many of our other souls.

Definition and Overview

Ghost

(*Gast, Gest, Geist, Keist, Geest.* 'Ghost' is the modern English form of the old Germanic word.)

Some of the old Germanic languages (Anglo-Saxon, Frisian, Old Saxon, Old High German) split the concept of Ahma into two, with their Ahma-related words applying primarily to 'breath' (including the Divine Breath), and another word *Gast, Geist, etc.* applying more to spirits and wights, though there was some parallel usage. Ghost-words applied to the inner spirit of a person, to spirit-beings such as ghosts, and to physical but otherworldly supernatural beings such as dragons, wights, and monsters (e.g. Grendel, called an *ellor-gast*, an alien spirit, in Anglo-Saxon, even though he was a physical being). In these languages, the Christian Holy Spirit was called Holy Ghost, *Halig Gast, Heilige Geist, etc.*

In my conceptualization of Heathen soul lore, our Ghost and Ahma souls are intimately related in this way: Ahma is the sacred breath, the unchanging and formless material of spirit, while Ghost is Ahma's hama or soul-skin, a pod that shapes and encloses our formless Ahma into a personal being with its own character: our Ghost. While, as I see it, Ahma is united with the impersonal, undifferentiated sacred power out of which everything flows, Ghost interacts with personal Deities and with the mundane world of Midgard on a person-to-person level, while still accessing the powers of our Ahma spirit.

Though the Ghost is a Life-soul, conferring life through the breath, it can also act as a Wander-Soul through temporary flight from the body during trance, dreams, coma, and near-death experiences, while remaining linked to the body through slow, deep breathing.

Definition and Overview

As we inhale our first breath when we are born, our Ahma enclosed within our Ghost rides in upon our breath and takes root within us. After death, when we 'give up the Ghost', our Ghost may join our closest Deities in their God-Homes. If it cannot fully let go of earthly life, it may wander as a haunt on the edges of Midgard. If our Ghost during life does not feel attached to any Deities nor drawn to haunt Midgard, then according to my understanding, it will likely dissolve its shape and revert to the undifferentiated Ahma state after death.

Hama

(*Hama, hamr, hamo*. *Hama* is the Anglo-Saxon term. Rhymes with 'Mama'.)

This word means 'a covering'. Hama is our human shape, a gift of the Gods: a shaped soul-energy which arises within the womb and placenta where a newly-conceived child lies. It holds the pattern of our physical body, and guides its formation during our growth in the womb. Hama also provides the pattern which guides the energies that heal and restore our body after injury or illness. The *hamingja* (ha-ming-ya) is a spirit of luck which is attached to the structures of the womb (placenta, caul, afterbirth), is born with us, accompanies us during life, and governs the nature of our luck.

In my understanding, Hama consists of three parts, given to Ask and Embla when humans were first formed from trees. *La* or *Lö* is the spiritual energy of the blood which invigorates our body. *Læti* refers to our ability to take physical action, to speak, and to engage in social behavior. *Litr* is our unique physical appearance, including the light of our souls shining through our body and our face, our countenance. Our *Lichama* or Lich-Hama is our living body, the combination of our Lich, our physical body, plus our Hama soul which governs the body and its many abilities.

After death the Hama decomposes along with the Lich, as it releases into the ambient energy of life, unless, as is told in chilling folk-tales, it re-animates its body to become a Draugr, an animated corpse.

Aldr

(*Ealdor, Eldi, Alds*. Aldr is the Old Norse term. Pronounced 'AHL-dur.)

The word Aldr stems from the root **al* and *alan*, meaning 'to nourish.' It is a life-soul which channels spiritual energy to nourish and heal our Hama and our living body, our Lichama, nurturing it over many years so that it lives long and reaches old age. The word 'old' is derived from this root, as are words for life-span and for an age of time. A word for 'killer' in Anglo-Saxon was *ealdor-bana* or Aldr-bane; likewise there is the Old Norse phrase for killers, *aldrs synjuðu*, meaning 'Aldr-snatchers', showing that Aldr is necessary to maintain life.

As the Hama shapes and empowers our physical body and life in space, Aldr governs our 'body and life in time'. It is shaped and given to us by the Norns when we are born, drawn from the Well of Wyrd, and is linked with our ørlög and wyrd, the patterns that shape and are shaped by our life-events. Aldr triggers time-dependent physical changes such as puberty and menopause, and governs the timing of events related to our ørlög throughout our lifetime.

During life Aldr weaves its own hama or soul-skin, like a cloak or a cocoon, made up of all the deeds and events of our lives. This soul-skin is called our Werold ('man-age'): it is our own personal world, made up of our cumulative experiences and deeds over our whole lifetime. It is because of Aldr that we humans have the ability to view our life as a meaningful whole, our life-span as an entity woven within the dimensions of Time and Wyrd.

Saiwalo

(*Saiwala, Seola, Siola, Sawol, Seula, Sele, Sela, Sal.* Saiwalo is the Proto-Germanic word. Pronounced 'SIGH-wa-low'.)

This is the word that descended to become modern English 'soul', with similar words in all the other modern Germanic languages. In Heathen times Saiwalo was understood to be the soul which goes to Hel after death, where it continues existing as the 'shade'. Unlike most of the other souls, during life Saiwalo has little involvement in everyday Midgard activities and our personality, except for its role as a life-soul which keeps the body alive by its presence. When Saiwalo departs, the body is *sawol-leas*, soulless and dead.

In my perception of Heathen soul lore, Saiwalo is rooted in Hel, and sends out a phantom, a Dwimor, to ensoul a living person in Midgard (see Book I, Chapters 13, 14 and 16). This Dwimor serves as an alchemical matrix that holds together all our souls and body during life, and returns to its Saiwalo as a 'shade' after death. Saiwalo-Dwimor is one being, with Dwimor being a projection of its essence into the Midgard plane.

The word-root of 'Hel' means 'hidden, concealed'; Heathen Hel was not seen as a place specifically for punishment. Heathen Hel is the Hidden Land, told of in endless myths, folktales, fairy tales, fantasies, experienced in dreams and trance-work. It contains sources of benevolence, reunion, rootedness, distress, emptiness, neediness, riches, power, beauty, mystery, arcane knowledge. Its denizens are the Saiwalo souls who shape their surroundings through their powers of imaging and their experiences during life.

II. The Daemon Souls or Wander-Souls

Hugr

(Hugi, Hyge, Hugs, Hei, Hu. Hugr is the Old Norse word. Pronounced 'WHO-gr.').

Hugr is very closely related to the abilities and capacities of both the intellect and the heart. It resides around the heart where, under the influence of strong emotion or the raising of occult power, it wells up and swells within the breast until it bursts out as emotional expression or as magical power. Hugr is the soul which can most easily leave our physical body on its own errands, as is told in Norse folklore up until recent times, and can, rarely, appear as our Doppelgänger or in animal form at a distance from the body.

Hugr is associated particularly with domains of Thought that help us deal with everyday challenges of social and practical life, as opposed to the more abstract kinds of Thought associated with Ahma and Ghost. Hugr is a soul within us who loves, who has desires and longings, and the envy that can arise from these. Hugr has intentions, strong emotions and subtle thoughts. It is fully embedded in and focused on our life in Midgard, and serves as our 'inner warder,' subtly helping us resist social pressures, deception and manipulation by other people. It is, among

Definition and Overview

other things, a guardian of our personal boundaries. However, it may engage in manipulation of other people itself, in pursuit of its own desires, if it fails to develop self-restraint.

After death, Hugr sooner or later is likely to reincarnate, but a mature and seasoned afterlife Hugr may also spend time as an ancestral spirit, a *Dis* (female) or *Alf* (male) of our physical or spiritual line who offers guidance, rede and wisdom from the spirit-world to the living. An angry, envious, hateful or vengeful Hugr after death may become an afflicting spirit, given many names in folklore such as Hag, Murk-Elf, Night-mare, etc. It will seek to cause illness, nightmares, ill luck, accidents, elf-shot, and other such misfortunes for the living.

Mod

(*Moðr, Moths, Mot, Muat, Muot, Moet, Mut, Mood, Mo.* Mod is the word in Anglo-Saxon and Old Saxon. Pronounced 'mode'.)

Mod and Hugr souls have a great deal in common. Both of them are sources of strong emotion, courage, determination, strategic and practical thinking. Both of them can serve as inner rede-givers, offering insights and knowledge not available to our conscious minds. Both are involved with our intentions that lead to actions. Both can flood us with negative emotions such as rage, envy, or cruelty, or throw us into moods and tempers, good or bad. The two of them provide a great deal of what we experience as 'character' and 'personality' within ourselves and others.

Mod is especially associated with strength of body, mind and will-power, and is a characteristic of Thor, his sons Magni (Might) and Moði (Mod-y), and his daughter

Thruðr (Strength). Mod was also the word used to translate Latin *virtus* or 'virtue', in the sense of possessing some out-of-the-ordinary power, like the healing 'virtue' of herbs, or the power in a magical item.

Mod does not willingly leave the body as Hugr can do, but it can be weakened or removed from the body of humans and animals through the agency of illness, or by magical or supernatural means. Many medieval spells sought to restore mod-energy to an ill, lethargic, weak or depressed person or domestic animal by ousting the wight, witch or sorcerer that was afflicting their Mod-power.

There's reason to believe that Mod originated as a daemon, an elemental spirit of nature, an expression of natural power, and that some of these elemental spirits, ages ago, began to associate more and more closely with humans, animals, Deities, and wights. Gradually they became more integrated with their hosts, just as, on the physical level, micro-organisms like viruses and bacteria gradually integrated with our microbiome and even our genome, and during evolution changed our nature to a degree. In humans, through the influence of our other souls, over evolutionary time our inner Mod became more human-like, more integral to our 'soular-system', while still bearing within itself the power and wildness of its elemental roots.

Sefa

(*Sefa, seofa, sebo, sefi*. Sefa is the Old Norse and Anglo-Saxon word. Pronounced 'SAY-fah'.)

This word descends from or is closely related to several words with these meanings: the 'self', the ability of the self to sense and perceive what is around it, and kinship

Definition and Overview

and relationship. It is related to the name of the Norse Goddess Sjöfn, who promotes and protects love, affection, and relationships, and to the Goddess-name Sif, wife of Thor, whose name is related to 'sib' (sibling) and words for 'relative, relationship' in all the Germanic languages. In Old English, *sibb* meant 'kinship, relationship, love, friendship, peace, happiness'. Proto-Germanic **sibja* meant literally 'one's own', a blood relation. Sib-related words indicating 'relationship' occur in all the old and modern Germanic languages.

The basic meanings I derive for Sefa are (1) "our self, with its abilities to sense, notice, perceive and understand, and (2) those who are connected to our self through relationship, love and affection." Further meanings of this word are related to awareness, noticing, paying attention to, as well as soothing and quieting. These are all faculties of our Self that are needed to promote strong relationships between people who understand one another well, pay attention to and care for one another.

I associate the word 'caring' in all its meanings with Sefa, along with the perceptive insights that are gained from sincerely caring about others. A nutshell-meaning of Sefa, to me, is 'the one who cares' within ourselves, whether that caring is related to people or other beings or things, or to any kind of situation or idea that one may care about. This includes the meaning of 'cares' as 'worries, sorrows, concerns,' as well as the meaning of caring *for* someone or something, and caring *about* anything. Sefa-soul includes the energy and the link between our self and whatever we care about, whether concrete (like another person, or the environment) or abstract (like the ideas of justice, beauty, kindness, honor).

Definition and Overview

Sefa is not a daemon-soul, but as it is closely linked with Hugr and Mod, I include it with these other two souls as a group.

Associated spirits

There are many fascinating accounts throughout the lore of Germanic lands and peoples, relating to spirits or wights which accompany some or all humans, and who are associated with peoples' kinship lines, household, land, crops, crafts, paranormal powers, activities of many kinds. They are a major source of the luck or ill-luck that affects human lives. Much has been written about them elsewhere, both by academic scholars and by practicing Heathens. Though I mention these spirits from time to time in my soul lore studies, they are not a primary focus of my work, simply because there is already so much for me to explore regarding our own inherent souls.

Soul-Footholds

In my understanding, our souls have what I call footholds in our physical body and its life-processes: places where that soul interfaces especially powerfully with our physical life. Here is a review of each soul's foothold in the body.

The work in this book focuses heavily on detecting sensations within our physical and soul-bodies, the energies that make up our totality, and using those energy-sensations as a way to learn about and work with our souls. Understanding how and where our various souls connect with our physical body is very helpful for this pursuit.

Ferah fills our entire body with its etheric life-substance. I think the channels of energy that are identified in Eastern

Definition and Overview

systems as Qi and Prana run through this Ferah-substance, as do our sensations and many of our instinctual reactions. Our perceptions, both physical-sensory and metaphysical, are also linked with our Ferah.

Ahma and Ghost have their foothold in our breath, lungs and diaphragm, while Ghost-Mind hovers over our brain and interpenetrates it. Note that important aspects of what we call "mind" are probably distributed all around our body, as recent research is exploring (see, for example, Verny's *The Embodied Mind*). This is one good reason for taking the approach I do with the exercises of this book, as we sense the effects of our souls, by paying attention to body-like feelings, as well as more psychological and spiritual approaches. But our Ghost-Mind, I believe, is most attuned with the aspects of "mind" that are located in our brain.

Hama is integrally connected with its creation, our Lich-Hama or living body, and especially with the blood, hair, skin and outer appearance. It shows itself in the activities, skills and abilities of our body, including our voice, body language, expressions, behavior and personal characteristics.

Aldr's foothold lies in our bone marrow, including the marrow-like material of our brain, and in the many fluids of our body, whose subtle energies are held within the body by our Ealdoryard, the Aldr's boundary that coincides with our physical exterior. Many of our body fluids are regulated by cycles of time: the rise and fall in levels of hormones, neurotransmitters, digestive / reproductive /

immune-related fluids, the fluids that bathe and nourish our brain, spinal column and bone marrow, and many others. These are heavily influenced by diurnal, lunar and seasonal cycles and by our age and stage of life. They are among the means by which Aldr influences our physical body and our body-in-time; they are Aldr's foothold in our body. The fluids ruled by Aldr symbolically mirror Aldr's source in the waters of the Norns' Well.

Aldr is also a soul which feeds nourishment to our body, especially the spiritual and energetic nourishment contained in food that is close to its natural state. Emotional nourishment is gained through all the work that humans do together to grow, obtain, prepare, celebrate, and share the food and drink. These aspects of soulful nourishment work together to optimize our life-span, vitality and wellbeing.

Mod is seated in our solar plexus and abdomen, meshed with our gut microbiome and with the powerful energy centers in this region. Mod gives us strength and vigor at all levels: physical, mental, emotional, spiritual. The interactive processes of digestion, metabolism, energy production, muscles and tendons, reproductive system, and immune system all influence and are influenced by the state of our Mod. Mod can express its power through the gaze of the eyes, as we see in Thor's intense, fiery gaze, the fierce gaze of wild beasts, and the deep wells of wisdom seen in Frigg's eyes.

Sefa resides in the heart, and **Hugr** in the breast, around and in the heart. (Note that ancient cultures around the world considered that 'thought' happens in the heart, not the brain. See, for example, Lockett's extensive discussion

Definition and Overview

of this in Chapters 2 and 3 of *Anglo-Saxon Psychologies.*) Hugr and Sefa are also associated with our organs of perception, our brain, and the many biochemical processes that generate and are generated by our emotions. With their focus on relationship and kinship, and Hugr's root in desire, these souls are heavily invested in the body's involvement with sexuality, mating, reproduction, parenting, and family dynamics.

Saiwalo-Dwimor, in my perception, has no actual physical connection with the body, except in the sense that in phantom form it is the image of our body. Dwimor is the metaphysical (non-physical) matrix which attracts and holds together the other souls and their energies during Midgard life.

With this review under our belts, let's proceed to a discussion of the approaches, tools and skills needed for experiential exploration of our souls.

Foundations of Experiential Exploration

Chapter 2

As we pursue a deeper understanding of the souls, we immerse ourselves in unfamiliar worlds with unfamiliar beings.

2. Foundations of Experiential Exploration

Methods for learning

First, it's important to establish your personal methods of learning, and these methods are going to include some that are not standard academic fare. Yes, there's study involved as you read and evaluate this book and the foregoing one, but that's only the beginning. The real challenge is taking these ideas, exploring and testing them, and transmuting them, through the alchemy of your own essence, into something that is part of the structure of your own lived experience. Each person who does this is going to have different experiences and come out in a unique place: their own landscape of the souls.

You can see from this that we won't be dealing with 'right or wrong answers'; such attitudes are beyond pointless for soul lore study. In fact, they will massively get in our way! We are not seeking 'certainty or absolute, irrefutable truth' here. *We are seeking understanding, self-knowledge, and experience. We are pursuing wisdom*, which must include experience and insight as well as intellectual knowledge.

Insisting on 'Certainty', within intangible realms such as spirituality and religion, establishes a person in a specific spot in the knowledge-landscape, their own certainty-fortress. Forever afterwards they will be defending that fortress against all threats, challenges, and new insights that might try, and perhaps succeed, in knocking down their throne of certainty. It's a miserable, stressful way to live, and turns a person into a closed, defensive box. (Of course, what I say about certainty here applies in 'fuzzy' realms like soul lore, religion, relationships, and the humanities. When it comes to building a bridge, you do want 'certainty' that the girders are going to hold up!)

'Understanding', as opposed to 'certainty', is delighted by the chance to explore, expand, reach new horizons, test out new perspectives, cogitate on new ideas. There is no way to threaten 'understanding': everything that comes its way is food for its nourishment and growth, even though the stretching and growth involved can sometimes be uncomfortable. 'Understanding' in deep, experiential ways, rather than dogmatic certainty, is what we are seeking through our study of soul lore.

So, how do we pursue our course here? We have to use study methods that are suited to our purpose. We begin with intellectual study, reading what I provided in Book I, and anything else you wish along those lines. We ponder and question until what we've read seems reasonably clear.

Then comes the real work, innermost work, where we first explore and test the ideas within the reality of our own soul-landscape. Then, if the ideas prove valid to us, we begin the work of incorporating the realities behind the ideas into our lived experience, our deep understanding, our storehouse of insightful wisdom.

The most essential ability: Imagination

For the first step of studying, we need our rational faculties. For the inner-work, the main bulk of our learning here, our imagination is essential. Imagination is the ability of our mind to perceive and mentally work with anything that is not physically there with us at this moment in time. Planning for tomorrow, buying a thoughtful gift for someone, envisioning how that new paint will look in your living room: a great deal of our mental activity every day relies on our imagination; it is an essential tool for human activity, inner or outer.

Imagination is something else, too: it is a sensory-organ system. This latter strength of the imagination is naturally strong in children, and is often squashed out of them and denied by modern culture. When we have an experience of Deity, of beauty, of insight or intuition, a premonition, a sense of danger, an experience that we long to capture in a song, poem or painting, we are sensing currents of being, of subtle energy, and translating them into modalities that mean something to us.

All of these things come to us through the sensing abilities of our imagination, in the same way that light reflecting off objects comes through our eyes, and our ears pick up audible vibrations. The raw vibrations of light and the audible spectrum are not something that our conscious mind can interpret directly; these things have to go through our eyes and ears and be processed by the relevant parts of our brain and body, before this light and sound make sense to us.

In the same way, the 'other senses' of our imagination pick up subtle vibrations in our spiritual / non-physical surroundings, and our imagination processes them into intelligibility, as our brain does with vibrations in the visible and audible spectra. Our eyes and ears and brain are culturally-trained to interpret what we see and hear in culturally determined ways, and the same goes for the sensory system of our imagination.

We need our imaginations to do this work of coming to understand our souls: imagination as a mental ability, as powerful as rational thought or more so, and imagination as a sensory system. We train our rational thinking and observational abilities well in schools and colleges and everyday work and living. (At least, it's supposed to work that way...) Our imaginations are equally powerful, but often have not been trained and disciplined in appropriate ways. I don't mean 'disciplined' in the sense of constrained or suppressed, I mean 'disciplined' the way an athlete or musician or intellectual champion trains: working diligently to develop and focus all our abilities toward a challenging and highly-valued goal. As we pursue experiential soul lore study, we'll also be training our primary interface between the physical and metaphysical worlds: our powerful imaginations.

Critical thinking and critical knowing

A word about critical thinking, which is an essential rational ability for living a well-balanced life, in touch with and interactive with the real physical and social worlds. Critical thinking begins its development in toddlers, with their incessant quest to test and explore everything around them through all their senses, including the sense of taste, since everything they encounter is put into their mouth! As they do this, they begin to develop their capacities for evaluation and judgement: this tastes great, that is awful, this thing burns, that thing will fall on me if I try to climb it, doing this is so much fun, doing that will result in somebody yelling at me.

Critical thinking depends on our ability to cross-check our own ideas and notions with what is actually going on in the real, physical and social worlds, which in turn depends on being physically and informationally in touch and interactive with these worlds.

Our imagination, or the suite of abilities I call our 'imaginarium', needs to develop its own version of critical thinking in the same ways: by exploring and testing our metaphysical environments and learning from actual, lived experiences and interactions there. It's important to realize that metaphysical events are not actually happening 'in our imagination', any more than real-life interactions are actually happening 'in our brain'.

Our perceptions, interpretations, judgements and reactions are indeed happening in our brain (and the rest of our body), but they are reactions to real things and real beings 'out there' in the real world where our physical body lives and takes action. Even though we cannot know, precisely, how well our brain images correspond to whatever is out there, nevertheless over time we build functional connections between our perceptions and responses, and whatever is happening in the fields of existence outside our body and mind.

The same is true in the metaphysical space-times that we perceive through our imaginarium and through our souls directly. Instead of the physical objects we experience in the physical world, in metaphysical worlds we encounter forms and flows of subtle energies, which our imaginarium can learn to sense and interpret just as our brain, sensory and nervous systems do with the physical world. Through experience and through pondering clearly and honestly upon our experiences, we develop a faculty of 'critical knowing' that serves our imaginarium, just as critical thinking serves us in our rational interactions with the 'real world out there.'

"We really don't / can't know anything about the soul…."

This is a common phrase used in religious and non-religious discussions about souls and other abstract matters. As we study soul lore, I'd really like us to dump this attitude! Yes, in a sense it is true: true that we can't objectively 'prove' things about souls, Deities, afterlife, and related matters. And it is also wise to avoid that know-it-all, sacred-certainty attitude that tries to force its own views onto other people's understandings and experiences.

Foundations of Experiential Exploration

But I'll tell you this: insisting that "We really can't know anything about souls, Deities, etc…" *is* a sacred-certainty attitude that some people try to push onto other people. People can be know-it-alls about *uncertainty* just as they can be about specific beliefs. They can feel so positive that it is impossible to know anything, that they close themselves off from other avenues of knowing, and push others to close themselves off, too. This attitude is highly counterproductive in studying soul lore and other sacred matters, and the whole issue comes down to the meaning of 'to know.'

In modern life, rooted in the age of scientific enlightenment, we tend to equate 'knowledge' with 'proven, objective truth.' Certainly, proven objective truth is an important part of the overall field of 'what knowledge is', but that is not all that 'knowledge' consists of. Knowledge is also 'gnosis', a closely related Greek word that is used in philosophy and religion to mean 'knowing through personal experience.'

People often react to this concept by pointing out how easy it is to misunderstand, or to fool ourselves and others, when it comes to our own perceptions and reactions about other people and situations, for example. People may interpret gnosis to mean "knowing through personal feelings". Like, "I just know that this person is the right spouse for me"…and then this turns out not to be the case. Our 'knowledge' is then shown to be flawed, and this cuts down our confidence in our own knowing. I'm sure we've all had sad experiences of this kind of 'knowing'. But this is not the kind of knowledge that I'm talking about, either.

Foundations of Experiential Exploration

Knowledge as skilled experience

The kind of knowledge I'm talking about can be illustrated by using the example of a personal skill that you have, any kind of practical skill, like carpentry, gardening, baby-expertise, mountain climbing, cooking, playing a musical instrument, hang-gliding, pottery, whatever. You learn a lot about this area of skill from other people, and you learn even more on your own, by trial and error and by constant practice. You can tell when you're on the right track because your skill clearly improves, and when you're on the wrong track, it stagnates.

What is it that causes this skill to develop in you, personally, in your own unique way? It is *personal experience* that makes it happen, and *there is no other way* that can make your own skill develop and increase. Only you, doing the work day by day, can create your own level of skill.

A skilled potter's hands have learned to express the soul's inspiration into the material world.

Foundations of Experiential Exploration

This skill and experience that you gain through your own practice, year by year, your inner recognition of your own skill and your trust in it, is the same kind of knowledge that you need for learning and putting into practice the knowledge of your souls. The only way we can come to know our own souls is through personal experience. There is no other way. No amount of lecturing, analysis and study will get you past the first stage of developing your skill, the beginner stage of gaining basic knowledge of the field.

Other people (like me) telling you things about the souls only gives you a place to start thinking about it all. It offers you the view of a path ahead of you, but only you can walk that path and make it your own. Only you can build your skill as a soul-explorer, and only you can reach that state of inner trust in your own proven skill at doing this, proven by the way you live your daily life, year after year, as a person aware of and true to their own souls.

I've been pursuing soul lore and trying to live in accord with it for enough years now, that I am able to trust my own skill, experience, knowledge, in regard to soulful living, and am able to share this confidence with others. Have I reached any kind of finish-point, any place to stop learning and say 'I'm done'? Have I "perfected myself"? No, far from it! This will never happen. There is always more learning and growing to be done, and the more we grow, the more we become aware of how much more learning lies ahead of us. But that knowledge need not shake our confidence in ourselves: our confidence that we are on a worthwhile spiritual path, and are doing well with our pursuit of experience and knowledge along that path.

I'll give an example of this inner trust and confidence in my connection with my souls. When I sat down to write these chapters about a personal approach to soul lore, I didn't know what I was going to write. First, I would wander aimlessly around for awhile, staring into space and letting something germinate within me that I didn't yet recognize. Then I sat down to write, and 'writing happened.' I was as interested to see what came out of it, as anyone else might have been!

Before my inner growth of trust in my own soul-knowledge, I would have felt anxious about not having a writing plan, an outline, something to get started with. I would have tried to take a logical, objective, academic approach, as I do when I write about my more analytical soul lore research. That is intellectual knowledge, and clearly that has its place, it is needed too. I relied heavily on that approach for a substantial part of Book I. But for this book, whichever soul I was working on came forward in a more gnostic way to guide my writing of these experiential soul lore guidelines, 'experiential' being the key word.

I have this new-found confidence that I don't have to wrestle with or plan what to write, I will just 'know.' Which doesn't mean it's perfect. Once it's written, it needs to be fine-tuned, better organized and clarified, to make sure I'm communicating clearly. But the first, more spontaneous draft is always on the right track in terms of offering knowledge about the soul in question, knowledge that I often didn't know I knew, until I wrote it! This form of 'just knowing' is based on years of personal experience and learning, and on sharing with and learning from others as well. It is not the "I just know it" of wishful thinking or of motivations hidden from myself and others.

Basic premises of Soul-Craft

When we pursue soul lore on the basis of personal experience, we need to start off with some basic premises or assumptions: this is proper philosophical technique. These premises correspond to the basic material that we seek to be skillful with, in the examples of personal skills that I gave earlier, like wood, plants, babies, mountains, food, musical instruments, gliders, potting clay. Premises provide the starting point and the 'raw material' for our work.

Our most basic premise here is that *'souls exist'*, and more, *'my own souls exist'*. Then: *'I am capable of knowing and interacting consciously with my own souls.'* A further premise for us is that *'my souls can be understood and experienced in the context of Heathen traditions, beliefs and practices.'*

So, this corresponds to us selecting the basic medium for our craft, our skill. This is what we work with: our souls and our conscious awareness. The context for our work, the setting for our craft, is Heathen tradition and belief, brought into the modern world. Then, there's knowledge to be learned from other skilled people, as we begin to learn the skill for ourselves. You may choose to regard me as one of those people to learn from, and there are many others around, to learn from as well.

As you become more familiar with the basics of your craft, you begin testing and shaping what you're learning, putting it into your own context, developing your own vision. Then comes steady practice, and trial and error. This is where you shape your craft to your own vision, learning from your mistakes, refining your vision of where you're going with this. As your practice continues and your confidence increases, you begin to take ownership of your skill, your craft, your vision, and you reach for mastery.

And how are you tested? Of what does your 'master-piece' consist, to show your growing mastery of soul-lore and practice? *Your master-piece is yourself and your life,* lived day by day: your deeds, your thoughts and words, your attitudes and behavior, your choices, your aspirations, your accomplishments, your giving to the world around you.

You're not trying to live up to other people's standards and expectations now. You're developing your own standards and expectations, based on your growing knowledge of your own souls: what they can be, what they can do, what they need in order to thrive, what they can give to the world. You and all your souls together are creating a vision and bringing it into being, and that vision-in-action is not based on wishful thinking but on hard work, experience, knowledge, skill, confidence, mastery.

To return to an earlier point I made, you cannot achieve all this if you are accompanied by a constant chorus of voices, from inside and outside yourself, that chants at you: "You really can't know anything about the soul...."! Resist and overcome this! Build up your own knowledge and awareness, and trust in your own experience and wisdom, in the true and soulful life you live, that results from your growing practice and mastery of soul lore.

Your Daybook

If you've pursued any kind of esoteric, spiritual, or psychological work in your life, you'll be familiar with some of the methods we need to use: meditation, journaling, trance-work, active imagination, dream-work, rune-craft, divination, spaecraft, automatic writing. I'm not going to go into detail on all of these; they are each subjects for entire libraries of books! I encourage you to apply any of these skills that you have, and learn more (there are many good Heathen and other books on these subjects), and apply your new learning, too. I will make specific references to using these various skills as we move through the lessons, but now I am going to emphasize two of them as we begin our study: journaling and active meditation.

Soul lore is complex and complicated, profound and life-changing, and it will stimulate your inner growth to a degree that you may find hard to imagine, at first. At least, this is how it is with me, and I assume for you as well. The learning process may (or may not) start out slowly at first, until you begin really processing the unfamiliar perspectives involved. Then, it may take off like a rocket.

For these reasons, it is really essential for you to keep a soul lore journal, or Daybook, as I like to call it ('journal' comes from the French word for 'day': *jour*). This is the place to record your questions, confusions, insights, experiences, aspirations. These things will multiply, transform, link up with each other in unexpected ways. There is an endless landscape of learning ahead of you! And just like any explorer, it's important to keep a map and records of where you've come from and what you've learned along the way.

Souls are like fractals and holograms, and multidimensional works of art and craft. They are like mathematical 'fuzzy sets' and multidimensional Venn diagrams. You learn something about a soul, and three months later, when you're studying a different soul, you have a sudden mega-enlightenment about how both these souls interact together and how they've shaped and expressed themselves in a big way in your life, that you never saw before. So you go back to the insights about the first soul that you wrote in your Daybook, and see that, yes, those clues were there, but you didn't see them at first. And now you see clues linking up with a third soul, or a different part of your life or character, and have another explosion of insight. Suddenly you remember a life-shaping moment in your childhood that you'd totally forgotten about. Which souls were involved with that, and how did it affect them? What was the result of that rune-casting you did, to ask about your Hugr-soul? Will you remember all these things, if you don't record them?

Only by using your Daybook can you keep track of and interrelate all these complexities. Otherwise it's all going to float off to wherever dreams go when you wake up. You need that Daybook! You don't need to write in it every day. Write in it when you have insights and experiences you need to remember, perplexities and issues you need to work through, new learnings to record, new connections to follow through all their complexities.

Use your Daybook as a process of digestion, digesting new knowledge and previously hidden knowledge and experience. It's useful to undertake some of this process of digestion by yourself, first, working in your Daybook to help you make some preliminary sense out of it. Then you may want to share this with others who walk the path with you, where shared explorations further promote your learning process.

The other way that your Daybook can serve as an essential tool is as a place for written conversations between your conscious mind and your souls, and between one soul and another. Find a quiet time and space, open your Daybook, and write a question, wish, concern or whatever. Then wait quietly until some response enters or arises in your mind, and write it down without any second-guessing or editing or criticizing it. There's a lot you can learn this way!

Your Daybook can be a physical notebook, a word-processor that takes typing or dictation, or a recording device. In addition to writing, you may want to add other media: drawings, photographs, songs and poems, etc., that also express the experiences and insights you want to record.

Preliminary exercise: Where are you starting from?

For your first exercise in studying Heathen soul lore, get your Daybook notebook or set up your e-file. Then start writing about two subjects:

1. What is your current understanding about what a soul is? Where does your understanding of this come from? How much of it consists of your own ideas and insights, and how much comes from what you were taught and simply accepted? How much comes from rebelling against whatever you were taught, and taking the opposite point of view? If you currently don't much believe there is such a thing as a soul, these questions apply equally well. Why do you believe that souls *don't* exist? Where does this perception come from? Was it taught to you, did you absorb it from those around you, did you think carefully

and reach this conclusion? What kind of emotional baggage is attached to whatever your ideas about souls are?

2. What do you want to achieve by studying Heathen soul lore? What are your hopes and aspirations?

Focused awareness

I'm actually not going to say anything here about 'how' to meditate. I figure many of you are experienced with this already, and even those who aren't, if you're interested in soul lore, you probably have enough familiarity with briefly achieving a quiet state of mind to get started. Each of our study modules is going to call for somewhat different approaches to 'meditation', anyway, so we'll talk about these as we go along.

The main reason we'll take various different approaches to meditation is because each of our souls has its own way of 'meditating', that is, of entering into a focused state that intensifies its sense of itself and its powers. Some of our souls are strongest in intellectual pondering or cogitating, sometimes called discursive meditation. Some do the transcendental-state-of-cosmic-being thing. Some are good with entering into a super-sensing of the natural environment and absorbing those sensations. One senses the flow of time, and ponders and absorbs the meaning of this. Some are good at trance-work and other occult practices requiring focus and clear mind. Some can reach (or be thrown into) ecstatic states where high-voltage power flows through, which can be useful, or can be disastrous, depending on how it is handled. Some can sink into our physical body and attune to its processes and needs. And it goes on. Please note: when I say

Foundations of Experiential Exploration

"different souls" I am not talking about "different people's souls." I am talking about your own multiple souls, as I discussed in Chapter 1 of this book.

So, we don't want to tie ourselves down to any particular method of meditation, nor to any particular definition of what it is. We'll just call it a way of focusing our mind, and our souls, and take it from there. What I want to emphasize here is that, just like using your Daybook, focused awareness is an essential tool for soul lore study, and you'll want to stay flexible about how you do this as we get to know our different souls.

Exercise 2-1. Thinking about soul-ideas.

Review the material in Chapter 1 of this book. There are some important basic concepts for you to consider here. One is my three-part definition of what 'a soul' is. What do you think of this definition? Does it make sense to you? Do you think it 'works' as a basis for studying souls? Do you think anything important is missing from this as a basic definition? Does it change anything about what you have thought, until now, to be the nature of a soul? Or does your idea of what a soul is, fit well with my definition? Look back at your responses to my questions in the preliminary exercise to respond to the last questions.

The second item to consider is my proposition that Heathen souls are not simply 'soul-parts' or functions such as 'thought', 'emotions', or 'memory'. My perception is that souls are full-blown entities, soul-persons, in their own right. Many of the souls have 'soul-parts' of their own, including thought, will, emotions, etc. Some of them have afterlives as independent beings, and some can potentially exit the living body and act independently at a distance.

The third unusual concept here follows from the second: in my approach to soul lore, I claim that we consist of multiple soul-beings who are all members of our personal 'soular system' or our *hiwscipe / hiw-ship:* our soul-household. I explore this concept in the final chapters of Book I, and return to it later in this book, as well.

Obviously, there is no requirement for you to accept any of these ideas, and it's hard for you to judge what you think about them until you know more, right? So, for now, let's approach it from the "for the sake of argument" perspective: let's say "these propositions *may* be true" and see where that takes us. It's actually really interesting to do this, and if you continue being interested, there's a long and fascinating path of spiritual adventure ahead of you!

Study participant experiences

<u>Sara Axtell:</u> *I have been "sitting with" the idea of multiple souls since I read Winifred's original articles some years ago, and I have grown into the idea. It has taken quite a while to get my head around the difference between a full soul and a soul part. I appreciate the resonance the idea has across different cultural knowledge systems.*

Exercise 2-2. Feeling and reacting to soul-ideas.

Before we begin this next exercise, I need to offer some precautions. If these ideas seem too creepy, strange, uncomfortable for you, you don't have to proceed with the following exercise of delving deeper into them. Do whatever is the right thing for you. If you're really interested in soul lore but want to take it in easy steps, more digestible bites, that's absolutely fine! Whenever you're starting to feel a bit overwhelmed by the strangeness, you can step back and buffer the impact by focusing on intellectual rather than experiential learning.

When we approach something as an intriguing intellectual idea, as a *possibility* rather than as an immediate personal experience, this helps ease us along at a more gentle pace. You can continue the readings, thinking about them, working in your Daybook, and discussing ideas with like-minded folks. As the new perspectives settle into your mind, you may be able to come back to the experiential exercises and find them more congenial to you. Always be aware of what is best for you, and follow that path.

In preparation for your next step, bear in mind your review of Chapter 1 and your responses to the previous exercise. Focus your awareness on your inner sensations and emotions, as they react to all of this material.

How do these ideas make you *feel?* Not what do you 'think' about them, but what 'feelings' do you have, what emotions, intuitions, and even bodily sensations might you feel, as you allow these ideas to float around in your field of consciousness, without intellectual judgement? Don't either accept or deny the ideas for now, just allow them to soak in as possibilities, potentials. Approach it the way you'd feel and sense the breeze, the sun, the bird calls, when you're standing outside on a pleasant day, without performing judgements and evaluations.

This exercise can be quite unsettling! You may have a lovely, spiritual experience, or you may feel unpleasant emotions like fear or distaste. You may have some odd body sensations: twitches, twinges, flushes or chills, dizziness, restlessness, aches that you didn't realize you had. It's really important here: make no judgements, and don't go off chasing your feelings in an intellectual, analytical way. Don't be overwhelmed by them, either. Don't blow them up, don't whack them down. Just sit with them. Let them be what they are. This is *you*, and your first obligation as a mature human being is to accept and honor who you are: warts, shiny bits, and all.

What you are doing now is *beginning to make a safe space, a clear space,* for your own souls to begin to step forward into your awareness: a meet-and-greet process! You probably have some experience with, or idea about, safe spaces and why people need them in order to communicate, build healthy relationships, and find peace of mind. Well, souls need this, too! You are laying the groundwork for communicating consciously with your souls, and for becoming aware of your soul-household, your *hiwscipe* or hiw-ship. There is no room for criticism and judgement, self-justification or self-shaming, hatred, fear, and avoidance in this safe space. There is only room for your whole soul-household, and your Self that arises out of them all, to feel valued and at home together.

I've said that you might have a lovely spiritual experience, or maybe an uncomfortable or perplexing one, but I haven't yet mentioned the most likely outcome the first time you try this: nothing happens, that you are aware of. This is okay; don't give up. You may need some time to get used to the whole idea and purpose of this exercise, and to practice it for awhile until you can feel comfortable and focused instead of self-conscious about pursuing it.

Even if you don't sense anything or have any specific 'experiences' or insights, you are *setting your intention* here:

Foundations of Experiential Exploration

an essential action for any kind of esoteric work. Your intention is to open your awareness, create a safe space and a comfortable form of practice, where all your souls and your everyday consciousness can interact together in full awareness. This exercise is the first step: opening the door into our deeper being, opening up some awareness-space within ourselves. We'll be doing a lot more of this as we go along.

Study participant experiences

<u>Sara Axtell</u>: *In this exercise, I found myself feeling several different souls, like I was experiencing a whole image (my self), with different threads of the image (souls) within the self in sharper relief at different points of the exercise.*

<u>My response</u> *to study participants on this exercise: About the matter of 'multiple souls' vs. 'soul parts', that's a good attitude you're taking, to wait and see. Some thoughts of mine about this. First, when it comes to non-physical entities, it's hard (for us physical beings, anyway) to discern any sharp or clear-cut boundaries between them, so it's hard to say whether we're looking at one being or more than one. Boundaries are fuzzy and overlap with each other, beings may pass through each other and come out changed on the other side. If this was all we had to go by, it might be easiest to just say that the question of 'one' or 'multiple' is irrelevant or meaningless when it comes to soul-beings.*

The first reason I started thinking about the possibility of multiple souls, rather than one soul with multiple parts, was when I was looking into the afterlife of the souls. Looking at traditional Heathen beliefs, we can see that they envisioned a number of possibilities: residence in a burial mound or grave, in

Hel, in Valhalla, in a cliff or mountain, afterlife as a ghost or a draugr, reincarnation, free-wheeling ancestral agents like Disir who come in dreams, etc. Scholars and others with a modern viewpoint simply assume that there is only one soul and it goes to only one of these afterlives. But are we sure about that?

This started me thinking about the possibility that we have more than one soul, that they come from different sources and go to different places in the afterlife, that some of them survive death and others don't, or only survive temporarily and then decay as the body does. And if they go off in different directions after the physical body dies, they can't be just 'parts' like body parts. Our liver can't live separately from our heart and our other organs, our organs couldn't survive and go off on their own, they're 100% dependent on being a part of our whole body. If our Hugr reincarnates, while our Saiwalo stays in Hel and our Ghost goes to the God-realms or wanders as a haunt, that couldn't happen if they were parts dependent upon a whole. It could only happen if they are independent beings.

Then when I started learning more about the souls, I saw how many of them have their own soul parts: thought, will, emotions, memory, etc. I started seeing how this could explain so many things about ourselves: inner conflicts, intending and wanting to do one thing, but doing something else instead, self-sabotage, things like 'talking ourselves out of something, or into something', hunches, second sight, conflicting desires and goals, etc. Having multiple soul-beings making up a soul household within us often seems, to me, like a better description of how we actually operate, than regarding ourselves as a unified whole who never experiences such pulls and tugs in different directions.

<u>Leif Höglund:</u> *Interesting point about organic interdependence. I've always seen the soul as a part of a matrix that extends between*

every being. We are a habitat for microorganisms, Earth is a habitat for us and other creatures, the universe is a habitat for the realms of the lore, etc. Like nesting dolls. After all, we can't live without the beings of our microbiomes, but they aren't exactly "us" either. If anything, this seems to be a line of thinking supporting multiple souls in one being rather than the opposite, but I think it might have further implications. Another thread to tack onto the Soul Lore corkboard...

<u>Laurie Sottilaro:</u> *Thank you for bringing up "talking yourself into something" etc. I was arguing with myself over something in the reading – I don't even remember what anymore – when I realized the ability to have the argument at all implied that the souls might be the arguing parties. Then I looked back over the descriptions and recognized some very familiar profiles... Glad that wasn't just me!*

Personal example

I'll share here what the experience of sensing all my souls feels like to me, to give an example and to set the stage for our final exercise in this chapter. Your experience may — probably will — be totally different than what I share here!

I feel like I'm swimming in the ocean. There are cool spots and warm spots in the water, that the waves and currents move around. Shadows come and go across the sun, the wind ripples the waves. Light, movement, warmth, and coolness fluctuate; boundaries are vague and blurry. It's hard to see clearly what things are. There are currents, deep ones and shallow ones. Strange creatures swim by. All of these things: light and shadow, currents and pressures, temperatures, creatures, all of them are strange presences, mysteries of the deep. This is a mysterious, potentially scary place, not a place that "I" control. Yet still I feel at home here, in my own element, alive and vigorous, snorting water through my nose and feeling the salt burn, feeling the pressure of the water upon my chest as I breathe.

These are not images that I'm viewing from a distance, as an observer. These are *sensations* I'm feeling in my body and souls. My imagination translates these sensations into the perception of 'swimming in the ocean': "I *feel like* I'm swimming in the ocean." Really, the feelings are inexpressible, and I have to use similes as I do in my description above.

The ocean, all the blurry, powerful, fluctuating, mysterious nature of it, is my total 'soular system'. What I perceive as my own body, swimming in the ocean, is my conscious sense of myself. This image shows that, far from containing my souls within my body and my conscious self ("I have a soul"), my body and my conscious self are smaller beings floating in the great ocean of my own 'soular system'. "I-the-person" arise from the surging and swaying of all my souls together, all these fluctuating presences meeting in the center and condensing into me-the-person.

My 'Self' is a little body of condensed matter, floating in a sea of beings.

The role of our sensory-organ analogs

We each seem to have a 'primary sense' through which our imagination-senses can most easily reach us. For many, the primary sense is vision: people see visions, see the colors of auras, see visual patterns and extract meaning from them, are clairvoyant. For many others, the primary sense is hearing: hearing or perceiving verbal messages and knowledge from otherworlds, being greatly inspired through music and the sounds of nature, being clairaudient. For myself, as may be apparent from what I described above, my primary senses are touch and taste.

Though I have many spiritual experiences that come through any or all of my bodily senses, strange as it may seem, my most powerful and enlightening ones come through my sense of touch, of body-like sensation, as I described above. And often when I am trying to sense something that lies beneath the surface of everyday appearance, I find myself opening my mouth and trying to taste the air at the back of my throat, where the air feeds in from my nasal passages, at the same time as it comes in through my mouth. I think some scenting animals, like dogs, do this too, and I've read that the various species of cattle, wild and tame, do also: smelling through nose and mouth, taste-smell, together. What I pick up this way doesn't seem like 'scent' or 'taste', and isn't anything I can put into words, but it's closer to these than to anything else, and it 'tells me things'. In the personal example I gave above, I not only used the sense of touch, taste and sight, but also proprioception: the sense of how my body was oriented in space, being tossed around by the waves and currents.

Exercise 2-3. Your sensation-strengths.

I invite you to consider the experiences you have while you are practicing Exercise 2-2, and discern which of your senses your imagination reaches you through most strongly. This is useful to know, one more thing to add to the process of knowing yourself better. Once you know which sense is strongest, you can choose to work to make it more clear and strong. Likewise, if you wish, you can work to strengthen the senses that are less tightly linked with your imagination-senses. The more ways our awareness is linked with our imagination-senses, the more richly and broadly we can perceive other worlds and beings, and our souls who interact with them all.

Your Soul-Habitat

Each of our souls has a 'habitat' where it is most at home, and most in touch with its own powers. It's helpful to enter consciously into these habitats as we begin to explore each of our souls, which means first discovering what those habitats are. As we proceed with our soul-explorations, I'll offer exercises designed for this purpose.

Consolidation

Now we've got some preliminaries and preparations under our belts. We've talked about the importance of our imagination as a sensory system: a way of intaking, processing and presenting metaphysical information to our conscious mind. We've talked about strengthening the

Foundations of Experiential Exploration

links between our experience of our physical senses, and the analog-senses of our imagination. This enhances our ability to explore, experience, and interpret the metaphysical realms similarly to the way we do in the physical realm: by using our senses, and the brain / body processes that allow us to interpret them and use them to build more complex ideas.

The way our brain functions to handle our physical senses is analogous to the way our imagination functions to handle our metaphysical senses. And just as with our brain and our intellect, our imagination needs education, training, practice, clarifying, focusing. Esoteric work of many kinds, and disciplined work with creative arts and crafts of all kinds, are excellent ways to make this happen. But without clear awareness of what is going on in the outer world and in our own inner world, the abilities of both our intellect and our imagination are diminished and wasted. Thus, we've started using ways to focus our awareness and our imaginations, and we'll continue doing that as we go along.

Your toolbox is building here: focused awareness, imagination-in-training, sensory and analog-sensory awareness, and your Daybook to record it all and make some sense out of all the pieces! You've given some serious thought to what your starting position is, your current understanding of what a soul is, and what you want to achieve by pursuing this course of study.

You've started (or continued) opening some awareness-space within you, making room to begin an expanded experience and understanding of your souls. And you've allowed some safe space and quiet time to process the emotions and feelings that are related to all these activities of soul exploration. This is an important part of healthy soul-working, and you'll want to continue doing these foundational exercises for as long as you need them, even as you proceed further in our course of study.

As you encounter new and unfamiliar souls in our upcoming studies, you may want to go back and repeat these practices of expanding awareness-space, and maintaining a safe, reassuring space and practice for emotional processing. Trusted Heathen friends, other insightful friends and family members can be very helpful here, too, as well as study groups.

....And more Daybook!

And don't forget your Daybook! It's a great space for working through issues, and you'll find that seemingly unrelated issues and events happening in your everyday life will in all likelihood turn out to be related to the soul you are currently working with. Now that you're beginning to work with your actual souls, it's important to also pay attention to what's happening in your everyday life. Our souls, or most of them, are very much involved in our everyday life, are actors in our life, and are affected by events in our life. It's very likely that as you work on each of the souls in turn, issues, events, insights relating to that soul will occur in your daily life: your actions, decisions, reactions, relationships, experiences. Don't ignore this; be aware! If you're not working through these things in your Daybook, you may not fully realize and remember the extent to which your soul-work and your everyday life are overlapping. You'll lose many opportunities for deep learning.

Foundations of Experiential Exploration

Each soul you are working with will be trying to open communication with you in many different ways, and everyday life is a primary one. This is a major and essential avenue for learning about your souls. Maintaining awareness of what is going on within you and around you, and working in your Daybook, are the means to carry out this task. Each day, when you have a few minutes to think, look at the events and pattern of your day to see how the soul you are working with might be involved or reflected there, and note this in your Daybook.

Some Esoteric schools of study, and monastic communities of various religions, recommend doing a daily review of your actions at night, just before you go to sleep. This is a good practice for soul-working as well: sift through the events and actions of the day, and consider how the soul you are currently working with was involved and impacted.

Foundations of Experiential Exploration

The Eihwaz Rune Poem

ᛇ

The Yew has a rough exterior,
Holds firmly to the earth,
Warder of the Fire,
Upheld by its roots,
Wynn (gladness) on the estate.
(my translation)

The Eihwaz or Eoh rune is considered by modern Heathens to represent life, death, and rebirth, and to extend as the Worldtree Yggdrasil between the overworlds and underworlds, with Midgard in the middle. Some of us consider it to represent the magical staff of esoteric workers such as the Seer/ess, and it also represents protection in the form of a longbow made of Yew. For our purposes here, I like to focus on the Yew's role as Warder / Herder / Keeper (*hierde* in Anglo-Saxon) of the Fire, in this case the mysterious fire that wards the Hidden Lands and their mysteries. Thus, Yew is the warder of the fire which itself wards the Hidden Lands, the domains of our souls and their mysteries. As you proceed on this path of soul exploration, keep hold of this rune, with the firm support it offers, and seek the *wynn*, the joy and gladness, that its secret powers and knowledge bring to your 'estate', your unique life-time-space that you occupy here in our world of Midgard.

Chapter 3

3. Exploring your Ferah Soul

{Primary runes in the bind-rune above: Kenaz as the fire, plus three tree-runes: Birch, Oak, and Ash; the latter two from the Anglo-Frisian Futhork.}

Background reading in Book I: Chapter 3, and the section on "The Ferah-Saiwalo Polarity" in Chapter 15. Alternatively, refer to the articles on my website entitled "Born of Trees and Thunder: The Ferah Soul;" and "What Happened to Heathen Saiwalo Soul?"

Now it's time to delve into the mysteries of the first soul on our list, the Ferah. I suggest you review the material listed above, to refresh your memory in preparation for these exercises. Take your time reviewing, and let the ideas begin to settle into your awareness. You are getting to know a seemingly unfamiliar being now, a great being within which your conscious self, mind, body, and life-force are imbedded, as they are with all our souls.

Join your Ferah in its habitat

Each of our souls has its own characteristics and, I might say, its own 'habitat' where it feels at home, where it is in its strength and competence. Joining that soul in its 'habitat', as well as you can, really facilitates communication between you. Ferah is powerful in Nature, in the flows of life and being that encompass Nature. It is strong in trees and animals, in mountains and forests, in lightning and thunder, in Fire and Earth, and in the life-energy that flows through all of us on this Mother Earth and links us together as the *Feorh-cynn,* the Kindred of Ferah. Ferah is very strong in humans, too. The ancient Saxons called human beings *firibarn:* children of Ferah, and referred to 'the folk' as *firihi.* Ferah life-force flows through us all.

Spending as much time as you can outside in natural surroundings and natural habitat, and especially spending time in the presence of trees and mountains, will stimulate and open your awareness of your Ferah, and promote communication between you. When you can't be outside, but want to connect with Ferah, meditate and focus your imaginarium on natural scenes and powers, and the life-force itself that flows through all living beings. A Ferah-and-Thor meditation or communion is a great thing to do during a thunderstorm, too, even if you (sensibly) don't go outside for it!

Exercise 3-1: Ancient roots

In Book I, Chapter 3, I show how the word "Ferah" and its siblings and forebears go all the way back to the Proto-Indo-European (PIE) language, a time before any of the European languages had branched off on their own. Ferah is truly ancient, as words go! Then, on top of that, the word is directly linked to the PIE Thunder God, *Perkwunos* or *Perkwunas,* and to powerful, ancient Earth-Deities.

Does this great age for the name, and the being, of one of your souls mean something to you? Does it deepen your sense of connection with your oldest roots: ancestors, nature, evolution, ancient Deities? Is this something that is important to you, or not so much? Explore this meaning, if it is meaningful to you.

What do you think about the idea of humans being shaped from trees? What is your interpretation of this, and what does it mean to you?

Study participant experiences

<u>Laurie Sottilaro:</u> *It took me a while to understand this question; it seemed a given to me that we would have the same soul composition as men all the way back to the first Homo sapiens, so why would this be a big deal? Then I realized it was that I was gaining the same _understanding_ as they had that was the big deal. And yes, it is one. Especially as a shamanic practitioner – I'm starting to work with one of the same tools they used. Just wow. Again especially working with ancestral helper spirits – they'll know exactly what I'm doing, with at least less need for explanation. And perhaps I'll better understand what they're talking about as well.*

My response: The realization that, by studying the roots of the old words, I was coming closer to what ancient people understood about the souls was so thrilling for me, too! Words shape thoughts and understandings, thoughts shape words. The words we use today are coordinated with how we think today, and that is influenced by so many cultural factors. What were the thoughts, the understandings, about the souls in people from a very different world and culture, using very different words?

That's why I've based my whole work on ancient words in context in the original writings, and on etymologies, rather than starting with modern ideas about 'what the soul is' and then just looking up words in old-language dictionaries to pick out the best fit. I wanted to *let them tell me* how they thought, not have me tell them, or have other modern people tell me about them. Agreed, that the evidence is very far from being clear and definitive, but there are still meaty clues that can lead us down paths of discovery, as we are doing now. And that is the whole point of all this work: for each of us to discover our own souls.

Sara Axtell: This is my favorite story from the lore (about humans being shaped from trees). I see it on many levels, including a literal level. To me, what is important about stories is the teachings that they give us. The teaching of this story–about our relatedness with trees–is a such a gift. I like to think about our tree-ancestors and tree-kin, how deeply they know the places where they grow, how they are connected through their root systems to other of their kin, and through them to other places, and depths of knowing.

I like to wonder about what that transformation must have been like, as sap quickened into blood, and roots loosened from the soil. A sense of wonder at how they could come to know different places more directly, and share their knowledge in different ways, *through story and song. But also a deep grief, at losing that deep knowledge of and connection to their place.*

So what you wrote, Winifred, about the knowledge and connection that the Ferah has to the rhythms and patterns of the land really resonates for me. Of course, our Ferah souls long for that deep knowledge of the places where we are living! For me, that kind of knowing and connection and inquiry bring the simple joy that you talked about.

<u>Leif Höglund:</u> *The linguistic history confirms what I already sensed within me: a deep-rooted connection with nature and ancient humans. This concept speaks to a broad web of interconnectivity between myself, other humans, other living beings, the ancestors, the gods, and likely more that I'm not even aware of. It is a rather transcendent feeling. I think the desire to return to a simpler, more primal lifestyle is just as connected to this interconnectivity as it is a response to the overwhelming changes that have come with industrialization and post-industrial society. Science can perform miracles that we should be grateful for; it is easy to romanticize the past when you're vaccinated against smallpox. But there's still such profound dissatisfaction. Our physical health is better than ever, but we are emotionally and spiritually bereft. I think this internal call to return to nature makes living entirely divorced from it feel extremely alien and unhealthy for both the individual and the society.*

I think it (humans arising from trees) is a very potent allegory, but isn't literal. The more I use the tree as a model for the soul-being, the deeper it becomes. The balance between stability/Earth in the roots and freedom air in the branches; the strength of drawing water and nutrients up against the pull of gravity; deciduous trees modelling the seasonal life cycle; trees as a nutritional center for the whole ecosystem, from soil stability to literally feeding and sheltering local wildlife; filtering our air to make it breathable, even when we pollute it. It isn't just that we are both upright, it's that the tree reaches out into a network that connects a whole community of beings, just as I spoke of in the previous exercise. The tree is the civil servant, the volunteer, the ecologist, the trash collector, and the castle in one.

I have recently become aware of the Recompose movement, which implements a form of human composting. Properly processed in a controlled version of the decay process, the body can create a truly stunning soil. I am opting to donate my soil to a local nature preserve– perhaps this is my Ferah-soul calling me home.

Exercise 3-2: Ancient Deities

Thor Thunder-God (ancient Perkwunos), his Mother Fjǫrgyn Earth-Goddess, and Frigg's father Fjǫrgynn, are all related to our Ferah soul through the congruence of all their names and functions. Nothing more is known of Fjǫrgynn than his name and relation to Frigg, but this name gives us some pretty obvious clues. He's likely to be the brother of Fjǫrgyn, and likely to have been her husband, too, at some point lost in time. They must be an ancient, powerful pair of Earth Deities, or an Earth and Sky-Powers Deity-pair.

As you work with your Ferah soul, tune in to all these Deities through focused awareness, using any technique you choose. Get a sense of how the power or energy emanating from these Deities is similar to the energy of your Ferah soul. When I do this I get a sense of 'flavor': they all have a similar 'energy-flavor', though the flavor I taste from the Deities is stronger than that from my own Ferah. There are also some subtle differences in their energy-flavors, which I like to explore and try to understand more clearly.

Do you sense connections, in some way, between your Ferah and these Deities? Do you sense the presence of elemental Fire and Earth here? Explore these connections and their implications for the nature, power, and potential of your Ferah soul.

Study participant experiences

Laurie Sottilaro: All of these connections can help with the growth of the Ferah soul, but for me some of them present ways "in" that could potentially help in connecting with the Ferah soul, and maintaining that connection. Ideally and ultimately, I'd like to be able to slip in and out of that connection with ease and fluidity, but for now I wait respectfully for admission. As for the growth and power implications – I'd like to get a better idea of what my Ferah wants before I start thinking about that.

Leif Höglund: I feel the energies differently while hiking. It feels much more personal between myself and the gods, rather than feeling myself as a representative of my family. The quiet makes me feel alone in the best way, but I can never get lonely; the entire world around me is alive. So much around us now isn't, and I find it pretty gloomy. The gods found me the first time I hiked alone, and it always feels like meeting up with old friends.

My response: I think that longing you speak of, for a closer connection with Nature that most of us feel, relates to our Ferah soul most of all. We can't go back in Time, and most of us can't revert to 'primitive' living. But we all have access to our Ferah soul once we recognize it and choose to live with it consciously. And our Ferah soul reaches back through Time, and is rooted in

Nature, including the Nature that is no longer on our physical Earth. This is what I talk about in my article on "Landwights and Human Ecology": the landwights connect the beings and ecosystems that no longer exist on the physical earth, with landscapes and features that do exist on physical earth. They mediate an energetic flow between the ecosystems and beings that Earth has 'breathed back into her Soul', that no longer exist on Earth, with the–however damaged, but still alive–landscapes and ecosystems which she has 'breathed out' of her Soul into our present time and space. I think that our Ferah-soul participates in Earth's breathing in and out of this life-force and life-forms, and recognizes, in a very deep way, what is going on.

Exercise 3-3: Your Ferah-habitat

Using what you've learned from the Ferah chapter in Book I, and the previous exercises, begin to explore, through meditation and through real-world experiences as much as you can, what your own Ferah's preferred soul-habitat is like. It's likely to be some kind of natural setting, but it could also be some kind of temple or other sacred place, and of course, it could be a combination of the two. It could also be a place that represents your ancestral ties and traditions. Let your mind wander through landscapes of the imagination, while holding to your awareness of your Ferah soul. Allow your Ferah to guide you to the place it considers 'home', and explore this place using all the powers of your imagination. As you continue with the next reading and exercises focused on Ferah, you may refine your understanding of its habitat.

Study participant experiences

<u>Leif Höglund:</u> As for my internal Ferah-habitat, it's somewhere deep in the woods. It's dark, quiet, and smells like damp moss and pitch.

One can spend time with other people, with pets, and all sorts of living creatures that make us feel more connected to the living world. It is not the same, however, as going out into the forest. The forest itself can feel simultaneously empty and full. Within it, one is both entirely alone, and deeply, intrinsically inside of and part of a vast and intricate ecological web. We are no longer in the world that humans construct to separate ourselves from the rest of nature – we are no longer out in a safe, open, space. We are in the hands of our senses, our ancient primate ancestors, and the gods. The forest brings a certain awareness to the Ferah and attunes one with it, and I think that to those of us who have suppressed or avoided our Ferah, it can be overwhelming and a little terrifying to realize the true, vast freedom conferred by the Ferah-soul. To know that you could just gather some tools, walk into the woods, and never come out, or any other such "new beginning" scares the souls out of some folks. The quiet contemplation of your Ferah's connection with the forest is an overwhelming and anxiety-provoking experience when it has been ignored and suppressed, but this doesn't have to be a stagnant relationship.

Ferah's sensory awareness

We've talked a lot about senses and sensations, and there's a purpose to this. When looking at our holism of body and souls, our Ferah soul itself is the locus where our senses function. Ferah fills the body as an etheric substance, and both our physical senses, and the analog-sensorium of our imagination, flow through this Ferah-substance as well as flowing through our body and brain. Our experience of the world is, or should be, a full-body experience of all our senses, physical and metaphysical. And in this full-body experience, our Ferah soul is our foundational actor, sensor, and responder. Thus, we grow ever more attuned to the physical world and to the metaphysical worlds, and our Ferah grows in power, experience, confidence, and wisdom. This is how humans are designed to be, and it is very clearly how animals are, too, in their own distinctive ways. All of us together are the Feorh-cynn, the Kindred of the Ferah.

These days, we live too much of our lives in spaces that limit our sensory awareness and our mental and nervous-system faculties that process, interpret, and are stimulated by this sensory awareness. Our visual and auditory senses are over-stimulated by all the forms of media and communication we use, while our other senses are hardly used at all when we are in cyberspace and other forms of remote media like television and telephones.

Relying on cyberspace, people don't learn the arts of reading body language, nor the subtle art of scent-signaling. Don't learn the arts of conversation, either, nor critical thinking. Critical thinking as we think of it today is mostly applied to abstract matters, but the ability itself begins and is founded upon the ability and training of our physical senses to observe, identify, discern, discriminate, sort, test, evaluate, accept or reject, and respond to challenges posed by physical objects, persons, and experiences in the outside world. Becoming more detached from the demands of living in the physical world, our critical thinking abilities likewise become distorted through the loss of our physical-world foundations.

This situation has been taken to extremes as we've socially isolated during the Covid-19 pandemic, and people's joy in getting together personally, face to face, when we can do so signals a resurgence of our need to use our full sensorium together: hugs, back-slaps, body language, smell, sharing tastes and glances, sweaty work-out friends, grubby kids, loud chatter, the lot. This is how we've evolved, body and brain together: our senses are the interface linking physical world to body, body to brain, brain back to body, body back to physical world. All of these transactions occur by going through our Ferah.

Our senses are the key to experiential learning in the real, physical world. The senses of our imagination, our analog-senses, are key to experiential learning in the metaphysical worlds. As much as some of our physical senses are atrophying as we depend more and more on cyberspace, the problem is even worse in metaphysical space due to lack of training and practice for our own imaginative skills. Cyberspace is imaginative space, true; yet a lot of it does not heavily exercise our own imagination. Stuff is fed to us; we don't do a lot of the cooking. This is in sharp contrast to reading or listening to fiction (without visuals), for example, where our own imaginations are challenged to come up with what the characters, landscapes, situations, surroundings look like, sound like, feel like, smell like, etc.

So, for many of us in modern life, parts of our sensorium are under-active, and other parts are over-active. Over-activity reaches its height when people are subjected to traumatic experiences, and suffer from PTSD and related injuries as a result. Traumatic experiences and existential threats are imprinted into Ferah's sensory-substance, destabilizing it and causing Ferah to throw out over-reactive signals when faced with everyday activities that normally would not be threatening.

Study participant experiences

<u>Sara Axtell:</u> *What resonates for me most deeply is the connection of the Ferah to nature. To the land and the cycles and rhythms of the land. That connection is the medicine that will heal the reactivities, and then that healing radiates out to our other souls as well. Another area of self-study that this lesson brings up is about my relationships with the gods. I realize that I am not very god-oriented. I have had a strong relationship with Freyja since I was quite young, and certainly connect with others (Frigg, Eir, Odin) on occasion. But I am much more oriented to my relationships with land.*

The ideas that I want to continue to sit with are about the close relationship of Ferah and Lich in our experience of physical sensation and emotion. I want to think more about injuries to the Ferah, both from our personal experience and from our collective cultural experiences of being cut-off from Ferah's rhythms. I like what you are saying about time in nature, and connection to the land's rhythms helping to heal.

<u>My response:</u> *I do think that Heathen soul lore can offer useful insights into both personal psychology, and societal phenomena. Your (and others') sense that healing Ferah through contact with Nature applies very well to this, and I think that a lot of the general uneasy sense that something's wrong comes from a subliminal sense of the growing ecological problems.*

Exploring Ferah

About not being very God-oriented, I get the impression that many Heathens feel this way, are more drawn to the ancestors and / or wights, while still honoring the Deities appropriately. I think this tendency is also shown in history, where long after conversion, people may have left the old Deities behind, but not the wights and the ancestors.

<u>Sara Axtell:</u> *I want to think more about the role of the Mod in healing. I am not sure I understand that yet.*

<u>My response:</u> When it comes to healing the Ferah, specifically, the qualities that are needed from Mod are courage, strong will, and determination. These qualities offer a good counterbalance if Ferah has become hypersensitive and overreactive due to traumatic life experiences. Such a Ferah feels threatened at every turn, overreacting to everything with anxiety and fear. Mod, and Mod's patrons Thor and his children, can step in as protective powers of your soul household, giving Ferah a sense of protection, a sense that someone has Ferah's back!

People whose Ferahs need this kind of healing will do well to work on.....I don't exactly know what to call this yet....maybe "mingling" or "inter-absorbing" their Ferah and Mod souls' energies. Ferah needs more than protection in order to heal: it needs to absorb and learn to use the qualities of courage, strength and determination that Mod can share with it.

We should be aware that this combination of Ferah and Mod can backfire if not handled properly. Unbalanced Mod can express itself as rage and savagery. Unbalanced Ferah can slip into slyness, deceit and cruelty as a defense against perceived helplessness. Both of them can fall into selfishness and self-absorption. These things do not add up to a happy combination!

Exploring Ferah

Most people won't be in that kind of extreme situation, of course, but it's wise to be aware of potential pitfalls and guard against them. The oversight and assistance of the Holy Ones is highly recommended, to ensure we are aware of weaknesses or bad habits of thought and behavior, and that we counterbalance and correct these flaws rather than enhancing them by allowing our souls to absorb each other's flaws instead of their strengths!

I hope this cautionary note doesn't make the Ferah healing process seem too fraught. The healing needs to be done, but it needs to be accompanied by self-awareness, and hopefully with feedback from trusted others, as well. But most of all, we need to trust in our own souls, in their innate desire for health and strength, for balance and the soul-companionship that a well-balanced soul-household can uniquely give.

One meaning or aspect of resilience fits well here. **Resilience is a sense of trust in our ability to handle things, to face the difficulties of life and rise to the challenges.** *Having trust in our resilience means trusting the sources and the channels of energy that we rely on to face our challenges; without sufficient energy and strength in some form, we can't do it. When our souls are in good condition, we can trust our souls, trust that their might and main are there for us to draw on, trust that we will be able to use this in the best way to deal with our challenges.*

In-depth soul-healing is a large topic of its own, that I won't attempt to any great extent here, where we are focused on learning the basics of who all our souls are. But soul-healing is something that I hope and pray other Heathens, trained and familiar with our Heathen souls and with other work ongoing in the Heathen community, will further develop and grow onward.

Exploring Ferah

Our Ferah is responsible for detecting and evaluating all physical and metaphysical sensory cues in our environment, and for deciding on appropriate responses (which can include ignoring irrelevant stimuli). It does not do that in a state of abstraction, away from our conscious mind. Our conscious mind's activities in this regard are part of Ferah's process.

Ferah unites all our senses, our body, our brain, with the flows of energy and information that circulate around us in our environment at every moment, including the energies of Deities, spirits, and beings of other worlds. Ferah is our master of ceremonies here, our ring-leader in this great circus of physical-metaphysical sensory life! If we had to rely simply on our conscious mind, our intellectual thought-processes, to run this whole show of sensing, evaluating and reacting to the entire physical and metaphysical sensory worlds out there, we would collapse within minutes! Our conscious mind and conscious learning and decision processes can only do so much of this massive knowledge-integration. We need our Ferah, and we need it to be healthy, experienced, wise, powerful: we need to be *feraht* Heathens.

Exercise 3-4: Nourishing Ferah

To do this work and stay healthy, Ferah needs to be properly nourished and cared for. Our physical bodies become weak and ill when poorly nourished and nurtured, and the same is true for our souls. For this exercise, enter into your Ferah-habitat and be still and receptive. Ask your Ferah to show you, cause you to richly sense and feel, what kind of nourishment and nurturing it needs, to be at its healthy and powerful best. Record what you learn in your

Daybook, and proceed with implementing what you've learned from your Ferah.

It's good to do this on a regular basis: check in with Ferah periodically to see whether its needs have changed, and whether your nurturing is being effective. As you proceed in doing this, you will become gradually more familiar with your Ferah, and be better able to understand its needs, its potentials, and how you can partner with it consciously instead of unwittingly getting in its way!

Study participant experiences

<u>Sara Axtell:</u> What keeps my Ferah nourished, healthy and well-resourced? Sitting in my backyard and watching birds, harvesting and gathering in the fall, cross-country skiing in the winter, dancing circle dances with my friends, going to see the cranes when they stop during their migration, cooking and eating fresh local foods, reading verse by my favorite poet who wrote about his orchard in western Norway. Anything that helps me to notice the land, and that allows me to feel fully present. Something that helps me to be immersed in what I am experiencing with my senses.

Ferah and Law

How do people come up with the idea of 'law' in the first place? What is the connection between what humans observe about the laws of nature, and the laws that humans come up with for ourselves? How much of human law is rooted in instinct (like perhaps the almost-universal laws against incest), and how much is invented by humans for various helpful or unhelpful purposes?

Exploring Ferah

There are three large areas of Law, in its broadest meaning, that Ferah is connected with: (1) the laws, patterns and rhythms of the natural world (for example, the law of gravity, or the laws of thermodynamics); plus (2) human social laws; plus (3) laws / customs / traditions that govern relations between humans, Deities and spirits. And there are Ferah-words that relate to each of these three.

The names of several kinds of trees, of natural phenomena, and the name of the life-force itself, are all derived from the root of *Ferah*. Then there is the word *firihi* meaning 'the folk' in Old Saxon. What is it that makes 'the folk' be a folk, an integrated group of people? It is their laws, customs, traditions, among other things like language, which indeed has its own language-laws itself. 'Ferah-soul' unites 'firihi-folk.' And finally, when a person is wise, pious, devout, strong in spiritual practice and spiritual connections, honoring the troth and commitments between themself and the Holy Ones, ancestors and other spiritual beings, that person is called *feraht*. Three words relating to Ferah, three domains of law: nature, society, religion. Law in its broad, life-supporting sense means creating and maintaining a structure of ethics, norms and behavior that supports our life as a healthy community of people, Nature, and the worlds of the spirit. There is more about Ferah and Law in one of the *Extra* sections at the end of this chapter, pp. 84-5.

Exercise 3-5: The path of priesthood

If you are on a path of priesthood, either public / group, or private / individual priesthood, or if you are a Heathen Law-Speaker or Thyle, study the section on "Ferah, Law and Priesthood" in Chapter 3 of Book I, or the website article on Ferah, and also the parts relating to Law and Sacrifice in one of the *Extra* sections at the end of this chapter, pp. 84-85. Consider which, if any, of the points discussed there, and above, have relevance to your path, and record your thoughts in your Daybook.

Exercise 3-6: Ferah and sacrifice

I talk about Ferah and sacrifice in Chapter 3 of Book I, and give a description of what Ferah-sacrifice means to me. What about you? As you're coming to know the nature of your Ferah soul, what are your thoughts about what sacrifice is, what the Ferah's role in sacrifice is, or should be, and what all of this means to you as a practicing Heathen? Take a look at the part about sacrifice and law in one of the *Extra* sections at the end of this chapter, pp. 84-85. Does that spark any thoughts in you? If the subject of sacrifice is not very meaningful to you, or if your idea of sacrifice is not really relevant to the Ferah soul, then skip this exercise.

Study participant experiences

<u>Laurie Sottilaro:</u> *My previous organization replaced "priest" with "sacar" based on the root word meaning "to make sacred." That's what a sacrifice really is – you give it to the gods, you put it into their realm, you make it sacred. As to how this relates to my Ferah... that's a question I'd like to come back to, after I'm more familiar with how all the souls work. I rather get the sense that sacrifice is the passage of something from the realm of Ferah to the realm of {something} but I don't know the other souls well enough to know who receives it and hands it to the gods. Thus, Ferah picks it up from Midgard, passes it to x, who hands it off to Asgard. No idea where that impression comes from.*

Exploring Ferah

<u>Leif Höglund:</u> Modern Heathen sacrifice, particularly in regard to Ferah is as follows: treating Nature as sacred life, and sacred space; providing both fiscal and temporal resources (to whatever degree possible) to organizations that protect living creatures, human or otherwise, maintain or encourage ecological responsibility, and that protect and facilitate civic education and engagement. These resources are far more sparse than food generally is in this country, and are just as meaningful to offer. Sacrificing food and cattle was one and the same with fiscal sacrifice. Acting as Warder of the Law, as well as a Warder of the Land is in line with respecting the spiritual world and the gifts the Gods have directly given us. I'd argue this is just as much a spiritual duty as the Blot.

Exercise 3-7: Afterlife of Ferah

What are your thoughts, or what is your sense, about the afterlife of Ferah? This is a subject I am still exploring myself; I feel there is a lot more to learn about it. Obviously, we don't and can't have 'objective' knowledge about this, any more than we can have 'objective' knowledge about the existence and nature of our souls. 'Subjective' knowledge, on the other hand, is accessible to all of us: this arises from subjective experience, and subjective experience is what we're pursuing here in our studies, along with whatever objective knowledge we can find. Modern Heathens are working toward modern understandings, both personal, and shared common understandings, about many aspects of our religion, and learning more about the afterlife, if any, of the souls is part of that great effort.

Study participant experiences

<u>Laurie Sottilaro:</u> *My thoughts on the afterlife of the Ferah... I was really hoping you could tell me! But I sense a return to its own kind for a time (a different inflection of "the trees") to get grounded again and "remember who I am" when alone, to become a whole being again after being part of something for so long (reminder of when my band broke up and it took me a little while to pick my guitar back up and find my voice as a solo again). Then on to the next round.*

<u>Leif Höglund:</u> *I'd think, from my subjective experience of Ferah (which I've worked with for years under other names), that this Soul-Being or Soul-Part becomes a wight. In my opinion, it is too heavily associated with trees and other parts of the Natural realm to become another entity, such as one of the ancestors.*

Exercise 3-8: Ferah during your childhood

Read the section on "Development and Psychology of the Ferah" in Chapter 3 of Book I. I see Ferah as being a very strong, up-front soul during the active years of our childhood. I had a great enlightenment experience when I realized this, realized that so many of my treasured childhood experiences and memories were rooted in Ferah and its interface with Nature. What I recognize now as my 'Ferah-Habitat' was, in my childhood, the treasure of my life, both inner life and outer life, though I could not have put all this into words.

Spend some time attuning with your Ferah in its habitat. Then, travel back in memory to your childhood, if this is a safe thing for you to do. If it is not, please ignore

Exploring Ferah

this exercise. But if it is safe for you, ask your Ferah to guide you toward memories where it played a big role, had a great influence in your experience of life.

There are several layers to the purpose of this exercise. One is to recognize your own Ferah and the role it plays in your life. Another is to enter into the joy that Ferah can bring: the simple joyfulness of being a child, filled with the bubbling energy of Life itself. I hope that you had such experiences as a child, and can find them again in this exercise. I also hope that if you have lost access to that simple joy in life, or didn't have the opportunity to experience it, you decide now in partnership with your Ferah to rediscover this path of delight, and walk it anew.

Study participant experiences

<u>Leif Höglund:</u> *My Ferah soul feels restless as a child. I want to explore, read, and learn new things. The world is so interesting; isn't it such a shame to let it become so stale? The best part of living is the exploration, of the self, of the world, of everything. Learn to keep it novel and interesting. Life's more fun that way.*

Summary of Ferah, with further meditations

Here is a short summary of the Ferah, and some guidelines for focusing or meditating on Ferah. These are 'chunks' of Ferah characteristics for you to consider and meditate on, one by one, in the process of becoming more familiar with this soul.

Ferah is life-force, sparked by lightning, grounded in trees and Earth, permeated by the vibrations of thunder.

Exploring Ferah

Our heartbeat and all the electrochemical and biomagnetic activities of our body reflect these powers.

Ferah is a subtle substance that fills our body. Our senses, sensations and feelings, and our instincts related to these things, are located in this substance as well as in our physical body and brain. Ferah, body and brain (and imagination) work together to pick up, process, interpret, and react to all our senses, sensations, feelings, and instincts related to these.

Ferah is a being with thoughts, understanding, emotions, wisdom. Our reactions to the stimuli we sense around us are the work of Ferah, who guides us in this way as we navigate life in the physical and social worlds.

Ferah is not our only guiding soul, not the only soul who participates in our everyday life. *Ferah's guidance and participation relate especially to these things:* our use of our senses and how we react to what we sense. Our perceptions of the laws, rhythms, and patterns of nature and natural life, including the life force that flows through us and all living beings. Our perception and interactions with the norms, laws, customs of our society. Our willingness to enter into relationships with our Deities, to follow a path of Heathen-style piety and devotion towards Deities and natural powers.

I suggest rereading the section *Development and Psychology of the Ferah* in the Ferah chapter of Book I, paying attention to the role of Ferah in childhood, and the distortions that Ferah can develop when it is mistreated or not well-nurtured. With its highly-developed environmental sensing functions, if Ferah is exposed to a damaging environment (especially during defenseless childhood), our Ferah, and we ourselves along with it, can

Exploring Ferah

develop excessive fears and phobias, become hyperalert and overreactive, and develop negative coping mechanisms to deal with these problems, such as slyness, cruelty, deceptiveness, withdrawal, neuroses, etc. These are important matters to meditate upon, to better understand ourselves and our life, but I realize that for some of us these issues may not feel safe to enter into more deeply. Use your own judgement about what is the wise course for you. Don't meditate on matters in this paragraph if you feel it would be harmful for you.

If you do pursue meditation on the preceding paragraph, and find that you have significant damage to your Ferah, look through this summary and go back to the Ferah chapter in Book I, or the Ferah web article, and *pick out some of the strengths of Ferah that you can use as healing meditations.* For example, Ferah's connection with the life-force; with the invigorating and re-tuning vibrations of thunder; Ferah's deep connection with the forces and rhythms of Nature and with our Deities, especially those of Earth and Sky powers.

Perhaps the most healing activity you can do with your Ferah is *get to know it and value it.* All of us feel healing and renewal of life, when someone else takes the trouble to know us deeply, cares about us, about our character, our life-history, our challenges, and offers love and support for our healing. You can do this yourself, with your conscious mind offering this blessing to your wounded Ferah.

This is one way (among many) to understand Odin's sacrifice of himself to himself, hanging upon the Tree. Ferah is connected with trees, with sacrifice, with Deities, with suffering (through its sensing abilities which can be overwhelmed by suffering). It is also connected with

Exploring Ferah

powerful life-force and with wisdom, both of them great supports for the healing process. By offering 'your conscious self' to 'your Ferah self' in service for healing, you recreate one kind of power that Odin the healer generates for us, hanging upon the Tree of Life.

As we grow throughout our lives, and especially as we strive to live good Heathen lives, our Ferah grows in power and wisdom. We become *feraht,* wise and powerful in the ways of our Ferah soul.

Focusing your awareness on Ferah

You can use these summary paragraphs as meditation-seeds in your quest to get to know your Ferah. Choose one, focus your awareness on it for as long as is useful, and record what you've learned in your Daybook. Then choose another paragraph to do the same. When you have worked through all of them (or as many as you choose), then begin meditation to get a sense of how they all fit together into a living, complex being.

Once you have done all this, you should be in a good position to begin to actually recognize this soul in yourself, and feel some ability to interact with it, get to know it, and work more consciously with it. Be sure to continue recording your insights in your Daybook. I think you can see what I mean, about our souls being complex beings. It really is useful to have our Daybook to keep track of all we're learning about them.

As you're working on these exercises, meditating and writing, you may very well find your Ferah 'writing notes to you' as you work in your Daybook. By this I mean that you will have a sudden understanding, not something you laboriously figured out, but an "Aha!" moment about

Ferah as you write. It is so great when that happens! Something inside you, some insight, just suddenly presents itself to your conscious mind, and the activity of writing often seems to stimulate such events. Your Ferah, or any of the other souls as you work on them, knows you're focusing on it as you write, and seizes the opportunity to communicate directly with you.

Extra: On trees, hierarchy and natural law.

Here is a longer study participant discussion of interest.

<u>Sara Axtell:</u> The times that I have been able to sit with Anishanaabe (a Native American tribe) teachers have made me very aware of the lens we have inherited from the western/Christian threads of our orlog that say that humans are at the top some kind of hierarchy in the natural world. (My understandings of Anishanaabe teachings is that they see it as the exact opposite–humans are the newcomers and so know the least, have to learn teachings of other beings.) When I tell our creation story, I talk about both what we gained in our transformation from trees to humans, and what we lost (rootedness, deep knowledge of place). This is why I love the concept of Ferah-kin. Similar to other kinships, we each contribute what we can and share in what we need.

So, my question is about the relational vs. hierarchical understandings of that story.

<u>My response:</u> I think that the old Heathens at the time the story appeared in writing did not see it as indicating any hierarchical arrangement of trees and people and other

beings. I think the main relational message in the story is the patronage–the gift-giving and taking responsibility–of the Gods toward humans, and this relationship is hierarchical, with the Gods on top. Norse Heathens at that time were very focused on relationships of patronage, obligation, loyalty, fealty, etc., and this story establishes the Gods' valuable patronage of human beings.

But the story itself is probably very old, and the word-relationships do lead us toward an understanding of connections between fjør / Ferah, and trees and other living beings, the Feorhcynn or Kindred of the Ferah. So I think the story is overtly about the hierarchical relationship between humans and Gods, but in a deeper, older layer, also about (non-hierarchical) interrelationships among humans and the beings of the natural world, though this is unspoken in the story. This latter conclusion is only partly based on the story itself, and based more on the study of ancient words, whose histories tell their own stories.

So far, I responded to your question, Sara, from the perspective of what I think the Heathens at the time of writing thought about the story, but didn't say much about my own view. And I have a number of views, but I'll just share one right now. I'm thinking about the lovely book I'm reading, "The Wood-Wide Web", by Merlin Sheldrake. It talks about the enormous and intricate web of fungal mycelia that link trees together into a communication network where the 'words and concepts' are chemical compounds that convey significant meanings to the members of the web.

When we look at tree-webs (forests) this way, we can see a lot more similarity between trees (and their mycelia-partners) and humans than might first be apparent. Both are interlinked by, and dependent upon their communication networks. Both are parts of ecological communities. We exhale CO_2, which trees and plants inhale, and breathe in the oxygen that they exhale. Both engage in competition for resources, and in cooperation, which Sheldrake discusses in his book.

Trees may be rooted in place, but they are very active beings. When I look at the story from this perspective, I see it like this: why don't we ask what the trees gained by transforming their substance into humans? You talked about this yourself, Sara, in response to an earlier exercise (3-1). Trees gained mobility, dexterity, and all the many qualities of humanity. Many people, including us here, see strong links between humans and trees. We can posit that there is a metaphysical web that unites humans and trees, where we are connected by something like metaphysical mycelia. The thing is, most of us don't know how to 'read' this connective network anymore. But what if this connection is somewhere in our metaphysical genome, inherited from our tree-ancestors, waiting for us to learn how to use it through our Ferah souls? This would be the ultimate in relatedness!

As far as a hierarchy of wisdom, I think that humans, trees and other beings all have high potentials for their own forms of wisdom. But trees, rooted in place and living long, maybe have more time and attention to spend on their pursuit of wisdom than people often do, when we spend so much time and energy on non-wisdom-producing activities!

Exploring Ferah

Here are people perching in the aerial roots of a huge Balete tree. This is a nice illustration of the idea of humans and trees sharing a 'root system' of communication between them: the Feorhcynn or living-kindreds in close touch with each other. The people look almost like fruits on the tree-roots. In our own mythology, we can indeed be considered 'fruits' or offspring of the trees.

Extra: A discussion on Ferah and Magic

This is a discussion with Cat Heath, author of the excellent Heathen book Elves, Witches & Gods: Spinning Old Heathen Magic in the Modern Day. *Her insights on the relation between Ferah and magic are well worth reading.*

<u>Cat:</u> (In Book I) You say Ferah is located in the chest, which is helpful. But you also say it's connected with various types of magic too. I have always felt/had an awareness of/ability to manipulate – I guess you could say it's a kind of buzzing, almost electrical-feeling energy. I feel it in trees, plants, other people and animals. It kind of reminds me of the

Exploring Ferah

sensation I get before and during a storm, (only less diffuse, obviously). It's what I work with the most when I am engaging in witchcraft, and have always seen its diffuse forms as a kind of static in the air. Living beings are about the only beings that appear "solid" to me, unless working magic, and then they become more "blurry"/static-obscured. Is this the kind of energy of Ferah? If not, could you describe how Ferah feels (in terms of bodily sensations) to you? I think it would be really helpful for tuning in.

<u>My response:</u> As far as Ferah's location–the Anglo-Saxon words locate it primarily in the chest, but the Old Saxon writings express it most often as "filling" the whole body, and that is how I feel it. I very much think that your description of electric-energy sensing is indeed your Ferah. You're sensing it in all the beings and phenomena through which Ferah flows–trees, animals, people, weather. Ferah-soul partakes of the energies of lightning, thunder, storm, and the earthing of those fire-powers into solid objects, bodies, earth, rock, nature in general.

Human and animal Ferahs come into being during conception, an event that I liken to atomic fusion, and at death they trigger the separation of all our souls through a flash of atomic fission. In between those times, Ferahs can use the same energy for transformation, which I assume is what you do with your magic–weaving that electric/atomic power of transformation into and through the materials and actions you work with to raise and direct your magic.

Another way this energy works, that you pick up so well, is a form of non-verbal communication between us, the entities of nature, Deities, wights. I liken it to the way plants and fungi communicate with each other through chemical signals in the air and soil, and perhaps through other modes as well. It's sort of a floating or tingling awareness that touches our metaphysical nerve-ends, our sensors. I think this fits in well with your description of static electricity. I liken it to being within a magnetic field, where my attention is drawn toward the most powerful magnets. I think this is what happened when the Gods transformed the trees into Ask and Embla: the trees were calling the Gods' attention in the same way, electromagnetically, and responded with those same energies to participate in their own transformation.

You may find it interesting, if you haven't already done so, to use the same sensation-awareness to explore some of the other domains of Ferah's power and interest:

– 'Law' and other types of patterns and rhythms within nature, within humans, and human behavior in societies. How might these feelings we've been talking about relate to the weaving of law-like patterns as they affect our behavior toward each other, toward the Deities, toward nature, toward frith and other patterns that are woven, or that fail to be woven, among us all? This is the broad domain where the *feraht* soul, the wise and devout soul, interacts with the *Feorh-cynn* and the *firihi*, the folk / the community that we are a part of. We often say that some action "feels right, or feels wrong." Is this Ferah, communicating, through our feelings, about lawful or unlawful action, according to its perspectives?

– 'Sacrifice'. What is this, really, in energetic terms? What makes something a 'sacrifice'? What are its effects, short term and long term? How might we re-envision 'sacrifice'

Exploring Ferah

in modern Heathenry, in the context of soul lore and other understandings of our relationships with the Deities, wights, ancestors, and others to whom we might make willing sacrifices? When we feel an impetus toward making a sacrifice, or are willing to listen to a request for sacrifice from others, these urges come through our Ferah soul. How does your Ferah soul 'feel' when you think about sacrifice? What does it do to your energy on various levels?

Think about connections between Law and Sacrifice. I believe they are there, and are important, for us: the Firihi, the Feorhcynn, who must learn to live in balance with one another and with the Earth. Which means there are natural and social Laws we must follow, sacrifices we must make, to achieve the *feraht* goals of the greater good.

I totally think you are on the right track with your Ferah-sensing. Perhaps you have trouble realizing that, precisely because you are so imbedded in it, it is so natural to you. I had that kind of a reaction when I suddenly woke up to my own Ferah, realizing how very 'there' it has been for my whole life, without my seeing it for what it was. It can be, literally, hard to see the forest for the trees!

<u>Cat:</u> Your words really helped to clarify a number of things I've experienced and wondered about for many years, but never had the words for. (An effect your work keeps having on me!)

If what I am experiencing with this sensation is indeed Ferah (and your response suggests that it very well may be), I don't know that I experience it in only my chest or only filling my body. I feel like there is an ebb and flow I notice within this force. When it has ebbed, it's like it goes back to its home in my chest. But when it's in flow, or

Exploring Ferah

recognizes a similar force in another, then it's like it awakens and flares in response, spreading through my body. I feel a similar effect when in ritual.

I didn't initially relate this to communication, but thinking on it, you're absolutely right. There have been times when I've communicated with trees (for example), by putting my hands against the trunk and feeling for the "electrical" feeling force within them. I then ask my questions (using a mixture of verbal communication and allowing images of what I'm asking to flow to them), then "read" the flares and ebbs in that energy. On occasion, I get imagery from them too.

One question I do have though, regards magic. When I work magic, generally what I am doing is imbuing what I create with that living, "electrical" quality (as well as giving the gifts of breath, color / heat / sometimes blood, and incantation / sense / purpose). I guess my question is, that when you refer to Ferah as being like atomic fusion, do you mean that this is something that may continue to grow if given the right conditions vs there being a finite amount of Ferah per person? Because while some magic can leave me feeling tired for a few days afterwards (especially those that involve moving my Hugr out of my body as opposed to my Ghost), something like imbuing a candle or amulet with that possible Ferah energy seems to put it into a flow state. It seems a little more like that stanza from Havamal where we find the words, "one word found another word for me, one deed found another deed for me." Has this been your experience too?

I find myself thinking about Ferah as a connecting force and the collective pattern we weave with our feorh-cynn quite often, and my thoughts often do line up with this

Exploring Ferah

idea of law as layers of action we set down, essentially co-creating / weaving the shape of what we have to work with in the future. I work at sensing and...sinking into this collective pattern quite often and suspect Ferah plays a major role in how I practice "going under the cloak."

<u>My response:</u> That's a really good description you give, of the energy that connects the Feorh-cynn, the energy we all share and can tune into. Your Ferah senses it especially strongly, and is also able to make use of it in a targeted, deliberate way. You sense that electrical force more clearly than I do, and are able to make targeted use of it, as you describe in these and other paragraphs. For me, it's more of a 'knowing' that it's there, a form of deep trust or faith, perhaps, energy that is felt in and through the heart, rather than the magician's ability to sense and manipulate it in the outer world. That's why you are the seidhkona / witch / mage, and I am the philosopher, mystic and spaewife! We both make use of these Ferah-energies, but feel and express them in different ways.

What you say here sounds to me like more evidence of your great facility with Ferah-energy--the ease with which you can tune into it, let it flow through you cleanly in the directions you choose, and continue to be connected with its life-giving forces even when you are not actively doing magic. I think that one reason you are so good at this, and that it flows so smoothly for you, is because both your Hama and your Mod are closely involved and tuned into your Ferah work. Instead of different souls pulling different ways, each wanting to focus on their own modalities and interests, yours are seriously pulling together.

Exploring Ferah

Mod, like Ferah, is connected to the energetic flows of nature, and my sense is that Mod's energy is potentially unlimited if we can keep the flow clear and unobstructed. The problem is, we often can't—Mod can be a difficult soul and often gets in its own way, as well as in the way of our other souls. I experience that a lot, myself. In your case, Mod may be actively supporting Ferah's activities, which gives your Ferah another huge source of energy to draw on, while it may be that your Hugr and Mod are less in tune, and Mod-energy is less available to your Hugr when it fares forth.

It also sounds to me like the La-energy of your Hama is very powerful and present to you, enabling you to magically give La's powers of color / heat / blood to your work. (See Chapter 6 in Book I for more about this.) Then breath brings in Ahma / Ghost, and purpose brings in Mod and / or Hugr. So many of your souls are working together here; this is a blessing and facilitates your magic enormously! It seems to me that this confluence of magical energies would indeed enable the energy to keep going, especially if you bring in the Deities, Elves, etc, as you write about in your book. But it does sound like a primary source of your magical activity and flow is your Ferah and its apparently unobstructed access to the flows of Ferah through natural entities and phenomena.

Exploring Ferah

These exposed roots show how the roots of separate trees mingle together underground, communicating with each other through mycelia and chemical signals. We too, as members of the Feorhcynn, and in a sense the spiritual descendants of trees, have hidden roots embedded in metaphysical layers of nature. We can learn to sense through these root-organs, and to communicate through them in nonverbal ways. Note the similarity between the root-patterns here, and the patterns in the image on the next page.

Exploring Ferah

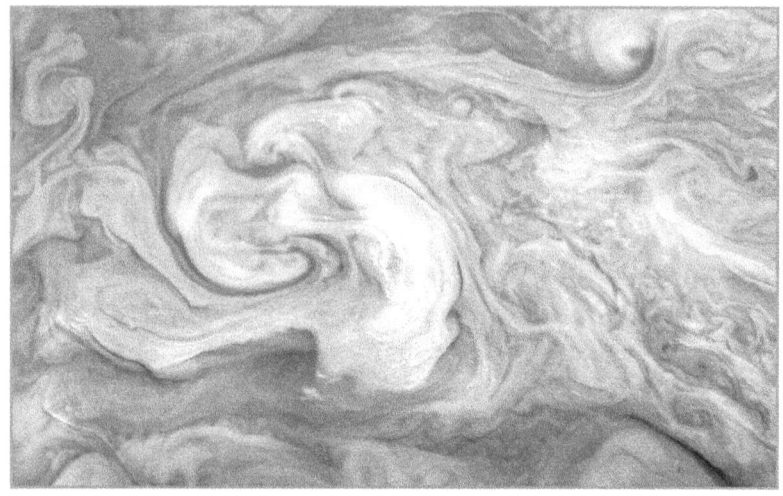

These swirling patterns of Jupiter's weather formations illustrate the swirling of Ahma's patterns that fill the roots of the cosmos. They are also interestingly similar to the root-patterns of trees. Here in these patterns, I see a representation of how Ahma begins to shape itself, or to be shaped by cosmic powers, into incipient individual beings.

Exploring Ahma and Ghost

Chapter 4

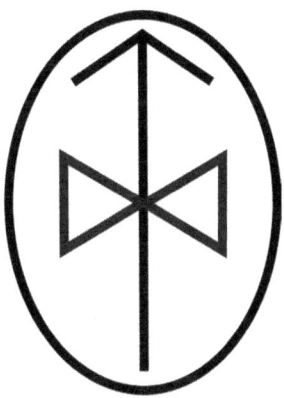

4. Exploring your Ahma and Ghost Souls

{Primary runes in the bind-rune above: Dagaz, Ansuz, Tiwaz, Kenaz.}

Background reading in Book I: Chapter 4, and Chapter 5 except for the section on Wode. Alternatively, read the web articles titled "Ǫnd, Ahma, Ghost and Breath: Their Basic Meanings," and "Ghost Rider: Ahma, Ghost and Wode in Action."

The Natures of Ahma, Ghost, and Deities

I will start out here with a quick summary of the main points about Ahma and Ghost, from Book I. I want to make clear to you which part of what I present here is drawn from ancient Heathen understanding, and which part is my own modern interpretation.

In some ancient languages (Old Norse and Gothic), they used Ǫnd and Ahma to signify all these things: our breath, divine breath and spirit, our own indwelling spirit, other disembodied spirits and wights existing in the environment of Midgard, and some of our intellectual and creative processes. They had Ghost-related words, but they were more descriptive, rather than used as terms for actual beings. Modern Scandinavian languages use *and*-related words for the same purposes: breath, inner spirit, and outer, independent spirits.

In some other ancient languages (Anglo-Saxon, Frisian, Old Saxon, Old High German), they used Ghost-related words to indicate spirits: the divine spirit, spirit embodied within us, and disembodied outside us. They rarely used these ghost-words to mean 'breath.' They had words related to Ahma and Ǫnd, such as Athom and Æðm, and these words usually meant breath, sometimes meant divine spirit. Modern German and Dutch continue with descendants of the same words and meanings (such as Atem for breath, Geist for all types of spirit, in modern German), while modern English has lost the ancient 'breath' word, and applies 'ghost' primarily to outer, disembodied spirits.

In a nutshell, those are the ancient Heathen understandings of these words: Ahma / Ǫnd / Athom, and Ghost, and their various related words. In my soul lore study I've taken these meanings further, wanting to adapt them to a modern context and general Western understandings of what 'spirit' means, while at the same time wanting to keep this adaptation rooted in Heathen lore and meaning. I've also spent years exploring my own spirit in a Heathen context, and I bring what I've learned into my presentation of Heathen soul lore.

So, the results of my adaptation are as follows. I use the Gothic word Ahma to designate the sacred breath-spirit, which I see emanating as a mist from the meeting of the polarities, Fire and Ice, in the center of Ginnungagap. I consider that our own Ahma-spirit, and the Ahma-spirits of the Deities and other beings, all emanate from Ginnungagap. This Ahma is the primal substance-energy of Spirit. It is beyond 'personality' and beyond the drives that influence us here in Midgard. Ahma is pure Potential out of which all spirit-infused Being arises.

As I see it, our Ghost is a soul-skin, a *hama*, that wraps a portion of Ahma within it, turning Ahma into a personal being with its own 'shape': our Ghost. This 'shape' gives Ghost a sense of personhood, with the characteristics, abilities and limitations that pertain to personal beings. I see the Deities in the same light: they are personal, personified Deities because their own Ahma, their limitless Spirit, is wrapped in a godly soul-skin or *hama*, shaping them as personal beings. Thus, our Ghost soul and the personal Deities have this in common: we are all made of unshaped Ahma-spirit wrapped within a shaping Ghost-hama.

In the photo-montage on the following page, the Earth is superimposed against the gigantic storm-patterns of Jupiter's atmosphere. The globe of the Earth represents our Ghost, a defined shape with its own nature and characteristics. The background photo of storm patterns represents Ahma: the surging, billowing movements of Spirit / potentiality within Ginnungagap and Mist-Home, that are not enclosed or limited by shaped, individual beingness.

The difference I see between us and the Deities is that their Ahma is not tightly enclosed within their Ghosts: their Ghosts are porous, elastic, and expansive. The Deities can shift with ease between a state of unbounded Ahma-Spirit, and a state of being a Ghost, a personal spirit-being. This easily-shifting nature of the Deities means that in our own spiritual practice, we can encounter them either way: either as personal Deities, or as unshaped spiritual power / essence / being. Both ways are true to their nature!

I will say that, when we approach them as a living human, the Deities *seem* able to shift from one state to another. In truth, I suspect they exist in all states at once, simultaneously, but it is hard for us to perceive and interact with such multidimensional fluidity. We encounter them in the form we expect or intend: it is our shift of intention, desire, expectation, or spiritual readiness, that causes their apparent shift of soul-shape. We actually just come toward them from a different angle, so to speak, shifting our perceptions of what they are.

Exercise 4-1: Becoming aware of Ahma's habitat

If you've done pretty much any kind of formal meditation, then ways of becoming aware of your Ahma, your transcendent spirit, will probably be familiar to you, and you can build on that. What we're seeking here is your own Ahma-Habitat, just as I suggested you find the 'habitat' where your Ferah soul is strong, clear, at home in its own place.

Still your mind, your senses, soften your breath. Let your imagination free to find a place of stillness, a place where the sacred breath of being is all that exists.

As you rest in this serene stillness, open up a space within your being. Realize that this space is not empty, it is full to the brim of something that you have no words for. Rest in a sense of passive knowing, not active seeking. Rest. Breathe. Sense the undefinable fullness.

Perhaps your senses will respond to this fullness; perhaps your emotions and feelings will respond. You might sense light or color, or tones of music. You might feel love, relaxation, quiet joy, a sense of beauty. You might feel longing and yearning, a distant sense of sadness. You might feel that you are almost 'there' and then it keeps slipping away from you. You might have goosebumps on your skin. It's hard to predict how you will react.

Keep your focus on the emptiness that is really fullness, on the silence that falls after all the echoes drift away. After awhile, after one session or several, let your Ahma hand you a key: a key to its habitat. Let knowledge of this key gently arise into your mind. The key will be something like a token, a reminder, a cue, that will help you return more easily to this state of mystical Ahma-fullness.

This key could be a sense or a feeling, a color or a song, a scene in your mind, a memory, a rune or galdor, a word or name, something material or something immaterial. None of these things are actually part of Ahma itself, they are only tokens or signifiers, aids on your path to seek a full experience of Ahma. You won't need this token after awhile, and you don't need to ask for one now if you don't want or need one.

All of this activity may not happen right away, and you don't want to push it or struggle toward it. Instead of 'trying to reach Ahma', look at it as 'making an opportunity for Ahma awareness to arise within you.' That opportunity you are making, that space within yourself, will fill with Ahma without you straining for it. Just rest gently and let it happen. Again. And again. Let it fill your life with sacred breath, let it breathe its power through you and out into the world.

Study participant experiences

Dale Wood: Because this was my first time trying to find my Ferah or Ahma soul, I initially went looking for it in the woods behind where I live, but it wasn't there. It was where I least expected….. mostly because I didn't know what to expect. Here is what happened: In the minds eye I stepped out my door to go into the woods, rounded the corner, blinked, (or at least that's what it felt like), and was standing in a stone tunnel with stairs going down. I saw the flickering glow of what looked like candle light and followed it. I'm not sure if this is the oil burner tech in me, but when I think of Ferah and Ahma's relationship I think of a flame. You need 3 things to a good and healthy fire. First is the Spark, (Ferah). Second is the air, in this case Ahma is the air feeding the flame. I came to the bottom of the stairs and stood before my Ferah soul. It was thin and wavered in some undetected draft. Definitely not clear, and not the strongest. I began to concentrate on my breathing and cascading like a stream down from the tunnel behind me was Ahma. It appeared prismatic breeze of light and wind and swirled around the circular room, counter clockwise, and clockwise before flowing to the center. Ahma geysered up from under my Ferah soul, and what was once a flame impinging on its own self grew and stood straight up to attention illuminating itself bright as the sun. A pillar of light, in the middle of the circular room, deep below the ground.

<u>Leif Höglund:</u> *My Ahma/Ghost habitat is full the way space is full. More dense in some areas than others, often highly dispersed to the point of extreme lightness. It is ever expanding, and I know that the substances within it are not totally massless, because I physically feel the expansion in my mind. My Ghost presses against my shape to push outward to the wider Ahma. It is the universe within me, and the universe without me.*

<u>Laurie Sottilaro:</u> *You said this would be hard to write about, and you really weren't kidding. If I find a way to express this, I'll come back to it, but I did want to share one line that jumped out at me*

as I was working on this. I think it was instruction, but who can say? "To enter the emptiness, you must first be empty yourself."

<u>My response:</u> It isn't surprising that it's so hard to write about explorations of Ahma: a soul that exists in realms beyond words. About the only way one can do this is to approach it sideways, or through symbols and similes, artistic expression, and through the Deities and spirits, too. The important thing is the experience itself, and our own personal knowledge that grows from experience.

Awareness

Odin's gift of Ǫnd / Ahma / Spirit-Breath carries with it the faculty of consciousness, of awareness. Ahma itself, our transcendent Spirit, is pure consciousness. Not consciousness or awareness *of* anything; it is just *Awareness* itself without any subject (I, myself) or object (anything else) of awareness. *When your awareness rests in Ahma, there is nothing else to be aware of; Ahma / pure Spirit is everything and everywhere.* This is the state of awareness that many forms (though not all) of meditation try to lead us toward.

In my understanding of the gifts that Odin and his brothers gave to Ask and Embla, Odin's gift of Ǫnd was (and is, for each of us) our Ghost: our breath of life and our personal spirit-shape which encloses Ǫnd / Ahma within a soul-skin of personhood and personality. I perceive that Ahma is unshaped, unlimited, unbounded, while Ghost encloses Ahma within a shape, limited and bounded by the dimensions of our personhood. By doing this, Odin gives humans *personal consciousness:* the awareness of "Self" and

Exploring Ahma and Ghost

"Other" that is meaningless at the level of Ahma's pure awareness.

Ghost carries within it much of our sense of everyday, personal consciousness. When we 'lose consciousness' through fainting or coma, our Ghost loosens its connection with our body, including its connection with our brain and the physical awareness that happens through our brain and its interface with our other souls. Sometimes this condition leads to out-of-body and near-death experiences, experiences where we are aware and observant of what is around us (whether in the physical world, or elsewhere), while our brain and body are not showing signs that this awareness is happening, or is even physically possible. The one who is aware in this 'physically impossible way' is our Ghost.

Ghost is also the soul who travels during shamanic journeys or other trance-working that involves very deep trance with full loss of consciousness, as is described about some of the famous Finn-magicians in Norse lore, and described in lore of other cultures as well, including shamans, sages, yoga-adepts, saints, and profound mystics. When we are in a lighter trance, seeking knowledge, spaeworking or soul-faring, this is not likely to involve Ghost-travel: when our Ghost fares forth, we do lose consciousness, we faint and collapse. Obviously, in a light trance our Ghost is still involved through our consciousness, but it is not actually traveling away from our body. The lighter trance experiences, without full loss of consciousness, involve faring-forth of other souls, generally our Hugr, or if it involves shape-shifting our Ellor-Hama (alternate Hama) as well.

As long as we continue breathing, physically accessing Athom-breath, our Athom-Ghost is still connected enough to our body to keep the body alive. When brain-waves are not detected in the body but the body still lives, this means that the Ghost is elsewhere, fully absent from the body, connected only by this thin cord of breath / Athom to keep the body alive.

Our Soul-Spindle

I see our Ghost / 'Spirit', and our Saiwalo / 'Soul' as the two ends of the spindle upon which all our other souls and our Lich, our body, are wound. Ghost is the upper end of the spindle, with its true home in the God-Homes or divine realms, and Saiwalo is the lower end, with its home in Hel, the Womb of Souls. We ourselves, in our shape as ensouled personal beings, extend downwards from the God-Homes and the upper levels of the Tree, and upwards from Hel and the lower levels, meeting in the center in Midgard. This range of Worlds is where we are able to exist as personal beings and individual souls. When our awareness moves outside these realms, out into the realms of cosmogonic processes and of pure Ahma, 'individual personhood' is no longer a meaningful description for our state of awareness.

Continuing this analogy of ourselves as a spindle around which souls and body are wound, we can see the 'fleece', or the substance on the distaff, that is pulled out for twisting into thread, as Ahma itself, the spirit-mist-air floating above Ginnungagap, condensed from the energies of Fire and Ice meeting in the middle. Ahma is the Potential out of which all Being arises. Threads are twisted from the Ahma-fleece and wrapped around our personal spindle of Being, the spindle-shaft that is formed from Ghost and

Saiwalo meeting each other in the middle. These threads are our other souls, each twisted into its own characteristics of thickness, color, smoothness, and so forth, and out of them arise our sense of Selfhood, our Lich and its functions, and our soul-parts or individual functions of our souls.

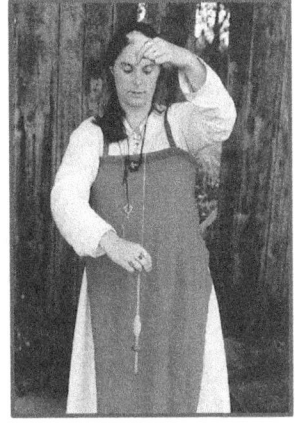

In Exercise 4-1, above, I outlined a meditation for you to connect with your Ahma soul. This is meant to give you a taste of pure Awareness (something you may already have experienced on your own), of the sacred breath moving through your being, into and out of the world, through you as an unobstructed gateway. A state where you-as-personal-being step out of the picture to leave a clear path for the experience and flow of sacred breath and the power of pure Awareness to take over. Now, in the following exercises, we'll turn first to experiencing the interface between Ahma and Ghost, and then to discovering the favored Habitat of your own Ghost.

Exercise 4-2: Tuning Ghost, Ahma and Lichama to the same wavelength.

Our Ghost is at its strongest and healthiest, its most creative and brilliant, when it is well-attuned with the energies of our Ahma, our transcendental Spirit. This attunement is fostered through breathing, and through understanding what breathing really represents for Ghost, Ahma, and Lichama, our living body.

Exploring Ahma and Ghost

Ghost is a soul-skin, like a pod or sack, which encloses and shapes Ahma within it. Though our Ghost is here in Midgard with our physical body most of the time, it also exists within a field of Ahma, outside of Space-Time, that overlaps our physical world. Within this field of Ahma / Ǫnd, our Ghost pulsates (kind of like a jellyfish in the ocean!), drawing ambient Ahma into and out of its Ghost-skin. This is our Athom-Ghost in the process of breathing Athom / Ahma / Ǫnd, the sacred breath, which gives our Ghost life. Our Ghost then stimulates our Lichama, our living body, to perform the same procedure with physical air, which gives our body life. Thus, as we breathe air in and out of our body, our Ghost breathes Ahma / Athom / Ǫnd in and out of its soul-skin. Both acts are necessary for us to remain alive.

For this exercise, I invite you to try to sense this double process happening. First, become still and fall into a comfortable, natural rhythm of breathing. Relax into this state for a little while. Then, as you continue to breathe comfortably, open your awareness and explore this: 'Someone' is actually 'breathing you'. There is a power surrounding and permeating you, and a force that draws that power rhythmically through your whole self, in and out.

If you wish, you can meditate to the sound of ocean waves (live, or recorded) to enhance your awareness of this rhythmic flow of breath. Try to set aside anything, any thoughts, emotions, reactions, that may be obstructing this life-giving flow. As you continue to feel like you are 'being breathed' by your Ahma and Ghost, you may also feel a desire to intone a God-name, a galdor or a song, the Ansuz rune, some other rune that presents itself to you, or simply hum or vibrate your voice. This desire to vibrate often arises naturally when we are in this state. Our Ahma and Ghost are tuning their vibrations together as we do this, and our Lichama instinctively wants to take part in this vibrational tuning. Throw out any inhibitions you might feel, and go with the flow!

This is a deeply revitalizing experience. The vibrations wash all through us, clearing away sludge, throwing open the windows of our Being to the fresh air of pure and beautiful Ahma. Giving yourself a Ghost-bath in this way for a few minutes every day will tune and clear your Ghost and its access to Ahma, as well as your body's access to your Athom-Ghost and the sacred, vitalizing breath that flows through it.

Study participant experiences

<u>Dale Wood</u>: *I'm standing in front of the pillar of light that was once a tiny candle flame in the middle of the room. How am I going to feel the dualistic movement? I stood in front the pillar for a long time feeling its warmth but not able to make it move with me or budge in the slightest. You're very correct with it being a little frustrating, but then it dawns on me. The point of view that my mind's eye is, is my Ghost! The Ghost encapsulates the Ferah and Ahma. Beam me up Scotty!*

I walk to the pillar of light and slowly walk into the column hands stretched out in front of me. The best way to describe the way it felt, I have heard before, but it was referring to anxiety. The term is electric flesh. It was hot and cold, lifting and crushing, expansion and contraction all at once, but it all came in the form of focus. It was in the strangest of ways very centering, and calming. No sense of anxiety, but focus. And for someone with ADHD, that's saying a lot.

Laurie Sottilaro: It felt very unstable, kind of like turbulence. I was only able to hold it for about a minute. It seemed like my ghost inhaled as I exhaled. Does that mean that I need to breathe out completely in order for my ghost to inhale completely? Try 2: I think my Ghost is toying with me. It's insisting on exhaling when I inhale and vice versa. Later efforts: I've spent a good amount of time trying to work with my Ghost as relates to Ahma, with mixed results. Most recently, I found my ghost effectively swimming in a field of Ahma, basically dancing in it. It invited me to join the dance.

I'm very befuddled by my ghost, it seems very playful and energetic, two things I wish I could be, and used to be before all this pain hit. However, while I can see the ghost doing this, I didn't feel anything in particular this time like I felt before when doing this exercise. It felt more like _I_ was supposed to breathe the Ahma, like my Ghost was inviting me to join the party. Oddly enough, this may be the most difficult thing I've attempted on the astral plane (?). This is very befuddling. I wonder why I'm having so much trouble?

My response: Well, this is rather amusing, Laurie, at least to read about......but that definitely does not mean that your exercise and experience is invalid. For all of our exercises, I don't think there are 'right' and 'wrong' ways to do them. All of them are based on my own experiences and insights, but I am not you, and your experiences are of the most significance for you.

Your Ghost's apparently contrary mode of breathing can be regarded in a number of different ways, and I suggest you test these out to see which applies best. 1) Why not? Why shouldn't your Ghost's and Lichama's breathing be this kind of in-and-out dance? Maybe this is natural for you. Or (2) possibly your Ghost

Exploring Ahma and Ghost

and your Lichama are out of sync with each other, and this could show up in various different aspects of your health and your life patterns. This push-me-pull-you pattern of breathing may be a signal for you to explore better ways to synchronize and coordinate between your Ghost and body / Lichama. Or 3) really, playfulness and humor are very valid modes of experience and learning; don't dismiss them, but follow to see where they lead. And enjoy the journey!

Exercise 4-3: Combine tuning with rune-galdor and with forms of art.

If you work with rune-galdors (rune-chanting), you will be familiar with this phenomenon, the flow of power through your voice-vibrations. You can experiment with combining your rune-galdor with your Ahma-Ghost-Lichama tuning. The power will then flow from the fields of Ahma, of divine inspiration, through your Ghost who, with the power of Ghost-Mind *(gastgehygd, gastgemynd)*, shapes that power into the rune you are working with. Then your Lichama galdors your rune into Midgard, backed by the power of Ahma, Ghost, and your powerful Ghost-Mind. (We will speak more of Ghost-Mind later.)

You can use the same process to feed inspiration and eloquence into your speaking, and beauty and power into your singing. All art is produced by the same process: (1) the flow of Ahma-Inspiration into our Ghost, (2) the shaping and directing of our vision by our creative Ghost-Mind, and (3) the expression of the result into Midgard by the power of our Lichama, our living, Hama-ensouled body, with its physical talents of expression and of making.

Exploring Ahma and Ghost

Experiment with the creative tuning process I describe here, applied through rune-galdor or through any inspired art, craft, or talent that you work with.

Study participant experiences

<u>Laurie Sottilaro:</u> *Okay, first time galdoring, and... goosebumps. Also my Ghost is still toying with me. Now it's like batting around balls of... I don't want to say that it's Ahma, but it's more or less just air... And I think the balls are made of itself. Dunno. Glad I can hold two things in mind at the same time though. I'll have to keep doing this and see how things change when perhaps my Ghost is in a little more of a cooperative state.*

<u>My response:</u> *I still think that your work with your Ghost is very promising, interesting and stimulating, but it matters more what you think about it, not me! If it were me, I would just hang out there and play, and not worry about analysis, evaluation, or even about thinking at all.*

The field of Ahma is a very different kind of place. Even though thoughts and ideas flow into us from there, before they flow through our Ghost-Mind they are not at all like our familiar shapes and patterns of thought. They're more like forms of energy that we don't even recognize as thoughts, until they've worked their way through our Ghost-Mind. The little air-balls you describe could well be such puffs of unshaped inspiration.

My take on your difficulty (I could easily be wrong, though) is that you're trying to navigate the fields of Ahma using your customary tools of Midgard-trained thought, awareness, perception. Those don't work well there. I think that your Ghost is trying to lead you into a different way of experiencing the pure being that is Ahma, trying to get you to approach it in ways that you're not accustomed to. Clearly, you are very experienced in

Exploring Ahma and Ghost

astral travel and working on other planes and so forth, and that's not what I'm talking about here. Those kinds of esoteric activities are truly 'work', purposeful and strenuous effort.

Experiencing Ahma is not 'work', it's the opposite of work, it's letting go. It's like the difference between swimming versus floating in the water: one is purposeful action, the other is letting go and conforming to the movement of the water around you, but it takes practice before we're comfortable with it. If you're getting tired and frustrated, let it go for now and go back to it whenever you're ready. But I still say, I think you are doing better than you think you are!

Exercise 4-4: Your Ghost-habitat.

The previous exercises have focused on your Ahma-Ghost-Lichama interface and interactions. Here we're going to just focus on your Ghost soul, on discovering its favored 'habitat' where it feels most at home. My perspective on the Ghost is that it is intimately linked with the Gods and Goddesses and their realms, whichever Deities and whichever religion one follows. For Heathens, we have a rich field of Deities from whom to choose, or who choose us, to form bonds of troth and friendship with our Ghost.

For people who are spiritual but who do not feel any closeness to personal Deities, or any sense that they exist, I believe that these people are most at home within their Ahma-soul. Ahma is non-personal; it is pure Spirit not shaped into personal being. Ahma is a state-of-being that is, I think, congenial to people whose beliefs and interests are more on the 'philosophical' side of spirituality than they are on the 'religious' side of spirituality. Their Ghost, with its Ghost-Mind, is still very much real and powerful within them, as it is within each of us. Perhaps, in some way I don't understand, their Ahma shapes their own Ghost, without the help of any Deities, and this is why these people do not feel connected to personal Deities. If this description applies to you, you may find that your most comfortable Ghost-Habitat is actually the field of Ahma that we've worked with in our previous exercises.

For those who do feel drawn to personal Deities, there are many choices in our Heathen pantheon, each with their own realm or God-Home towards which our Ghost may be drawn. Now, it can be confusing if we want to specifically find our Ghost-Habitat, because our souls other than our Ghost are also likely to have their own connections with our Holy Ones. We may feel drawn to and close to any number of our Deities, and the connections between us and each of the Deities could be due to any of our souls, not only Ghost. Our Hugr could be closely linked with one Deity, our Mod with another, and so forth. There is also no requirement that our Ghost (or any other soul) feel close to only one Deity.

So, to find our preferred Ghost-Habitat(s), we will want to enter into our Ghost-awareness and see what it is like. This will give us clues as to which God-realm is most compatible. Our Ghost is a channel for 'inspiration'; it leads the flow of divine inspiration through ourselves and out into Midgard.

What is it that most inspires you? What excites and elevates your Ghost with inspiration? This could honestly be anything; it doesn't need to be artistic or intellectual inspiration, though of course it may be that. It could be your love of, and dedication to, your family. It could be a love of order, that expresses itself in many ways in your life and gives you a sense of satisfaction and fulfillment when you achieve it. You could be inspired by physical challenges like mountain climbing or sports, by runes, by mysteries and trying to solve them, by preparing food and feeding people, by creating beauty in your garden and your home, by managing people well in your workplace, getting the job done and helping them find fulfillment in the process. Helping others to heal. Anything.

How does inspiration flow through you and express itself through you into the world? What area of life is it, that from within yourself (not imposed by other people) reaches out and challenges you to be the best that you can be?

This may not be something that can be answered during a half-hour meditation! These avenues of inspiration through your Ghost may well change over time, too, with some things being greatly inspiring in our younger years, and changing as we get older.

The practice of awareness that works for this exercise does not involve 'going elsewhere' in your mind. Rather, it is *being aware of your attitudes, feelings and choices during your daily activities, and your daydreams and thoughts, to detect the strongest flows of inspiration and see where they lead.* And (guess what!) working on this question: "What most inspires me?" is a great exercise for your Daybook! This exploration is an act of self-awareness that leads to deep understanding and personal growth. It also can point us toward specific Deities who in some way embody or oversee those fields of inspired activity.

Study participant experiences

Laurie Sottilaro: *After fiddling with this exercise over and over, and then pondering it even more, my family totem (fylgja?) Called me back to other space, and told me that I was indeed overthinking it. Apparently I built that place over many years, I've put a lot of energy into it, and now it's mine. I've asked if this was where I was going to wind up when I died, to which the response was "at first," and it would always be my home, at least as long as I maintained it.*

Personal example

It may come as no surprise that I am greatly inspired by soul lore and practice, by what is often called 'mysticism', and by philosophy that relates to these things. I feel personally close to almost all our Deities, and very close to a fairly large subset of them. I've worked with my own souls for long enough now, that I can understand pretty well which of my souls are drawn to which Deities, and why.

One of our Deities with whom I work most closely is also one of the most obscure, with only a few very brief mentions in the lore. This is Vør, the Goddess of Awareness, whom I see as a daughter of Frigg and Odin, offspring of their own great powers of awareness and wisdom. Frigg is a guide into the realms I want to explore: she tosses her spindle, and I follow its unrolling thread across the wide fields of Knowing. Another Great One with whom I work is Mimir and his Well of memory and inspiration, which inspired Odin himself. My preferred Ghost-Habitat is actually the Well of Mimir, which I experience as "World-Mind". Tuning in to these great

Presences is my way of placing my Ghost into its habitat: where it feels at home, where it deeply wants to be.

This painting shows a lake surrounded by rocky peaks, representing Mimir's Well of memory and inspiration, enclosed by Ymir's rocky bones that undergird all of Midgard. The Well is overshadowed by mighty clouds, representing the fields of Ahma, and also Ymir's heila or brains. I envision how our Thoughts and the inner movements of Ahma and Ghost, as they rise and fall between the Well and the sky and clouds, build up energy and substance as they move. In total, this shows a dynamic image of World-Mind in the process of perpetually coming into being and refining itself. (A Storm in the Rocky Mountains, by Albert Bierstadt.)

Ghost-Mind, Intellect

These subjects prepare us to turn to the next topic: Ghost's powers of Intellect and Mind. Inspiration flows from the fields of Ahma and into our Ghost, very often with inputs from the Holy Ones along the way. As it first flows into Ghost, inspiration is a brilliant, scintillating, but unshaped form of energy, just as Ahma is. It is the task of our Ghost, our spirit-shape with its powerful Mind, to shape that brilliant energy into something that is comprehensible and meaningful for humans living in Midgard.

What Ghost loves to do

Ghost loves this activity, loves to work and play with intellect, inspiration, mind. Some of our other, more practical and Midgard-life oriented souls with high intelligence of their own, can make great use of these Ghost-activities, bringing them into action in practical ways in Midgard.

Here's an example: some people's Ghosts love abstract mathematics. For these Ghosts, mathematics are a delightful game and an inspiration to explore ideas and insights, develop theories and structures of knowledge, and ideas of how they might be applied. But Ghost is not the one who will take that mathematical knowledge and actually build a bridge or a power grid or a computer system out of it. The Mod soul is likely to take the lead in such an activity, using its own great ability to harness abstract or disembodied energy and direct it toward a practical or strategic goal.

This can be seen as teamwork between a wild-haired, absent-minded professor who likes to shout 'Eureka!', and a laser-focused engineer who likes to say 'let's get down to business and make this work.' When they are able to understand and communicate with each other, and work together, great things happen!

To illustrate the flow of this example: Inspiration-energy flows from Ahma into Ghost. Ghost-Mind takes that energy and shapes it into a mental form, in this example, mathematics. Part of this form involves some intriguing, but perhaps impractical, ideas of how it might be used. Mod picks up this idea-energy from Ghost-Mind, concentrates and directs it in Mod's own ways, and applies it to a practical goal in the physical world. Obviously, any pursuit that involves action in the physical world is going to involve our Lichama, our ensouled physical body, including our ability to talk or write about it. And more often than not, our other souls also participate, depending on what we are doing and thinking about.

Thus, inspiration comes from Ahma into Ghost, is shaped by Ghost-Mind, then expressed directly from Ghost-Mind into Lichama, our living body. From Lichama, the inspiration flows out into the physical / social world. The flow of inspiration can be expressed in many different creative ways. Ghost can partner with our other souls and Lichama to create new inventions, new expressions of knowledge and feeling, new ways of doing things.

Ghost loves to play with ideas, and each person's Ghost has its own favorite kinds of ideas it likes to play with. I gave examples of mathematics, inventions, and of artistic creativity, but there are many, many more types of ideas that Ghost can get into. Ghost's love of 'mystery' is another big area, that can cover anything from fictional or real-life crime mystery, to philosophical pondering, to scientific research into unexplained phenomena, to esoteric studies, to enjoying puzzles, riddles and mental games.

Creativity and inspired intellect can reach into and enrich every corner of our personal lives and our lives shared with each other in community. I think it's clear from what I've written that the more open and unobstructed the channels are between Ahma and Ghost on one end, and Lichama and our other souls on the other end, the better able we are to access and harness the flow of inspiration, creativity and creative intellect.

Study participant experiences

<u>Leif Höglund:</u> *My Ghost expresses itself through music, philosophy, meditating, debate, and learning for fun. Like every part of me, it's at the top of a mountain overlooking a crystal clear lake. It's also really important to me that a romantic partner and I have Ghosts that engage one another. It's important to me to have a relationship where the distance between my Ahma and their Ahma is a little less than with anyone else. A hard thing to come by for sure, but absolutely profound to experience.*

......I struggle far more to execute the ideas my Ahma/Ghost comes up with than I do coming up with them at all.

<u>My response:</u> *As for executing Ghost's ideas...yeah, I have to laugh there! That is so typical of Ghost...it's perfectly happy to settle into the realm of ideas and thoughts, create grand designs and structures of creativity or logic in our mind, and then do very little to bring it all into Midgard!*

This is where the Mod-soul is so useful, with its impetus toward action, achievement, and excellence in any realm of human activity. Ghost, Mod and Lich-Hama make an excellent team: Ghost comes up with the ideas, insights and creative impulses, Mod figures out how to express them and make them happen in This-World and gives us the energetic urge to do so, and Lich-Hama gives us the physical and social-interaction abilities through which to express all of this.

Disembodiment

I think you may have picked up on the fact that Ghost's talents are *disembodied*, not embodied in the physical world. Ghost needs our other souls and Lichama to express itself into Midgard. On its own, Ghost lives in abstract space: in the fields of Ahma, in the God-realms, in the world of ideas and thoughts. It is not strongly tied to Midgard on its own; it depends on our other souls and Lichama to anchor it in Midgard, or else it will go drifting off on its own into ethereal worlds.

Ahma, Ghost, and Saiwalo are the souls who have the easiest time of it when we go through the physical death-process. They are already so attached to their afterlife-realms, even during our physical life, that it isn't normally that hard for them to just let go of our body and settle into their natural habitats. Some of our other, more Midgard-oriented souls may put up a much bigger fight or struggle.

It does sometimes happen that the Ghost becomes a haunt in Midgard, when it refuses to let go even though it can't really hang on, either. This is part of the larger topic of soul-wounds and soul-healing in general, which is beyond the scope of this volume of soul lore. But to make just a brief reference to it: I think that when a Ghost becomes a haunt, it has lost its 'filling' of Ahma-Spirit-Breath. It's like a deflated balloon. It is no longer connected to life in Midgard through Athom / Breath, nor through the Lichama and the other souls, who all have their own fates after physical death. It has also lost its connection with the Deities, with the field of Ahma, and with the flow of inspiration which triggers intellect and creativity. This

Ghost-Haunt floats around in its own little world within the spirit-domains of Midgard, a shape without inner substance and without connection to its natural habitat. It's my sense that this cannot happen to Ghost, unless it somehow chooses that path, by refusing all of its other natural afterlife paths into the God-Realms or the field of Ahma.

Nurturing your Ghost

It is totally unnecessary for Ghost to suffer such a fate, and in fact Ghost has to struggle against its own nature if it chooses the path of the haunt after death. The lesson to learn here is to keep our Ghost healthy during life. Foster the activities of Ghost-Mind, allow it to play with ideas and thoughts, to develop and use its intellect in ways that it is drawn to, even when you don't see any 'good reasons' or 'practical applications' for it (though of course, practical applications are good, too). Just think about and learn about things that are interesting, for no other reason than because they're interesting. If you put those ideas to use at some point, fine; if you don't, that's fine too.

Ghost is an intellectual hobbyist, it likes to sit and tinker for hours with some abstract idea or thought or learning, detached from practical demands of everyday life. Give your Ghost some time for doing this, whenever you can. Allow inspiration, intellect, and creativity to flow richly through you and express themselves into the world in your own ways.

It's vitally important to create space and encouragement for children to engage in such activities as well, allowing their Ghost-Minds to expand and grow. I think that modern life does not encourage such development in children, doesn't encourage the activity of just letting thoughts and ideas and creative urges roam freely in a quiet, undemanding, nonjudgmental space-time. Heathens with a good understanding of our souls, and who are connected with children in any way, should work to counteract that trend. Especially by setting the example themselves: that is always the best way to teach children! There are so many enjoyable ways to allow intellect and creativity to run loose in an interactive environment between loving, insightful adults and lively, curious children.

If your Ghost is drawn to relate to the Deities in personal form, develop and foster those relationships, which will continue after physical life is over. If your Ghost is more drawn to abstract, impersonal Ahma / Spirit, work on keeping energy and consciousness flowing freely between your Ahma and your Ghost. In this situation, it seems likely that after death your Ghost will dissolve back into Ahma, since you will not need a Ghost-body with its personal characteristics and relationships in the afterlife. Thus, it behooves you to keep Ghost and Ahma closely integrated through spiritual practices such as Athom-work during life, so they can easily merge in the afterlife.

What I've described in the foregoing paragraphs are all ways to nourish Ghost, to keep it healthy and well-connected, rooted and balanced.

Exercise 4-5: Expressing your Ghost

Think about what I've written here and describe ways that your Ghost expresses itself in your life right now. Do you feel any urges or suppressed enthusiasm from your Ghost, to express itself in new ways that you haven't yet pursued?

Were there ways that your Ghost was more actively expressive in the past, that have kind of fallen out of your life now? What do you feel that your Ghost needs now, to thrive, be healthy and at its best?

Exercise 4-6: Choosing words for Ghost-practice

Study the section "Ghost and Mind", and Tables 6 and 7, in Chapter 4 of Book I, or the web article "Ǫnd, Ahma, Ghost and Breath". There are many terms described there, in different Germanic languages, for concepts such as thought, meditation, spiritual practice, intellectual abilities, sources of inspiration. These can be considered as soul-parts, faculties and attributes of your Ghost-soul. (Words relating to Ahma are also included here, since Ahma and Ghost are so closely related.) Choose some of these words that relate best to your understanding of your Ghost, or to things about your Ghost that you want to explore and develop. You can use these words to shape a Ghost-practice for yourself, and also as a checklist to make sure you are not overlooking any of Ghost's many abilities.

For this exercise, list the words you want to focus on now, and write about what they mean to you and how you will use them to shape your Ghost-practice at this time. If you have other words, in modern English or another language, that fit better for you than the ones in the tables, then write about them, instead.

Exercise 4-7: Fostering the Ghost of children

If you are presently associated with children as a relative, teacher, caregiver, family friend, what are some ideas that you could pursue with them, to promote their freewheeling exploration and growth of their own Ghosts, and yours along with theirs? Activities with children often inspire our own sense of creativity and exploration; it's a win-win endeavor!

Obviously, there is no need for you to actually use the rather intimidating word "Ghost" with children, unless you are working with them in an openly Heathen context and you think they would understand your explanation about it. But caution is recommended here; you don't want to scare the children instead of inspiring them! And of course, you could always use the more neutral term 'spirit' with them, instead, if you feel it's needed. For children, activities are more likely to capture their attention than long-winded explanations, so special terms such as 'ghost' may not be necessary. Just focus on activities.

Study participant experiences

Leif Höglund: *I think an important aspect of my Ghost development was my parents getting my brother and me involved in music education from a young age, and I played wind instruments for eight of my twelve years of music education, and was in chorus for another. Feeling the way the breath moves and the way you need to adjust your personal intonation to match the ensemble feels like a certain dissolution of the space between our Ahmas, and I think music education is an incredibly important part of childhood development, if it is possible to include it.*

Exploring Ahma and Ghost

This campfire sending out sparks in the wind illustrates the actions of Wode. Our Ghost-soul is made of Elemental Air and Fire, and when ignited by the power of Wode and Wind, it shoots out sparks and flares of fiery inspiration, or of wode-rage, in all directions.

Chapter 5

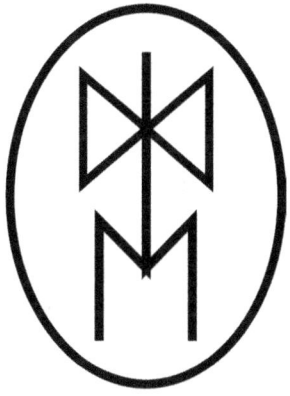

5. Ghost and Wode

{Primary runes in the bindrune above: Dagaz, Ehwaz, Sowilo, Eihwaz, Kenaz, Hagalaz, Gebo.}

Background reading: The section on Wode, in Chapter 5 of Book I, or in the web article "Ghost Rider."

Now, here we are on the subject of "Wode / Oðr". Unlike most of the soul topics that I cover here, I am not going to offer guidance into experiential learning of full-on Wode! It is too powerful, too potentially unbalancing, to pursue without solid training, and ideally with in-person guidance. If you have such a background, you can work on the ideas I discuss here on your own. But here we'll talk more about a general understanding of Wode and its effects and uses, how it can be trained, and I'll offer some suggested references for further learning. A lot of what I have to say about Wode is in the background reading listed above, and I won't repeat that material here.

Wode / Oðr is a form of inspiration. We can look at inspiration as a spectrum of energy, running from very slight, humdrum forms of inspiration like 'hey, let's go out for a walk now', to inspiration that is so intense and overwhelming that it runs into actual insanity, even though it is 'genius-level insanity.' There are any number of famous artists and other geniuses who are known to have ranged from mildly eccentric, to unhinged, to suicidally insane.

"Wode" describes the degree of inspiration at the higher end of this spectrum: a level of inspiration that can have profound impacts on our mental and physical health, our behavior and our conduct of life, depending on how it is controlled and directed.

Dysfunctions and imbalances of Ghost

All of our souls, except for Ahma, have potentially dysfunctional characteristics, as I mentioned about Ferah with its possible hyper-alertness, hyper-reactivity, hypersensitivity, fears and phobias, and negative coping mechanisms that arise from these, such as deceptiveness, cruelty, or withdrawal. For Ghost, its potential dysfunctions stem from excessive Wode, and / or from an inability to handle Wode. Severe problems that result from this can include mania and manic states, schizophrenia, psychosis, hallucinations, hysteria, obsessiveness. Seizures and other neurological dysfunctions, such as dizziness and fainting, can result from powerful wode that 'blows the circuits' of the nervous system, which is unable to handle that much spirit-power flowing through it.

Another potential dysfunction arises from the personality disorder that in old Norse lands was called 'berserker' personality, and referred to as *oðr*, or wode. I distinguish two forms of berserker behavior. One is the warrior's trance that leads to outstanding performance in battle, and resistance to injury and fear, at least until the battle is over. People in other very intense situations, such as life-saving rescue attempts or their own life-threatening circumstances, can enter this same kind of super-energized trance, as well. This type of berserker phenomenon can be of great benefit, as long as it is limited to temporary circumstances where that kind of ability is needed, and the wode 'stands down' when no longer needed. This is warrior-wode under control, loosed only under the appropriate circumstances.

But the sagas also tell of always-on berserkers, physically powerful and brutal people who were perpetually on the very edge of battle-rage, and how dangerous, predatory and exploitive these people were toward their own communities. This is clearly a form of sociopathy, devoid of empathy and respect toward cultural norms and ethical behavior. This is a state of perpetual berserker-wode-ness, with little or no personal attempt to control or direct it toward beneficial purposes.

These are extreme cases of an overabundance of uncontrolled wode. Much more commonly, all of us, I think, are subject to mild fixations of our Ghost-focus, very mild forms of wode. This happens when we get stuck in head-space, in our own little worlds, and don't want to leave: cyber-space, book-space, TV-space, game-space, hobby-space, creative space, sports-space, getting stuck on certain ideas or preoccupations. Someone tries to interrupt us, our duties and responsibilities intrude, and we get annoyed.

These are mini-wodes: minor fixations of Ghost's focus that it doesn't want to get out of, and minor reactions of irritation and impatience when we are nevertheless pulled out. Unfortunately, some people react with more than a mini-wode, spilling over into anger, blaming, harmful behavior, even rage and abuse, instead of mild irritation and annoyance.

Ghost likes to focus on its own interests, and it tends to be careless about competing matters, like our body's need for sleep and exercise, our family's (and our own) need for healthy family meals and time together, our job and home responsibilities, our social life, and the desires of our other souls. Ghost would like nothing better than to be allowed to focus where it wants and do its own thing, all the time! (I speak from long experience here…)

There are many factors in our lives that compete with this desire of Ghost, and in the long run, it is in Ghost's own best interests to live a well-balanced and disciplined life. This is Ghost's best defense against eventually becoming overwhelmed and seriously unbalanced by wode, while at the same time allowing a reasonable amount of time in our life for Ghost's interests, and its own growth into its mature powers. Ghost is a powerful and brilliant soul, with many gifts to give to us and to the world. But it should not be in sole charge of how we live our life as a whole; it very much needs to be counterbalanced by our Lichama and all our other souls.

Exploring Ghost and Wode

A note on creative Wode and substance abuse

(My response to a study group discussion on recovery.) The use of mind-altering substances, in all cultures, is one way that people access the energy of wode and the insight and creativity it can lead to. The problem, at least within our own modern culture, is that this particular pathway is so easily abused and has a whole lot of problems associated with it, problems that far outweigh, and eventually overwhelm, any creative flow that might be associated with it. And one of the problems is that people on this path become unconsciously trained to assume that this is the only way to reach, control, or shape their creativity. Then, when they step off that path and become clean, they feel they've lost that connection, or that route for wode to flow into their lives.

This is basically a good thing, because wode flowing in this way too easily turns into very negative forms, like frenzy, fury, mania, or dissociation from the everyday world. The use of substances, at least as it is currently done in our culture, blocks a person from being able to control and direct wode, and so it runs wild within us. But the last thing we want, is to apparently lose our creativity in the process of recovering from substance abuse.

For a person in recovery, it's entirely up to you, how much creative wode-flow you might want to invite into your life, and what form you'd like it to take. I would suggest: nurture your curiosity. Ghost can shape the inflowing wode in many different ways, and 'creative' projects in the form of arts or crafts is only one of those ways. Another big way is intellectual activity. Encourage

Exploring Ghost and Wode

your own curiosity by exploring new things, new areas of knowledge. Learn things! Things that fit in with the way your mind thinks. Maybe history? Some areas of science, where you can learn a bit about chemistry or astronomy or the science of weather, just for the sake of interest? Maybe problem-solving? Writing, just for yourself? Music? You might enjoy puzzles and brain games, or working with craft kits.

You don't need to soar off on wild flights of imagination if that's not your way. A quiet sense of satisfaction because you've solved some puzzling thing, or put something together, or learned some interesting new thing, works just as well to energize your Ghost and the flow of Wode that is right for who you are, at this time in your life.

The main thing is this: never assume that the full and beautiful creative expression of your Ghost depends on the use of any substances. Rather, it depends on getting to know your Ghost and its own healthy desires for creative expression.

Controlled development and use of Wode

Some of us seem to be mentally and neurologically prone to wode-ness, or drawn toward activities that involve wode-states. I mentioned earlier about artists and other creative or intellectual geniuses who sometimes cross the bounds of sanity, and about berserker-wode in its uncontrolled and its controlled states. There is also the form of wode that can lead to trance-working, altered states of consciousness, spirit-possession, second sight and prophecy, which again can happen in uncontrolled or in controlled ways. And the final form of intense wode that I'm aware of involves

Exploring Ghost and Wode

mystical experiences and ecstatic spiritual states, transcendent experiences of the God-Realms, the fields of Ahma, and profound explorations of phenomena that lie outside of Time and Space. All of these things I list here can offer priceless gifts to humanity, but can come at a high price to the individual giving it, being driven by wode up to, and at times over, the edge of sanity or of balanced living.

The solution for such individuals is not to reject or turn against their wode-inspired Ghost, which seriously backfires in most cases, anyway. The solution is to train themselves to manage wode, to nurture and develop their Ghost appropriately, and to live a healthy, well-balanced life that respects the needs of their Lichama and their other souls as well. This applies also to those of us whose Ghost is not overwhelmed with genius-level wode, but who want to develop our own Ghost-abilities to the highest level that works for us, without unbalancing the rest of our life.

I want to note something important here: if there isn't much of a flow of wode into our Ghost, our Ghost is going to be all over the map, not focused on excellence in one or a few areas, but just roaming around as a dilletante, having a taste of this and that, here and there. If there is too much wode flowing in, meaning more than we personally are able to handle, then Ghost becomes fixated and goes off the deep end. It's good to seek a happy medium. Let Ghost relax and have fun with its hobbies and interests, but also allow and encourage it to seek excellence in some area so it can develop its full powers, which requires training, experience, and a well-managed flow of wode.

Ghost-training is demanding and takes time; I can't cover it here in a few pages, nor do I have the necessary

Exploring Ghost and Wode

expertise to cover it fully. But I will offer suggestions for how you can go about it. The suggestions are pretty obvious, and the emphasis is on training and self-discipline. The purpose of this is not only to develop a specific ability — artistic, intellectual, esoteric, whatever — but *to control and channel the wode that pours into your Ghost,* ensuring that there is enough but not too much. Both focuses of training are equally important: skills, and wode-management. Skills are how you manage wode, while wode inspires you toward high achievement with whatever skills you work to develop. My suggestions here will also, I hope, be useful for parents and grandparents who are considering ways to foster the healthy development of their children's souls. Here are domains of action in Midgard life where Ghost and Wode play major roles.

Artistic Wode: This covers all forms of art: representational, literary, movement arts, music, drama, craft-work, etc. The key here is to pursue disciplined training in your art, whether through classes, apprenticeship, or self-training using resources provided by experts. Daily practice, even for brief periods, will have a cumulative and beneficial impact on your Ghost's abilities and your control of your wode.

Warrior-Wode: Considering how dangerous this is when uncontrolled, if you have a tendency in this direction, it's essential for you to pursue some kind of martial arts training that emphasizes not only martial skill, but also character development, ethical action, self-control, and if at all possible, management of spirit-energy such as *Qi / ki / chi*. (This is even more crucial for children, to develop their ethical sense and self-control right along with their physical abilities.)

As far as I know, the Eastern martial arts have more prospects for this type of enhanced training than other kinds, but I'm not very knowledgeable in this area anymore. (I did reach the highest level below black belt in Korean karate, but that was many years ago! But the class did offer ethical guidance and training in management of ki, very useful, and I enrolled my young, boxing-mad son in such classes as well, which did him a lot of good.)

Also in this category is the practice of turning warrior-wode energy toward the skills needed for emergency response and rescue, where physical ability, targeted skills, and laser-focus are essential. As you undergo training and experience in this area, consider the role of wode in powering and focusing your abilities on the job, and harness that wode to increase your effectiveness in a controlled way.

<u>Intellectual Wode:</u> Enhancing your Ghost's intellect may or may not result in any productive output. It isn't necessary that it do so, though it's fine if it does. Here you are developing the skills of abstract thinking, whether through rune-lore, various forms of philosophy, development of theories and ideas, scientific pursuits, history, languages, mathematics, mental challenges, or whatever route your Ghost takes.

You are training your skills just as much as an athlete does, but the results may or may not be very visible to others. You might write, teach, lecture, have a career in research, and these are very good ways to stimulate your Ghost and share your knowledge with others. But some people have jobs or careers that are not strongly focused on intellectual matters, yet they still love to learn and explore ideas unrelated to their employment. If that's you, then challenge yourself to become an expert in some area of knowledge you're interested in, just because you are interested. Like me, with Heathen soul lore! You don't have to have a paid job or career in some area, to become satisfyingly knowledgeable in it.

<u>Esoteric Wode:</u> I include here trancework and altered states of consciousness, seidh-work, oracular and rune work, magic of various kinds, and other types of wode-enhanced mind-states that are used in esoteric and magical contexts. There are a number of dangers and pitfalls inherent in this kind of work. We need to start slowly and carefully, pay heed to expert guidance, and be sensitive to our own reactions and the effects our work is having on ourselves and on others.

Here, I'd like to recommend several books that offer very useful training in this regard, the first two by Diana L. Paxson. My primary recommendation is *Trance-Portation: Learning to Navigate the Inner World*. This is in the form of step-by-step lessons; it offers precautions and excellent guidance, and I recommend it for training your Ghost and wode in matters of altered consciousness. Diana's *The Way of the Oracle: Recovering the Practices of the Past to Find the Answers of Today* is likewise an enlightening book. Another very relevant and useful reference for developing and directing esoteric wode is Cat Heath's *Elves, Witches & Gods: Spinning Old Heathen Magic in the Modern Day*. Josephine McCarthy's *Magical Healing* has good advice for maintaining and restoring physical and psychic health during strenuous esoteric work, as does her series on *Magical Knowledge*.

Mystical Wode: Finally we come to mystical wode, which bears some similarities to what I call Esoteric Wode, and some differences. The methods of both types of endeavor may be very similar, but there may be some differences in the aims. Mystical Wode is focused on direct personal contact with spiritual realities: Deities and their Realms, Ahma / unconstrained Spirit, spiritual beings such as ancestors, Landwights, and others, as well as with fundamental cosmogonic processes outside of our familiar Time and Space. The latter includes phenomena that in our belief are pictured as Ginnungagap, the Wells of Wyrd and Mimir, Hvergelmir, Ragnarök, how things happen in mythic Time and Space, the World-Tree / Yggdrasil, processes of wyrd and ørlög, the mystical roots of myth, and similar spiritual explorations.

This is a very personal endeavor; one's experiences are sometimes difficult to communicate and share, and there isn't much practical application for it, except that it eventually tends to reshape one's whole life and understanding!

When wode strikes in this area, its strongest form presents as mystical rapture, which is a phenomenon known in all religions that I am aware of, both major and off-the-beaten-track religions. A person may fall unconscious, as their Ghost is 'raptured' away to the God-realms, and they may receive revelations. Some sects 'speak in tongues.' In some religions, physical phenomena may occur, such as stigmata among mystical Christians, where the wounds of Christ's crucifixion appear on the

Exploring Ghost and Wode

body of the mystic, temporarily or permanently. Hindu yogis and Tibetan lamas are said to undergo paranormal physical phenomena, as are shamans, monks and nuns in many traditions. Inexplicable illnesses, often neurological in nature and sometimes including paranormal phenomena, often drive the inner growth of traditional shamans and mystics.

This degree of powerful wode flowing through mind and body is difficult for a person to handle, and sometimes occurs without their choice or wish for it. It's like a rushing torrent too strong to stand against. Milder forms of this wode, undertaken voluntarily, serve as a pathway to the Deities rather than as a hurtling torrent. Both lead to the realms of Spirit, but their level of power, difficulty, and life-disruption varies! Diana Paxson has another book that offers useful insights for handling some kinds of mystical wode: *The Essential Guide to Possession, Depossession, & Divine Relationships*.

Most modern Heathens have a good deal of experience interacting with our Deities, though this may not involve a heavy state of rapture-wode, but rather a lighter state of altered consciousness. Some of our Deities, such as—obviously—Woden / Odin, may be into wode-based relationships with humans, more than other Deities. Really, the best way to constructively work with mystical wode in our faith, is to work with whichever Deity is sending it your way. It's a personal thing between you and that Deity, and can be experienced in many different ways. An article of mine, *Earth, Water, Wind and Fire: Elemental Modes for Relating to the Deities*, offers some ideas for mystical explorations for our Ghost and our other souls as well.

It's essential to follow all the usual guidelines for Ghost-health and overall healthy and balanced lifestyle as you pursue these Ghost activities. Maintain sound friendships with mature Heathens and others who can keep you grounded and in touch with Midgard. Pay attention to your other souls, your Lichama, your family and friends, your job, everyday life. Use self-discipline to ensure that your explorations into mystical wode are neither overwhelming the rest of your life, nor drifting off into shapeless airhead-land, taking your brain along, too. Making use of your Daybook is an essential method to keep you on track with this.

Exercise 5-1: Evaluating wode in your life

Without throwing yourself headlong into a torrent of wode, consider whether and where wode has played any role in your life. In Chapter 4, you explored areas of inspiration in your life, and thought about ways you'd like to follow a personal Ghost-practice. Now, think about the role of wode in those things.

Is wode something you want to get into, to encourage more of in your life? If so, in what direction do you want to encourage it to flow, and what training and discipline will help with that?

Or do you feel you have about the right amount flowing in? Even if so, do you still need to consider more about what direction it is flowing, and what training would shape and empower it further?

Or is a lot of wode flowing into you, and you have trouble managing it? If that's the case, are there suggestions in this chapter, and in the recommended references, that might point you in a direction to manage it better?

Study participant experiences

<u>Laurie Sottilaro:</u> *As a trained shamanic practitioner, I'm somewhat familiar with wode. That energy can easily carry one away in Journey work, and it's happened to me more than once. Control is an important lesson. Arguably wode has come up in my professional life as well, in the form of the coder's trance. In this state, I could lose myself for hours while I worked on a given project. Since I plan to continue my shamanic Journey work, I do intend to continue working with wode. It's a uniquely creative energy, that almost fizzes. This takes meditation training, and a whole lot of focus.*

Whether I need to get more flowing in or not I'm not sure, but that seems to me to be something that changes day-to-day. It flows in, where it gets transformed into whatever is being done, or it gets used directly depending on the task. I do have signs of having too much flowing in, the ill health and occasionally the difficulty focusing. It takes energy to control energy, and I don't always have that basic level of energy. It can wreak havoc on me. Grounding and centering are incredibly important.

Chapter 6

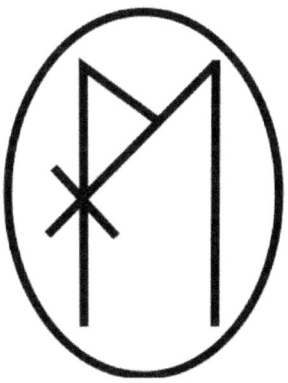

6. Exploring your Hama, Lich-Hama and Ellor-Hama

{Primary runes in the bind-rune above: Ehwaz, Raidho, Gebo, Laguz, Ior, Wunjo.}

Background reading: Chapter 6 in Book I, or my web article "The Shape of Being Human: The Hama Soul."

Our Hama is, as I understand it, the soul which shapes our physical body, our Lich, and confers on it the ability to speak and take action in Midgard. These two entities combined, our Lich and our Hama, are called the Lichama or Lich-Hama: the living body ensouled by Hama. Our Lichama provides a channel for our other souls to express themselves into Midgard; all Midgard activity of our other souls is dependent on Lichama. Our other souls also depend on Lichama for much of their information-input from the physical world. Lichama serves another vital function as well: it is a physical anchor for our other souls, holding them in Midgard and serving as a center of gravity for the Midgard life and activity of the souls.

The Hama consists of three parts: (1) the *La*, the spiritual energy of the blood that gives warmth and reflects in the health of the hair and skin; (2) the *Læti*, comprising our voice, physical actions, behavior and mannerisms, and (3) the *Litr*, our face and our total outward appearance, including the 'impression' we make. It is the Litr through which our souls shine, or fail to shine, into the Midgard plane.

Hama and Lichama are the basis of our ability to express ourselves: through our words and the intonations of our voice, through body language, gestures and actions, through facial expressions, and behavior in general, and through our scent, as well, though that is often covered up cosmetically in modern life. As our Hama shapes our physical body, it also shapes our social expression, our behavior, and our social persona. These comprise our *Litr* and *Læti:* our soul-infused, unique personal appearance, our unique voice, and our actions, mannerisms, behavior. The third part of Hama is the *La*, the spiritual energy of the Hama soul that is carried especially in the blood, the hair, and the warmth of the body.

All of our other souls need to go through Hama and Lichama in order to participate in our social persona's actions. Thus, the character of our Hama shapes the physical, Midgard expression of all our other souls. This is no small thing, and it leads us to consider how well our Hama, Lichama, and other souls mesh with each other, or fail to mesh well, and are thus prevented from full expression in Midgard.

I don't want to go into any detail about dysfunctions of the Hama, as I have with our other souls, because these dysfunctions are of a very sensitive and upsetting nature, having to do with handicaps that impact one's ability to take physical action, to express oneself, or to behave in expected ways in social contexts. There is an article of mine posted on my website, where I talk about a specific method of Hama-healing that includes a little guidance for using soul lore to help compensate for harm to one's Hama: *Disir, Hama and Hugr as Healing Partners.*

I don't mean to make light of these matters by suggesting that such compensations solve the problem; of course they don't, though there are many examples of truly heroic people who have developed amazing and empowering responses to their challenges. But if one is interested in applying soul lore to one's life in all possible ways, the article I mentioned above offers one suggested approach. I hope that other Heathens, who have more experience, knowledge and training in these areas than I do, might be able to see and develop other ways that soul lore could help one deal with such difficulties. A useful method for assessing and repairing day-to-day stresses and strains on the Hama and hamingja is offered in Cat Heath's book, *Elves, Witches & Gods: Spinning Old Heathen Magic in the Modern Day* (pp. 109-110).

Hama as a covering

Hama is a covering made of soul-stuff, full of soul-power, which shapes not only our physical body itself, but the abilities, behavior, expressions, and activities of our physical body and brain. It gives us a physical body which acts in physical space, and it gives us a 'social body', a social persona, which acts in social space.

Here's something to think about: in all of human history up to modern times, our physical body and its expressiveness has been the necessary medium for all of our social interactions. With the rise of writing, printed books, and later telecommunication, this began to change. Now, with the invention and takeover of cyberspace, much of our social interaction takes place with only minimal participation of our Lichama. We need our hands or our voice to input our words and pictures into cyberspace, we need our eyes and ears to receive input that others send us through cyberspace. But those are not actions we share with others, they are not physical interactions directly with other people. Instead, they are just our own interactions with machines.

Now, with the rise of various types of interactive video space, we do get a look at other's faces, hear their voices, but it is still not the same as physical presence and interaction, when it comes to our Hama soul. It's a question worth exploring: how much of our *Litr*, our *Wlite*, our soul-infused and soul-energized appearance, transfers over cyberspace, in comparison with face to face interaction?

Yes, we see each others' faces with our eyes, we hear their voices with our ears. It's certainly a huge improvement over social isolation, and it's great for getting together over long distances. I wonder how much is still missing, though, of the intangibles and the spiritual energies that our Hamas send out to, and pick up from, each other when we are face to face? This is a subject for future soul lore research! And for the first step toward this research, let's turn to our exercises now, to begin sensing our own Hama and learning more about it.

Exercise 6-1: Sensing your Hama

Focus your awareness and enter into a still space. Sense your Hama as a covering. Feel yourself covered in something: what is it? Skin, clothing, fur, blanket, shell, metal, camouflage, sand or grit, feathers, ornaments, bark, streamers, spikes, thorns, swirling winds, steam, ice, scales, tattoos....it could be anything. What do you perceive that your covering consists of? And why do you think your Hama takes that particular form of covering, or why does your awareness perceive that Hama takes this form?

What does this form of covering, or your perception of it, tell you about your Hama and yourself? Does it feel constrictive, protective, welcoming, irritating, defensive, offensive, reclusive, blatant, shining, beautiful? Does your Hama covering express your true self, or does it hide it?

Study participant experiences

<u>Laurie Sottilaro:</u> *My covering seemed to be a compound thing, like the dermis and epidermis. As I shifted form, the inner thick layer stayed the same but the outer went from smooth to furred, as it folded in on itself to produce the hairs. I suspect my Hama is malleable like this because I've been shifting shapes pretty freely since I was tiny, I learned how at seven years old. As I said, the structure of it seems to resemble human skin, which probably comes from my biology background. I doubt that's what it actually looks like. It seems like a cell wall on the outside, permeable somehow, but selectively. It feels very elastic, or plastic, I guess, because it doesn't feel tight at all. Given my propensity for masks, this probably makes a lot of sense, and both expresses my true self*

and its ability to shift (I have a tendency to wear metaphorical masks a lot), and conceals it in that it only has one form at a time. My Hama is amoebic; who knew?

<u>My response:</u> I hope you don't mind, Laurie, that I laughed in delight at your statement about your Hama being amoebic! Just like I laughed when I realized my Hama takes on the appearance of ugly-colored, greasy, smelly fur when I'm around people that I want to stay away from. I feel like Hama's creativity has a sense of humor to it that I find really amusing and delightful. As I think about this, I get the feeling that this humor, enjoyment and creativity is one more way that Hama can shape who we are and who we project out to others around us. Hama is a shapeshifter, and maybe one of its lessons to us is to be flexible, not go overboard in how seriously we take ourselves and the way we present ourselves to the world.

<u>Leif Höglund:</u> I am covered in thick dark soil of the deep woods. Slightly damp and pleasantly cool – I am made of decay. I am compost rebuilt and recycled over and over. From sun to earth, from earth to plant, from plant to animal, from animal to earth. It feels temporary, like the shroud keeps me from bursting out of my skin into some beyond. It is almost like a sapling pushing out into the morning light for the first time.

It is cool. It is quiet. My shroud is the texture of thick, wet moss. Springy. Absorbent. Temporary. So very temporary. Perhaps even in this lifetime.

I think I perceive my Hama this way because it is ultimately.. true? It's representative of thick, fertile loam. Which my corpse could create and recreate itself from. The Hama is more or less a shroud, which divides me from the greater world, thus death's removal of Hama is a removal of the division between system and surroundings.

I think me sensing the Hama that is so ephemeral is because I know I still have profound changes to undergo – my Hama will look and feel different at different times, and will eventually transform into something new, even if the soil is only a different texture.

My response: Your sense of your Hama is very sensuous and powerful, easy to sink into! I love what you say about recreating your Lich from loam, and your sense of Hama being a shroud that separates us as individuals from the whole system around us.

I've had somewhat similar experiences to what you mention: I call it incubation. When I feel like any of my souls need earth-work, earth-digestion and ripening, or other work, I turn myself over to our Landwight, the holder of our land here at Wynnwood. He takes me underground in spirit and wraps me in a clay cocoon, like a grub buried in the ground. It feels a lot like what you said about being swaddled in a heavy blanket. My soul's attention stays there as long as it needs to for the work. Sometimes I am very aware of the kinds of details you describe, other times it kind of feels like it's happening backstage, so to speak. But you know, I hadn't thought about these sensations belonging specifically to my Hama. So now I need to do this some more and explore that perspective!

Exercise 6-2: Sensing Hama-shifts

Repeat Exercise 6-1 periodically while you are in different moods and surroundings, and during or shortly after different kinds of activities and events in your life: negative, positive and neutral. Does your Hama change its covering under different circumstances? Whether it does or not, what does this tell you about yourself and how you react to, and deal with, the various circumstances of your life?

Study participant experiences

<u>Laurie Sottilaro:</u> *When I look at my Hama while exhausted I see no change. Two days later it seems much the same, but the edges are shimmery like they can't decide on a form. Another time it seemed tight. When I was hungry, the surface seemed more porous and diffuse.*

<u>Leif Höglund:</u>
– Tired while studying and having difficulties focusing, it felt like a heavy, gelatinous shroud.
– It feels flexible but durable, like a long rope of taffy. I've been getting things done since I woke up, no caffeine required.
– A thin dry film, with bubbles like those under a screen protector, never quite sitting right. Both tired and restless.
– Midway through yard work. Making great progress. Having a "no noise" afternoon. Hama feels like a warm fresh compost. Fine, damp, and dense.
– After taking a hot shower, lighting some candles, putting on a sweater, getting some tough phone calls done, I feel quite cozy and tired, at only 4:30. It feels heavy, but not uncomfortable, like an internal gravity. Or even, being swaddled in a giant weighted blanket.

Personal example

When I worked with the exercises I described above, I experienced my Hama as a fur covering, which changes its texture, color, and even its scent, under different circumstances, making it more appealing, or defensive, or other traits depending on what is needed at the moment. For example, defensive traits include the fur becoming very shiny, smooth and slick, so that incoming negativity slides off me, while other times porcupine quills appear amidst the fur to appear 'prickly' and unwelcoming. The fur may even take on an offensive scent, bristly texture and ugly color to ward off unwanted others from coming too close. My Hama-fur becomes more appealing by taking on a lovely honey-incense-forest scent, a thick, soft texture and rich color.

I might mention that our choices of clothing, hair styles, accessories, tattoos, piercings, our personal care including scents, and other ways of presenting our appearance are also ways that our Hama expresses itself. Hama can also change its size and density in response to our emotions, such as becoming very strong and firm when we feel sure of ourselves, and shrinking or becoming wavery when we are unsure or intimidated. Becoming aware of our own power to attract and repel, to invite and defend, and to send messages about who we are and where we stand through our Hama is very empowering, as well as interesting and fun, and I encourage you to pursue and strengthen these abilities!

Exercise 6-3: Shaping your Hama

Once you begin to recognize and know your Hama, you can consider deliberately modifying your Hama-covering under different circumstances, depending on what you want to subliminally present about yourself. Sometimes you might want your Hama to be warding and protective, other times shining and beautiful, warm and welcoming, strong and steady, factual and businesslike, open for interactions or closed for privacy and time to yourself, and so forth. Try playing with these possibilities through changes in the nature of your Hama-covering.

But I suggest you keep this in mind, too: your Hama and your other souls who work through Hama may have a clearer idea than you consciously have, about what kind of covering your Hama needs to shape for you in any given situation. There is a *lot* of traffic going through Hama: all the stuff coming in from the outer world, being evaluated by your Lichama, Hama, and Ferah, and responses being developed and sent out by them. Then your other souls are expressing themselves through Hama and Lichama, especially Hugr, Mod and Sefa, and there's lots of traffic going through Hama there, too. It gets very complex, there's stuff going on that's outside the scope of our conscious mind a lot of the time.

There may be occasions where deliberately modifying the shape of your Hama, as opposed to allowing your Hama and other souls to shape Hama as they think best, is the less effective approach. All of our souls have their own wisdom, their own experience, and it's wise to acknowledge that. Sometimes, it's good for us to train and manage our souls in certain ways, as I talked about with regard to Ghost and Wode in the previous chapter. Sometimes, it's best to step back and ask them to teach us what they know. The relations between our conscious mind and our souls should always be one of mutual respect and cooperative action.

Study participant experiences

<u>Leif Höglund:</u> I think that I most obviously feel the way I shift into different shapes whether I'm at work or home, on a date or with a

platonic friend, and so on. Recognizing the shifts and that they happen intentionally is easy for me – what isn't quite as easy is that some of these shifts have felt authentic and some haven't. Fortunately they've become more authentic as I've grown up, but this is a common trend that implies that there isn't something inauthentic about some amount of Hama flexibility, but rather implies the question of why one shifts their Hama or if they overstretch it. What are the factors in how flexible one's Hama is? Cultural influences, personal values/experiences, and internal reflection to be sure, but beyond that it becomes more vague. It's an interesting psychosocial mystery indeed.

<u>*My response:*</u> *That's an interesting mystery you bring up, about the flexibility of the Hama and its authenticity in different forms. It's worth some thought, to consider what 'authenticity' means in Hama's context. When Hama morphs, there's a reason for it. Is the authenticity that you're talking about really a matter of our own motives relating to the interaction we're engaging in? If so, this could be a matter involving Hugr, who sometimes works with Hama on shapeshifting. I think there's still a lot of exploration to be done on Hama in a modern Heathen context.*

The Ellor-Hama

I've long wondered about the alternate shape which in Norse folklore is referred to as being *hamrammr* or 'shape-strong', and is referred to in many other contexts as shape-shifting or astral / etheric travel in another form. Do we, or do some people, have two different Hamas, one the human Hama which shapes our natural body, and the other an alternate Hama with an animal shape or a shape with paranormal powers like a witch's flight? Or do we all have only one Hama, which for some people can morph into an alternate form?

I call this alternate form the Ellor-Hama, 'ellor' meaning 'strange, alien, other, Otherworldly' in Anglo-Saxon, to distinguish it from our natural, human-form Hama. (Pronounced EL-lor HAH-ma.) My original thought was that our human-form Hama would need to remain with our body at all times, since it is the shaper of our physical body. Wouldn't our Lich fall into shapelessness, if our Hama went off astrally somewhere and left it behind? Thus, I thought that if some people are shape-strong, they must have a second Hama, an Ellor-Hama. But I gradually began thinking differently about this, and doing the exercises I described above solidified these different thoughts (or shaped them!).

Our Hama shapes our physical body, yes. But our Lich has a good deal of stability on its own, as all matter does. The brief, temporary absence of our Hama morphing into an Ellor-Hama for a little while would probably have little effect on it. On the other hand, our non-material social 'shape' or persona, also shaped by our Hama, may not have the same kind of stability that our Lich does.

What this adds up to is a situation where a person may be able to shapeshift astrally or etherically and travel in that form, under the power of their own Hama, without substantially harming their Lich as long as this is not done for too long or too frequently. However, this absence or splitting of the Hama may well have a noticeable impact on the physical person's behavior and actions, which may appear quite strange and abnormal during the time that the Hama is away. This means that their 'social shape' changes, along with the shape of their etheric or astral body as they take on the Ellor-Hama.

Thus, with this theory, two things change: social 'shape' or behavior, and Hama shifting into Ellor-Hama, the human energy-shape taking on an altered form. One thing doesn't change: the Lich, the physical body. I think this description accords with many observations of paranormal phenomena, and lore and magic relating to shapeshifters. It also fits with words like *hamstolinn* or Hama-stolen, referring to people whose wits and behavior are perceived as being addled or abnormal with respect to the customary behavior of their culture. For a *hamstolinn* person, their behavioral 'shape' is different than what is expected, even though their physical shape would probably be considered 'normal'.

Evaluating Hama's communication

It's important to discern whether we are sending out mixed messages through contradictory aspects of our Hama, and how those mixed messages may be affecting our relationships with others and their reactions toward us. Once we gain some ability to perceive our own Hama and its changes, this opens up some very useful perceptions concerning these mixed messages that we all tend to send out to each other from time to time, very often without intending to.

One very common mixed message, that we often don't realize we are sending to others, is: "Come closer / back off." We want to be closer to some people, but past experiences, lack of trust, past behavioral patterns, etc., cause us to push them away at the same time that we want them closer. This has a very disruptive effect on relationships, especially when both / all people involved in the relationship are doing this, and the timing of each person's 'come closer' and 'back off' is not synchronized with the other person's! Thus, when one person wants to be closer, the other one wants to back off, and vice versa. This generates misunderstandings, hurt feelings, and worse, and can occur in all our personal relationships, including between children and parents. This is just one example of the many mixed messages we may be sending out, and picking up from others.

Exercise 6-4: Are you sending mixed messages?

Use what you have learned from the previous Hama exercises to watch your own behavior toward others, and discern whether your Hama is sending such mixed messages. Your Hama might, for example, take the form of something that is attractive or beautiful, but also has a threatening or uncomfortable quality to it, like prickles or needles underneath lovely fur or fabric, or a beautiful covering that contains an irritant or poison embedded in it. Perhaps a seductive shape, clothed in such horrible, clashing colors that it makes others take a step back, just when they were going to step forward! Or a rapidly changing Hama that doesn't settle on one kind of message but keeps shifting back and forth. Really, it could be anything.

Use your soul-intuition to observe your Hama and other people's Hamas, and watch how they respond to each other. There is a great deal that can be learned from this! It's often difficult to make such observations at the same time as your interactions with other people; there are too many things to pay attention to at once. Another way to go about this is to review the interaction later, in your memory and imagination. As you do this, as you set the scene in your mind, tune into your Hama and ask it to appear in this memory-scene in the covering or appearance that it was using during the transaction.

Your Hama may also be able to perceive the other person's Hama as you construct the memory-scene, which can be very enlightening. Keep this important point in mind, though: your and your Hama's perceptions of the other person's Hama are just that: *your* perception. This perception is valid and important, because this is what your Hama was picking up on and reacting to during the interaction. But your perception of the other person's Hama may not be what they were actually sending out, or intending to send out.

Once you've sorted out as much as you can from this memory-exercise, it's best to go back and have a conversation with the other person, and do some cross-checking about what they thought was going on between you. Then use this information to fine-tune your and your Hama's perceptions for future interactions with that person.

"Come closer / back off" is just one of many mixed messages that we may send out. Other examples include "I'm competent / I'm incompetent"; "I'm willing / unwilling"; "I care / I don't care"; "I'm listening / not listening"; and many others.

One thing I like about approaching this matter through our Hama, is that it helps to defuse the natural defensiveness that we all feel when anyone (including ourself) criticizes us or suggests that we're doing something wrong. If we're unconsciously sending messages that we don't truly want to send, and someone points this out to us, we may well react defensively or deny it.

However, if we've learned to enjoy perceiving and playing with our Hama, and the realizations about our behavior come about as a result of this Hama-play, we are less likely to be defensive and in denial. Instead, we can be intrigued and challenged, and enjoy designing a new Hama for ourself, one that is more in line with what we truly want to communicate.

Taking this approach turns an insight that might otherwise seem threatening and uncomfortable, into an enjoyable challenge to our creativity. I might mention that these are enjoyable exercises or activities to share with children. You may learn a good deal yourself, by such sharing: kid's Hamas are very creative and flexible!

When we have designed our changed Hama, we need to follow up by keeping it in place during our daily interactions that are relevant to the new Hama (there are likely to be other situations in daily life that have no relevance to the new Hama, that need a different one).

Changes in physical appearance, such as clothing, colors, hairstyle, etc., can reinforce the Hama changes we are working on. Physical changes such as our posture, volume of our voice, eye contact, and many others also go along with this. Our Hama, appearance, actions and behavior are all interconnected. When we want to change these things, we can start with any one of them, and those changes will influence all the other areas of our Hama.

A word about Hamingja

In Norse folklore, Hamingja is both a form of luck-energy, and a spirit who bears and gives that luck to the person with

Exploring Hama

whom it is associated. As with Hama, Hamingja is considered to reside in the womb / caul / afterbirth. It accompanies the child it was born with throughout life, as long as nothing dire occurs to destroy its luck or its connection to the person. The Hamingja-spirit is the link between flows of hamingja-luck energy in the environment, and our physical / metaphysical body and souls, especially Hama.

I believe that our Hama-soul and our accompanying Hamingja-spirit are closely related. Both of them come into being within the womb when a child is conceived, as I understand it, embedded within the tissues of the womb itself. Both have strong influence on the child as it gestates, and continue to do so throughout its life. But one of them is a personal soul, one of the members of the person's soular system or soul-household, while the other, the Hamingja, is an accompanying spirit that is not a member of our soular system. While of great interest and relevance, the Hamingja spirit is not a subject of the present study, which is focused on our inherent souls.

Summary

Hama is deeply involved with our appearance, body language, speech, behavior, physical activity, and with how all of these phenomena shape us as interactive social beings in Midgard. Hama is equally involved in perceiving and interpreting all of these things that other people around us, in our social space, are doing. In addition to our physical appearance, Hama takes on different metaphysical or subliminal appearances in response to different situations and conditions we may be in at any given time. We can learn to discern these shifts in ourselves and others, through our Hama soul, and learn to consciously control them in ourselves so as to communicate more clearly and respond more appropriately to any given situation.

Exploring Hama

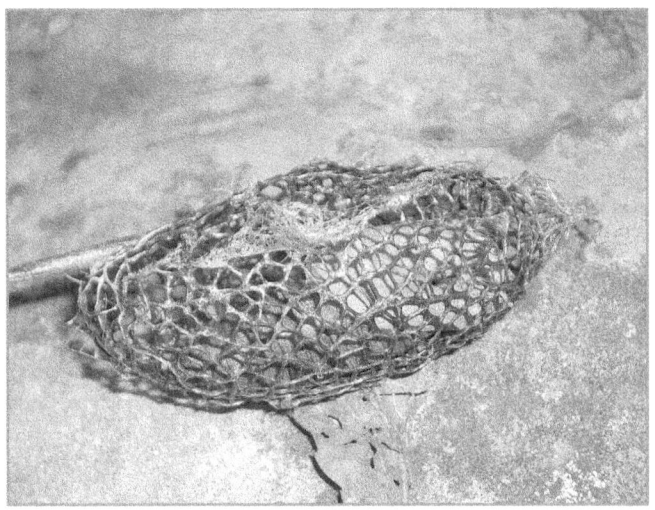

This interesting cocoon represents the Hama enwrapping our Lich (physical body) inside itself. The Hama-cocoon influences how we present ourselves and how others perceive us.

The leaves and bark of the Alder tree have multiple medicinal uses. Aldr is a healer in tree-form, as well as in soul-form!

Chapter 7

7. Exploring your Aldr, Ørlög, Werold

{Primary runes in the bind-rune above: Perthro, Laguz, Jera, Nauthiz, Ingwaz, Eihwaz, Ac / Oak.}

Background reading: Chapter 7 in Book I, or my web article "Aldr and Orlay: Weaving a World."

Aldr-Wita

Our Aldr soul is, among other things, a channel for nourishing spiritual energies to flow into our Lich. This inflowing nourishment is contained within our *Ealdorgeard* or Ealdor-yard, an energetic construct that maps onto our physical body, where our Ealdoryard energetically overlaps with our Lich-Hama and Ferah. Both Aldr and Ferah sense, and are affected by, the states of wellbeing and health, or of illness and suffering, of our Lichama. For those who work within a shamanic mindset, the Ealdoryard is

Exploring Aldr

often the location where energy-intrusions or 'worms' and other illness-causing wights make their lairs, impacting Lichama and Ferah through the Aldr soul. Grief and suffering deeply affect the Aldr, and over the long term, can cause erosion of this soul, limiting its ability to funnel spiritual nourishment into us, and leading into a vicious cycle of suffering, illness and inner loss.

Aldr-Wita, discussed in Chapter 7 of Book I, is a term I offer for a Heathen-oriented path of spiritual and physical health. Rune-work, herbalism and natural remedies, spiritual and magical healing, adjusting our lifestyle to the rhythms of nature and our true physical needs, healthy living on all levels of being, the support of a Heathen community as well as family, friends, and other communities: these are tools of Aldr-Wita, of integrated spiritual-physical health and nourishment.

Exercise 7-1: Aldr-flow

Sit quietly and try to sense an inflow of nourishing energy within yourself. Spend time getting to know how this flow feels, feeding life-energy into every cell. Use one or more of your analog-senses to help you sense the energy of your Ealdor-yard, and how it feeds and supports your Lichama.

Once you've become familiar with this flow, use your inner senses and imagination to scan your body, checking to see whether there are any areas that are poorly nourished or blocked from your Aldr-power. I find the sense of taste to be most helpful here: I go through my Lich (body) section by section in my imagination, and remain alert to how my taste-sense changes as I move my imagination around. If the flavor diminishes, or becomes less pleasant, that's an indication of problems with Aldr flow. Of course, any of your senses can be used, this is just an example.

Visual scanning shows changes in color and intensity of light; auditory scanning might pick up changes in tone as your body hums to you, or sense harmony or disharmony. Feeling-sensation can sense temperature and texture differences, vibrations, and comfort or discomfort; scent works the same as taste, as I described above. Proprioception (the sense of how your body is oriented in space) may tell you that some part of your Aldr is outside its natural space, is too large or small, or is oriented in the wrong direction. The result is a distorted Ealdoryard.

All of the components of our body are connected in some way with our emotions and thoughts: they are connected physiologically, and energetically, as is studied in Traditional Chinese Medicine, in Indian Ayurveda, in Western Vitalism and the four Humors, etc. Take note of what emotions and thoughts come to you, as you're scanning each area of your body. These emotions and thoughts, and their connection with specific parts of your Lichama, are very much a necessary part of your Ealdoryard scanning. If you have shamanic healing skills and experience, you may want to look for intrusions as you scan your Lich and Ealdoryard in this way, as well.

Study participant experiences

Laurie Sottilaro: *My Aldr is a mess. Let me get that out there right now. It's full of holes, or spots so thin as to seem such, and over the years I've been constantly trying to defend it. I gave up a few years ago, when I got this latest illness, and it's still looking pretty ratty. I've worked with my Aldr quite a lot, but never knew it had a name. I have lots of methods to refresh it, mostly drawing from the Earth or Sun in one form or another, but I find assimilating that energy can be difficult. It's almost like it's tuned a half-step off from the other energy, I have to repattern it in order to absorb it, and that's draining. Interestingly enough, my Aldr is very thin where my sensation has been lost. It also gets thin between my solar plexus and heart.*

<u>My comment:</u> *I've found after years of experimenting that my diet makes all the difference in my energy level and my Ealdoryard, more difference than anything else I try. We're all different in the kinds of food that are good or bad for us; I don't think 'one size fits all'. We each need to experiment and see which foods need to be avoided, and which ones emphasized.*

This goes along very strongly with our Aldr soul, who is in charge of our nourishment and the energy we gain from it. By 'nourishment' I don't mean exactly 'the food we eat', but rather 'what we holistically do with the food (and other sources of nourishment) we consume'. If the food is useless or bad for us, it isn't 'nourishment'. We each need to figure out what is most nourishing to us on all levels, and commit to pursuing that way of living, to honor our Aldr and help it give us a long, well-shaped, productive life-span, productive in our own personal ways, whether that is visible to others or not.

As for the thinness of your Aldr between your heart and solar plexus.....in my understanding, the heart is the seat of our Hugr, and the solar plexus and gut is the seat of our Mod soul and mod-power. Thinned energy between those areas may be a clue that your Hugr and Mod are out of touch with each other. You show a very active Hugr in your writing here in your soul lore studies, but it's clear that all of your difficulties have affected your mod-power, your strength and energy, might and main. It might be worth exploring this relationship more.

This also relates, in part, to what I wrote above. I consider that a main foothold of our Mod is in our microbiome and gut, which relates again to diet and nourishment. We each have a unique microbiome, with unique requirements for 'care and feeding' of it. Our microbiome / mod-root is involved not only with nourishment, but with our immune system, nervous system, endocrine system....really, everything. You might want to focus more on Mod and Aldr working together.

Exercise 7-2: Healing Aldr-flow

If you find areas where your Aldr-flow is having difficulties, consider the list of Aldr-Wita tools I mentioned above, and any others you may be familiar with. I will say that I find the theories and techniques of traditional Eastern forms of medicine to be helpful, along with Western forms of energy medicine. I find flower essences (this is not the same as aromatherapy, which is also good), which each target specific meridians, power-centers, and organs, to be especially helpful. Plus they are completely safe, not very expensive because they're used in such small doses, and you can make some of them yourself, depending on the plants that grow where you live.

But of course, there are also more traditionally Heathen ways to enhance Aldr-flow, including Rune-work, diet, physical activity, and bringing your lifestyle more into conformity with natural rhythms of Earth-time, as it is expressed where you live. Josephine McCarthy's book on *Magical Healing* offers many good ideas for this work, including homeopathy and flower essences. Her focus is on healing oneself, as an esoteric practitioner at risk from health impacts of one's work, rather than on becoming a healer of other people. Cat Heath's book on Heathen magic likewise has very useful guidelines.

Aldr, Ørlög, and the Ordeal

The term ørlög or orlay refers to the influence that past deeds and events have on the present, and holds implications for how these two, past and present, influence future events and experiences. As I understand it, our ørlög or orlay gives our Aldr and our life-span substance and dimension within the domain of Time, as our Lich gives us substance and dimension in Space. Ørlög does this through the property of 'continuity', which is the analog in Time of the property of 'shape' in Space. Our Lichama gives us our physical shape, and holds that shape in space. Our ørlög is the stream of continuity through Time that links us in the present moment with the past, both our personal ørlög and past, and that of kin-lines, culture, species: all the influences that shape our personal and collective ørlög.

This linkage and continuity through time gives us our time-body, which is our Werold: the totality of our lifetime's experiences and deeds. The linkage or 'glue' that holds our time-body together is ørlög: both the ørlög we lay down with our deeds and choices in this life, and the ørlög of the past that still influences us in the present.

The ørlög from the past and the present lays the foundations for 'what shall be' in the future, the tugs, pulls and pushes we feel toward choosing or moving toward one path rather than another. Every choice we make opens up some new choices, and closes down some others; thus our ørlög, working through our Aldr-soul, continually shapes our Werold, our experience of our life-span.

Exploring Aldr

All of this adds up to the 'ordeal' of life itself: "ordeal" meaning *'the primal roots of a given ordeal-circumstance: the ørlög, the weaving of wyrd, which has been dealt out for me to face here and now, in this place, in this time.'* An 'ordeal' has the connotation of a struggle, a challenge, and it is that, but it is more. It is fateful, it is a weaving of wyrd, a drawing-together of the strands of our life into a nexus-point of deep significance. Much of our past has gone into reaching this nexus-point of the ordeal, and much will lead forth from its outcome, that will shape our time to come.

In my understanding of Heathen philosophy, life itself is an ordeal in this sense: a complex, patterned knot or nexus of strands of ørlög, arising from the past, gathered together in the present, and shaping the future to come. The ordeal of life is a challenge and a struggle, indeed, but more than that, it shapes the whole pattern of our Being, and shapes the meaning that our life holds. Our purpose in life is not to avoid or escape true Heathen ordeals, but to rise to the challenge they offer: the challenge not only to meet the ordeal successfully, but to use it as a vehicle to emerge from the ordeal with greater soul-qualities than we had when we went into it.

The stream of ørlög, with the ordeals it brings and the continuity it bears, gives our existence shape and meaning, links us with the past and draws us toward the future. Because of ørlög, our deeds and choices are not random, they have context, meaning, consequences, significance. They build upon each other to create the fabric of our Werold, our life in Time. For these reasons, I like to think of the old words *Aldar-beornum, Eldi-barn,* as meaning 'children of Time.' This is what we mortals are: Time-Children. We can use this knowledge to pattern our lives purposefully and meaningfully, or we can throw it away as we 'waste the time' of our lives.

Exercise 7-3: Being shaped by ørlög

Sit in silence and gather your awareness. You're an unborn, insubstantial consciousness floating deep within the dim, indistinct waters of the Well of Wyrd. Somewhere in the distance, you hear an eerie chanting: the Norns are singing, gathering together the strands of your Aldr soul, wrapping them around the spindle of yourself. Your lack of substance begins to fill with these strands, as your ørlög is spun by the Norns.

How do these ørlög strands feel? Do they give you shape and substance? A sense of direction, or a sense of challenges? What are the colors of these strands, or what do you sense about them with your other senses? Do they constrict you? Can you see how a band of constriction could be turned into a thread to weave into the tapestry of your life, your Werold? Can constrictions or limitations be transformed into resources, life-experience, wisdom, under the stern benevolence of the rune Need and the gaze of the Norns?

Now move forward in time, to some significant event in your childhood (as long as this is safe for you). Keep that time in your awareness, and non-judgmentally examine the ørlög-strands that played into this event: strands that came from recent or distant past, strands that might be pulling you forward in time, in a certain direction.

You can repeat this exercise as a life-and-ørlog review, working through your full life up until now. This will take a long time, and shouldn't be rushed; you can do it over the course of a year or more, and of course it is an

Exploring Aldr

ongoing exercise, being aware of ørlög and your Werold for as long as you are alive. Keep a record of your findings in your Daybook; you will find, I believe, that your whole life history and meaning of your life and Werold takes on shape and substance through these exercises.

This is the "Tale of Your Aldr", and the "Weaving of your Werold," that you are examining honestly and with compassion here: learning from it, growing in wisdom, gaining insights into yourself, your choices and their consequences. This activity, extended toward others as well, helps you increase in compassion, acceptance, and understanding toward other people as well as toward yourself. Perhaps most importantly, when you begin to have a true sense of how ørlög has shaped your life in the past, you can begin to make choices about future actions and directions with a fuller awareness of how ørlög works in your own life.

If you feel drawn to serious, in-depth astrology, such as evolutionary or psychological astrology, such knowledge can point you in helpful directions for understanding how ørlög has worked in your life. The planets and signs can, and have been, interpreted by modern Heathens using Heathen symbology. Just as one example, I find that Saturn can well be regarded as Urðr or Wyrd, herself: the 'Norn of What-Is', of the past which is shaping the present.

Mapping the complex factors of yourself, and perhaps your parents and other close kin and loved ones as well, through the deeps of astrological time and space is, I have found, very enlightening when we're working to understand ørlög and wyrd in our lives. Both astrology and Aldr focus on our life in time, the timing of events in our lives, the sequences, causes, consequences and influences of experiences and deeds. Serious, in-depth astrology is indeed a helpful tool for understanding more about our Aldr and Werold.

Study participant experiences

<u>Laurie Sottilaro:</u> *I didn't expect the hundreds of vivid, bright lines that fed into my creation. That's what I think I watched, as the more threads fed into it, the bigger I got. Finally there was enough to sustain life. It was truly bizarre. The threads were of varying colors, and varying textures. Some felt like silk, some felt like guitar wire. I moved forward to a particular riding accident I had, and what I saw was very interesting. They were threads coming from myself, from the horse, from my trainer and the clinician, from the sky (weather I think), and from spirits that surrounded me. All of them fed into my being thrown, and my landing.*

What I found particularly interesting is the variance of saturation of color over time. Sometimes the colors were greyed, other times they were bright again. I expected a continuous desaturation, but that's not what I got. There just seemed to be times of brighter and lesser color, possibly indicating how well I was living my Ørlög. There were constrictions, but rather than feeling tight or restraining, they gave me form and supported that form.

<u>My response:</u> *I like what you wrote about the strands being more shaping and supporting, than being constricting. This is how I see it, too; I think this is a wise way to view our own ørlög, and to view the Norns who help us shape that ørlög before and during our lives. Hard and difficult parts of our ørlög help us grow our character and inner strength, and our compassion toward others*

who similarly struggle. This is part of human experience, human growth and development.

Weaving a Werold

Our Werold is our lifetime and everything it contains: all our thoughts and deeds, choices and experiences. We may think of everything that has happened with us up until now as 'the past', but in fact, it is the Werold we have woven, the garment or soul-skin of our Aldr soul. What is past is not 'gone', but still here with us, transformed for better or for worse by how we deal with all the matters of our life. Our Hama creates our Lich, our body in space, day by day from the time of our conception until our death. What we do, what we eat, what we think and feel, what happens to us, the passage of time: all of these affect the ongoing, day by day shaping of our Lich, our body in space. In the same way, our Aldr weaves our Werold, our body in time, day by day, out of life-experience and orlay. This is the tale of our life, woven from a myriad of threads.

It is worthwhile to learn to see your Werold as a tapestry of threads. Some of these threads were spun by yourself, others were spun by the Norns, and by people who have influenced you or touched your life significantly, for good or for ill. Others are spun by the society and culture we live in, by the history of our kin and culture, and by many other factors, such as genetics. We do not have full control over every one of the threads of ørlög we are handed in this life, but what we can choose is how to pattern those threads into our Aldr-tapestry.

Exploring Aldr

A tapestry depiction of the Roman Pomona, Goddess of Fruit. We might view her as Idunna, instead, with her holy apples or fruits that nourish the Aldrs of the Deities and extend their life-span.

Exercise 7-4: Your Werold as a work of art

Can you draw or paint what your tapestry looks like, the colors and patterns that are woven there? Can you embroider or weave something that looks like it? Or use any other form of art? A tapestry is a visual thing, but you might perceive your Werold more like a song, or a piece of instrumental music, or a roughly-textured, complex sculpture, or a garden with flowers and weeds. Try to render your Aldr's soul-garment, your life woven into Time and Wyrd, into a form of art. If you don't have the artistic skills for this (though it is worth doing even if you don't think it's very good and don't want to show it to anyone), then work in your imagination.

Personal example

I'll give an example of my own. I've gone through many iterations of this exercise at different times of my life; they've all been different. The first time happened in a dream, during a time when I was going through difficult changes in my life. In my dream I held a very beautiful vase made of blown glass, iridescent with rainbow colors, admiring it as I walked. But then I stumbled and dropped the vase, which broke into thousands of colored pieces, many more colors than it had had, before. I was upset at the loss; I started sadly picking up the pieces of glass, and then had the idea of making a mosaic out of them.

I was in a cave, dimly lit by fire or torches, and I started pressing pieces of broken glass into the moist clay wall of the cave. I eventually filled the whole wall with this mosaic, a rich tapestry of dark and bright colors and swirling patterns, lit by flickering firelight. I couldn't see the whole pattern, some of it was tantalizingly obscure, but I loved this beautiful, expressive mosaic as a whole. The glass vase had been a lovely, small container, shaping my perceived desire for a simple, beautiful life-pattern. But this broke, and what I made out of the pieces turned out to be much larger, grander, more complex and far-reaching, reflecting my real inner life more accurately than the lovely little vase ever did.

I return in my imagination, from time to time, to this cave with my firelit mosaic; each time it seems richer and deeper, extending into darkness on either end, endlessly fascinating even though I could not express in words what it means to me. It is my Aldr who loves this mosaic! I think that the cave where it lies is close to the Well of Wyrd; it is the water from this Well which seeps through and moistens the cave wall, allowing it to accept and hold the pieces of my mosaic. I feel that this is a subtle gift of help from the Norns, supporting my efforts to understand my Aldr, my Werold, and how they relate to the Norns and Wyrd.

Study participant experiences
<u>Laurie Sottilaro:</u> *I actually didn't perceive a pattern I could draw, it was all a mass of colors, some blending others clashing. Each thread looked glass-like, and it was woven less into a tapestry and more like a sheath. It was truly a bewildering display, I may have to watch over time to see a pattern. The lack of one was quite surprising. You'd think the colors would blend into mud, but instead each was... think strands of stones, some bright like emeralds and sapphires, some more like aventurine, and some dark like lapis or sodalite.*

Nourishment as ørlög

We've talked about Aldr as the nourisher, and we've talked about Aldr's connection with ørlög and with time. Now let's put them all together, and look at how our physical Lich, our body, reflects in many ways the metaphysical ørlög that we are born with and that continues to accumulate throughout our lifetime.

First, nourishment and our Lich. Our Lich is made out of what we eat, drink and breathe, throughout our life. We inherit some kinds of ørlög through our genes and the reproductive cells from our parents, and the environment of our mother's womb and body, including the emotional and spiritual environment, which in turn is affected by her own life circumstances and the people around her. Our family and environmental inheritance continues to shape us during our childhood, and impacts our Lich, including our brain and all our complex body systems. It shapes us through the different kinds of 'nourishment'—physical, emotional, mental, spiritual, that are available to us in our environment. And equally, we are impacted by any lack of such nourishment, as well as inputs that are not nourishing, but are toxic or disruptive to the healthy functioning of our Lich and our souls.

All of these situations leave their traces in our Lich, our ørlög, and our souls, and spread out from us to those around us. In this way, our Lich is like the Well of Wyrd, with its layers of orlay that accumulate over time. And even more, it is like the Tree, which the Norns nourish by patting layers of ørlög-infused white mud from the Well onto its trunk, day by day helping the Tree grow its strong life-rings under the influence of ørlög. Our Ferah life-force soul is connected with trees. Our Aldr-soul, with the Werold it creates, and the Lich it nourishes, is also connected with trees through the great World-Tree and all it bears upon its boughs.

Exercise 7-5: Understanding nourishment

I've talked about, and implied, many kinds of nourishment that impact our Aldr and our Lich: physical nourishment in the form of healthy food and drink, and emotional nourishment like affection, love, a supportive environment. Mental nourishment like books, stories, art, a good education, a stimulating environment. Spiritual nourishment: contact with Deities and benevolent spirits, with the spirits in nature, sharing our experiences and insights with other spiritual people, learning and growing on spiritual levels.

And then there is anti-nourishment, toxins and disruptors in the things we ingest at these different levels, too. Toxins in our food, drink, and environmental exposures. Toxic or disruptive emotional and mental

Exploring Aldr

environments. Distorted and harmful spiritual teachings and practices, and exposure to harmful spiritual forces.

For this exercise, to the extent that it is safe for you, consider the kinds of nourishment, positive and negative, that you absorbed from your environment in childhood, and in your life up until now. How did that affect your Aldr, your Lich, and your other souls? How has it affected the expression of ørlög in your life?

How about now, your life today? How well are you nourishing your Lich, your Aldr, your other souls, on all levels? Are you providing good nourishment to others around you, especially children? Are you perhaps supplying forms of anti-nourishment to yourself and others? How might you change this?

Exercise 7-6: Exploring your Aldr's time-body

Enter stillness and awareness of your Aldr and ørlög, as you've learned to do through the preceding exercises. Now: can you sense ørlög from the far past, from your kin-line, your culture-line, or from past lives? Can you distinguish these threads from the threads of your personal ørlög in this life? Some strands come from you, some come from others, and from history itself. Can you sense how to integrate these different strands into your life-tapestry, working them now into a new pattern woven by your own will and wisdom? This is another exercise that will take a long time to accomplish, and is ongoing as your life proceeds.

If you wish to do this, and if it feels safe for you, look toward 'what may be' through the eyes of ørlög and Skuld, the Norn of 'What-Should-Be'. Future-ørlög appears to me like cords, thicker and thinner ropes, cords and threads, tied to different pieces of my already-woven tapestry and leading off in different directions. The thicker the rope, the stronger the pull on my orlay, drawing the whole pattern of my Werold off in that particular direction. Thinner threads, without much ørlög-power behind them, I can perhaps ignore or work around. Heavier ropes indicate a strong force of orlay, bound back in time to the past and present. They must be recognized and accepted for what they are: strong and possibly unchangeable influences on what is coming down the road for me.

This is a very difficult exercise, difficult to perceive and interpret, and even more difficult to change, if we wish to do so. At least, it is so for me. I seem to relate most strongly with Verðandi, the Norn of Becoming, and secondly with Wyrd / Urðr and her work of weaving the past into the present, whereas I feel little connection with Skuld and her domain of 'what should be'. Perhaps for others, this exercise is less difficult; I don't know. It is certainly daunting and unsettling, and you may wish to entirely skip the work I describe in this paragraph!

In closing

I've suggested enough work here to keep you busy for a long time, as is appropriate for the soul which governs our life in time! Time is what Aldr is all about: nourishing and extending our life in time, shaping the events of our life in time, connecting us to the past and to what may come in the future. These matters can be difficult to work with, both emotionally and conceptually. It's best to approach them in small pieces, with a supportive and non-judgmental attitude toward yourself. I've written a number of articles that relate to ørlög and wyrd, if you want to explore these matters further, which can be found on my website, *HeathenSoulLore.net*, and other Heathen authors have as well.

Chapter 8

8. Mod and Hugr: Motivating Forces

{Primary runes in the bind-rune above: Raidho, Uruz, Mannaz, Sowilo, Wunjo, Nauthiz, Ehwaz, Dagaz.}

Background reading: Chapters 8, 9, 10, 11 in Book I, or the articles on my website titled "Dances with Daemons: The Mod Soul;" "Hunting the Wild Hugr;" "Who is Hugr?," and "The Occult Activities of the Hugr."

Mod and Hugr have many similarities: their Midgard focus, their influence on our character, emotions, modes of thought, actions and reactions, and the connections between Mod's deep-root of Will, and Hugr's deep-roots of Desire, Longing, Yearning. These are primary motivating forces in our lives. Mod and Hugr can express themselves in very positive ways, and in negative ways, as well. One of the main things we do, as we grow and mature in Midgard life, is to become more aware of these souls as they express themselves through us into Midgard, and work on shaping their attitudes, actions and powers to work beneficially rather than counter-productively in our lives.

First, the context

I want to emphasize that, in my understanding of Heathen soul lore, these soul-forces that motivate us are not divided into Christian-influenced 'good versus bad' motivations or inner personas, pictured as the influence of devils / demons versus guardian angels. The psychologist Sigmund Freud, and many after him, divided our 'self' into a subconscious or Id, and a super-consciousness or Conscience, and pictured the human character and deeds as a battleground between Good and Evil, where everything we fear and hate is stuffed into our subconscious and invisibly influences us, while our Conscience struggles, and often fails, to counteract these tendencies.

These observations have some accuracy, because this view of Good versus Evil is the perspective of Western society, and that cultural influence shapes people's characters, ethics, thoughts and deeds. Medieval Christians believed in literal angels and demons influencing their inner choices, while modern, more secular people take a psychological approach; both of them base ethical systems upon their assumptions. But if you look at these approaches carefully, there is not that much difference between them, in the sense that they are both focused on an interpretation of Good versus Evil as the axis which shapes (or perhaps tortures) humans and the human world around us.

Mod and Hugr: Motivating Forces

My exploration of Heathen soul lore leads me in a different direction, toward different conclusions. I don't characterize Mod and its Will, Hugr and its Desires, as either 'good' or 'evil, bad'. These inner forces are what they are: I believe that Hugr and Mod are individual soul-beings within us, who should be respected and understood, just as we try to do with other people around us. I don't think they should be labeled, insulted, deformed, beaten into submission, or stuffed into a dark box and denied. Nor should they indulge themselves in orgies of self-gratification, exploitation of others, or uncontrolled envy and rage.

Just as with any member of a household or a community, there needs to be a balance between pursuing one's own will and desires, versus the needs of other people and the environment, including the rest of our own souls, our Lichama, and our relationships. In order to reach these understandings, our Mod and Hugr need to learn by example and experience, just as children do—that is, just as the Mod and Hugr within each child learn to do, or should learn.

It gives a great sense of inner freedom to leave behind this 'good versus evil or bad' dichotomy, and instead take a more nuanced approach to the soul-dynamics that lead to the development of our character, temperament and behavior. This approach can be considered as 'functional' rather than 'prescriptive', based on the Heathen idea of ethics as being something that humans develop, maintain, and adjust as necessary, based on the always-evolving needs and wellbeing of their community, rather than based on laws cast in stone.

So, this is the context within which I'd like us to explore the motivating forces of Mod and Hugr within ourselves: by taking an objective view of these powerful souls and how they shape our lives, with the understanding that there is always room for change, growth, development, and that self-knowledge and self-respect are the basis for a healthy and worthwhile life in any culture, place and time in the world.

Exercise 8-1: Observing your motivating forces

We're going to look at Will and Desire here, the roots of our motivations, and I want to emphasize taking an objective, non-judgmental position as you do this. The point of this exercise is to understand 'what is', within you: what is actually going on. If you impose value judgments at this point in the process, that will introduce distortions and lack of clarity in both the expressions of your motivations, and your reactions to them. Right now, you're like a scientist studying certain phenomena, in order to understand how they work.

I suggest pursuing this both during meditation, and as much as possible also during 'real time' in daily life. We'll start with meditation. Gather your awareness and open a space within your spiritual perception of your heart and throat, guts and jaws, and then your whole body. Sit quietly for awhile and allow any knowledge or feelings to arise within you, relating to wanting, willing, longing, wishing, needing. Write or record in your Daybook as this is going on, because there may be a long list, and it may be jumbled and confused.

Mod and Hugr: Motivating Forces

Work on refining and clarifying this list of inner drivers: ask your Hugr and Mod which are the most important, the most fundamental, the ones that shape and influence your other, more superficial desires and will. Try to reduce it to a short list, working in your Daybook, but remaining tuned in to Hugr and Mod.

The next step is to take one thing at a time, one underlying motivating force in your life, and explore how it has expressed itself throughout your life. How has it influenced your choices, actions, emotions, behavior?

Personal example

(This is longer than the other examples I give, reflecting how I trace one motivating force of my Hugr and Mod through the circumstances and choices of my life. Skip it if you want!)

Perhaps because I grew up as the daughter of a US diplomat, and thus moved to different countries every couple of years, and later moved and traveled a great deal during young adulthood, I've always had a longing for a particular sense of 'my own home'. I have an inner sense of the qualities that make up 'homey-ness' to me, and the determination to achieve such a place has been one of the drivers in my choice of career, in how I manage my finances, and many other choices, actions and patterns in my life. I've harnessed my Mod's Will and determination to work through many years of difficulties and sacrifices in order to pursue this desire of establishing a home. Sometimes this driving need has led to choices that overlooked other important factors of my life, leading me to decisions that, in hindsight, I might have made differently if I had been more aware of these matters.

Mod and Hugr: Motivating Forces

Further, I've come to realize that my true ideal home isn't even a physical place, so in addition to my efforts to obtain and maintain a physical home, I've worked for years to understand my own need for a metaphysical or spiritual home. Finding Heathenry and Heathen spiritual practices, and in earlier years my work in founding and leading Heathen organizations, has given me a deeper sense of spiritual homecoming.

Even so, there is always an inner longing for more, a longing to come closer to some unreachable ideal of 'true home'. This feeds into my care and deep concern about nature, habitat and the environment, which provides homes for all people, animals, landwights and other beings. I can never feel completely at home myself, when other people and beings are being made homeless all around us.

This perspective drove me toward my career in watershed management and landscape ecology, focused on improving and protecting habitat for other beings: helping them have homes, too. Due to many difficult circumstances, it took me almost two decades to achieve the university degrees that qualified me for this work. My Mod (though I did not recognize it by name at the time) kept me on track and didn't allow me to give up my goal, no matter how difficult the challenges.

Mod's Will was tuned in to Hugr's longing; both of them drove me powerfully, using not only determination but as much courage, strategic planning, intelligence, strength and stamina, and other qualities of Hugr and Mod as I could muster, to reach this goal. In this driven process, though, some other good things were overlooked, given up, chosen against, that maybe I would have done differently if I had been less driven, or driven in a different direction.

The stress and strain also had long-term impacts on my health. Some things were gained, some equally good things were lost or diminished. I can't say that these deeds of my Hugr and Mod were either 'good or bad' here; they led to choices based on my needs and values at the time, and they shaped my life accordingly.

This inner longing for myself and all beings to have true homes is a desire that can't ever be fully satisfied: it is a rooted part of my being that continues to shape many aspects of my life, my choices, actions and reactions, and my worldview. It even shapes little things that I enjoy and long for. For example, I love containers of many different kinds: pottery jugs and jars, decorative boxes, storage chests, and chests of drawers, from tiny to full-size. As a child, I loved dollhouses, aquariums, terrariums, large and fancy pet cages, and 'fairy houses' (well, I still do). All these containers are symbols of little 'homes', tempting me to acquire more things than I need or can afford and take care of, in my ongoing quest for the ideal quality of 'home'.

Observing Hugr and Mod

This is what we're working on here: coming to understand the roots of inner longings and desires, along with the will and determination to reach toward those desires, and seeing how these things have worked, and continue to work, to shape the circumstances of our life, our choices and actions.

We do this without blame or shame, criticism or guilt, without getting bogged down in regrets, resentments, justifications. We just observe, objectively and compassionately. As we do this, we are coming into awareness and recognition of our own Mod and Hugr.

Once we've learned this skill of honest and compassionate observation by practicing on ourselves (this must come first), we can apply it to enhance our understanding and improve our relationships with other people, with their Mod and Hugr souls, as well. This skill nourishes the deep growth of our own wisdom, compassion and understanding towards our self and toward others.

Exercise 8-2: Observing Mod and Hugr in action

At the beginning of the previous exercise, I mentioned that it's good to pursue learning about your Mod and Hugr in two ways: through deep thought focused on the exercise, but also through an underlying awareness as you go through your daily life. Once you've worked through some of your main drivers, your underlying desires and will, in the previous exercise, then it's time to extend that awareness while you are in action.

The first step in doing this is to try to be aware of what you learned through the previous exercise, and notice how it plays out in your daily life. As often as you can, briefly stop and ask yourself: what is motivating me to do / say / think this right now? When you do this, don't get into any long, meditative, analytical answers; you can't be interrupting yourself to that extent in the midst of your daily activities, and the deep-thought approach leads to one kind of awareness, but closes off other kinds.

For this daily-life exercise, when you ask yourself that question about what is motivating or driving you at the moment, let the knowledge 'appear' to you, without thinking and digging around the way you did in the previous exercise. Instead of 'thinking', open your awareness to how you're *feeling*: your senses and other-senses, your emotions, attitude and mood, how your body feels—tense or relaxed, 'in the flow' or feeling a lot of resistance, etc. These non-rational experiences will tell you things about your Hugr and Mod that you won't get from thinking. You don't need to do anything, at this point, with the insights you gain this way; you are simply building more levels of recognition and awareness of your Mod and Hugr, and how they shape your daily life and character.

Exercise 8-3: Wiliness and frustration

Up until now, we've been proceeding as though Hugr and Mod are transparent, reasonable and cooperative beings. And they usually are, as long as things are going their way! But as we well know, life is not always like that. Many circumstances occur, every day, that anger, frustrate, upset and disappoint us, making us feel that nothing is going our way, and that we have little control over our circumstances. These feelings are triggers that can flip Mod and Hugr into reactive stances of defensiveness and uncooperativeness. Other causes for such flipping are challenges to Hugr's established world-view or framework of thought, or to the underlying logic and acceptableness of Mod's driving motivations.

    How do Hugr and Mod react when they shift into defensive mode? This is something for each of us to explore for ourselves, but there are two very common stances to be aware of. Hugr tends to become wily and manipulative, to rationalize and excuse its words and actions, to practice self-deception (that is, misleading and working around our conscious awareness) and deception of others. Mod tends to behave with a lot of frustration, outrage, anger and acting out. I'll be exploring both of these tendencies in more detail later on, but let's begin with this starting point.

*Frustration can lead Mod and Hugr to act out
in pointless but destructive ways!
("Stalo," also called "Troll-Butting," by John Bauer.)*

Among the best and most important ways to get to know your Mod and Hugr is by recognizing their negative behaviors in yourself: what triggers those behaviors, and how do they manifest? It's quite challenging to pursue this, because Hugr and Mod are being defensive and will try to prevent you from becoming fully aware of what they / you are doing. They are protecting their own self-image, their self-justification for their actions, attitudes and reactions. They feel they have a 'right' to their reactions and behavior, and don't want to be called out. (Keep in mind: these are your own feelings and attitudes, too. It's very difficult to use the right words, when talking about our souls who are also, collectively, our Self! I hope I am being reasonably clear....)

So in fact, you are not going to confront Hugr and Mod and try to call them out; if you do, they'll just work around your conscious awareness and make things worse.

Mod and Hugr: Motivating Forces

All you need to do in this exercise is *simply observe what's happening within yourself when things go wrong during your day*, either due to outside events, or to your own negative thoughts and emotions (often both together).

Don't try, at this point, to change anything, don't put blame on yourself or others, and don't get caught up in your Mod-self's anger and frustration, or your Hugr-self's rationalizing, manipulation and self-justification. Just step back and look honestly at yourself / Mod / Hugr as if you were an outside observer. Again, this is going to be happening in the thick of your everyday tasks and activities; you won't have time or patience to analyze and meditate while it's happening. A fluid awareness and acknowledgement of what's happening is what you need.

So that's it, that's what you do here: just observe honestly and learn, without making excuses, rationalizing, laying blame, becoming angry and frustrated, or trying to confront and control Hugr and Mod.

Study participant experiences

<u>Leif Höglund:</u> *As somebody who struggles with anxiety, I find that my first defensive response is usually avoidance. As I work through this to try to find healthier, less self-destructive responses; however, I find that I do get frustrated when I hit obstacles, particularly when I am trying to focus on accomplishing a task and I am unable to.*

The wiliness. This is an existential threat to a Hugr like my own. It is a threat to the pious self-image I construct of myself, of maintaining and defending frith. Of what I consider ethical. Intellectually and philosophically, this is well moderated. Within my emotional capacity, though, it is the weakness I fear most. I respond fiercely and defiantly to false accusations. This has caused a lot of unnecessary strife.... It remains challenging. It will remain challenging. I must find ways for my Hugr to rise to it, and so far, it has.

The effects of honest observation

It seems like this constant observation would make your defensive Hugr and Mod really annoyed and even more prone to being frustrated and making excuses, but the funny thing is that it doesn't work that way, at least in my experience. What happens is that Hugr and Mod realize that you are actually honoring them by your effort to become aware of and understand them, including understanding what makes them upset, frustrated, angry, defensive, and how they express those things.

By becoming aware of them, but not dictating to them about how to behave, you are treating them as real beings worthy of respect. Once this foundation of respect is laid, which comes about with ongoing practice of honest and compassionate observation, then you have a basis for your Hugr, Mod, your conscious self, and your other souls too, to work together on making whatever changes you all agree on. There is now mutual trust and respect between your everyday consciousness and all your souls, which provides the necessary foundation and safe space for negotiations and the resulting actions and changes to take place.

Hugr and Mod want to be effective in your Midgard life, want to achieve their goals and desires. Once they understand that some behaviors are counterproductive, or don't fit well with the character and the life your whole soul-household is trying to create together, they become more willing to shift into a different mode of action. They come to value strength, courage and wisdom over defensiveness and frustration. All of the activity I've discussed here is part of building character: becoming a person with strong and well-developed souls and soul-powers, guided by wisdom, self-knowledge and self-respect.

We've laid the groundwork for a deeper understanding of these two souls, Mod and Hugr, who are so active and impactful in our Midgard life. Let's now pursue this in more detail, beginning with Mod.

Mod and Hugr: Motivating Forces

Arthur Rackham

This complex picture can spark all kinds of tales and wonderments: about why the rider is in these spooky woods, why the hidden wights of the forest are chasing him, what he seeks and desires, even why his horse seems to be blinded with ribbons. How and why did he get himself into this? This is the kind of perplexity we are often met with, when we try to decipher the motivations and desires of Hugr and Mod—our own souls, and those of others as well.

Chapter 9

9. Exploring your Mod Soul

{Primary runes in the bind-rune above: Ehwaz, Uruz, Sowilo, Tiwaz.}

Background reading: Chapter 8, and the section on the Modsefa in Chapter 12, both in Book I. Alternatively, the articles on my website "Dances with Daemons: The Mod Soul," and "Sefa: The Soul of Relationship."

The nature and strengths of Mod and mægen

Mod is Will and Power, and all that can be influenced by these things within our self and our life: our behavior and actions, our character and aims in life, our strengths and our abilities, and our drive toward excellence, in whatever fields of action we choose. Mod fuels these drives within us to take action, to survive, to thrive, and to achieve.

All of our souls consist of certain forms and flows of energy, which have various sources and express themselves in various ways within us and within our world of Midgard. Here, I want to look more deeply into the nature of Mod's energy, its mægen, and how it is shaped. Mod exists in three different but related forms. It is simply a form of energy, for one thing, and this comes across most clearly through the many medieval spells I've read, that seek to restore mod-energy to an ailing human or domestic animal, one who is weak, tired, lethargic, depressed, ill, unproductive, unable to take action. Let's look at this form, first.

Exercise 9-1: Sensing your Mod

In the exercises I offered in the previous chapter, about the motivating forces of Mod and Hugr, you worked on observing your behavioral patterns as a way to understand these two souls. Now we'll approach it from another direction: sensing Mod's energy within yourself.

Absorb the discussions about Mod I've offered in all the readings, then sit quietly and gather your awareness. Direct it toward sensing, feeling, recognizing your Mod. First, try to recognize where the core of your strength lies, within your body. There may be more than one core or wellspring of strength. I feel one core in my solar plexus, and a second one in my throat and jaws. The solar plexus is a natural power core of our body, and I assume that most people feel Mod-power here. The core I feel in my throat and jaws could be because I express much of my Mod-power through words and singing, but this is also where I

Exploring Mod

unconsciously suppress my Mod-power by clenching my jaws and tightening my neck. So throat, jaws and neck sometimes turn into a Mod-battleground for me!

There are often other mod-power centers within us, as well, including the pelvic region (encompassing genitals, womb and ovaries, sacroiliac, lower abdomen), thighs, hands. Eyes are a major avenue for expressing Mod. For example, very mod-powerful beings, like Thor and Jotnar, are sometimes seen to have flashing or burning eyes, as is seen near the end of *Thrymskviða* (Poetic Edda), when the giant Thrym pulls back the veil covering the person he thinks is his bride, Freya. Instead, this is Thor in disguise, come to retrieve his stolen Hammer, and Thrym cries out:

"Why are Freya's eyes so terrifying? It seems to me fire is burning from them." This is a showing-forth of Thor's mod-power through his gaze.

Most of the old, decorated Thor's Hammers that I have seen feature staring eyes, indicating Thor's powerful, mod-filled gaze. This one is an extreme example of staring eyes, and shows a full face, not just the eyes, as many other Hammers do.

If you are working to connect your Mod-soul with Thor and the Thorlings (his children) pay special attention to their gazes when you interact with them, and pay attention to what their gazes trigger within yourself. The monster

Exploring Mod

Grendel in *Beowulf* also showed a fiery gaze when he attacked Heorot: his Mod was in a state of ire, of rage, and an ugly light like fire shone in his eyes (ll. 726-7).

Secondary mod-centers can be anywhere, depending on where your Mod expresses its power, or wants to express its power. Be aware of any mod-power areas you might find, but for now focus on seeking the central Mod-core within you. This is likely to be in the same region of the body where Thor wears his *megingjörd*, his belt of megin- or mægen-power.

Once you feel this core of strength, try to sense your Mod-Will in the center of this core. Just relax and let it well up within you: any kind of sensation, thought, image, feeling, urge, emotion. I sense this as a rising-power, an uprush like a geyser or fountain, filling me with a sense of 'I want, I need, I must, I can, I Will.' When I feel this, I want to jump up and take action in some way, exert myself for some purpose, though I may not have anything specific in mind. This is its 'native form', I would say, the form it takes when Mod motivates me toward some action.

There's another form Mod-Will takes in me, that enables me to stand my ground when I need to (or when I stubbornly want to!). It's not an up-rushing geyser, but a consolidated, boulder-like feeling, heavy and rooted, not going to be moved. That's Mod's Will, too. I guess one could call these the Irresistible Force and the Immovable Object, which are both good descriptions of Mod!

We'll be working more on Mod's Will later on, but for now just try to get to know it a bit, from within yourself. Spend some time sensing strength and Will within you, exploring them with all your senses, thoughts and feelings. Are there any images that come to you, symbolizing these things? Could you express them artistically? Explore this in your Daybook.

Study participant experiences

Leif Höglund: *I feel Mod in my muscles, particularly in my upper arms all the way down to my hands, and its will burns with the heat of metal in the forge and the muscles of the smith. Malleable, strong, full of potential. It requires my body and other souls to be healthy to maintain its heat and focus. It is a spiritual metabolism, which transforms the energy of other souls and the body into a form that Mod can use and direct in its own right (as you point out). Mod is especially present when I'm doing food prep at work (I'm a line cook, who preps about half of the line's ingredients). I use a hammer to tenderize meat, quite literally. Cooking is something I love for people I love – including the people in the dining room. From a business perspective, this can be a challenging mindset. My Mod is most efficient when it outlines a strategy for itself ahead of time, rather than diverting energy from actually carrying out a task while it is already in progress.*

Laurie Sottilaro: *Two major takeaways. I'm a litterer, and my Mod is a puppy. I was unsure what I was going to find on this one and was rather surprised to find it doing well. My Mod resides in my center, and is apparently very flexible. Once I found it, it looked pretty transparent, so I decided to check it out and see what was going on. I do a lot of energy work, as in building (esoteric) constructs. Apparently I had a few that I left up. Since my Mod looked so transparent, I asked it to expand so I could look more closely, and it kind of took me into an alternate space where it turned into a column so I could see where all the linkages were. I was surprised to find it was my Mod that was supporting all those old (esoteric) projects, as well as my current ones. With that cleaned up, things looked a little better.*

And at that point, my Mod went from strained to somewhat puppy like, bouncing around and doing the equivalent of jumping up on me and licking my face. I was quite surprised. It was very glad to get attention, and even more so to get that clean-up. As I said, it appears to be very plastic in the original sense of the word. It's kind of chaotic in form, shifting with almost every thought to something that would be appropriate for that thought train. Apparently I mentally model things as part of my thinking process, and my Mod is the support for that.

Mod and Wode as states of being

As well as being strength and energy, mod is also a state of being, an ecstatic state that does not consist of love, peace and bliss, but of overpowering rage and determination to conquer, to achieve one's will by barreling through all obstacles. This is described in Old Norse as *Jotunmoði*, the mod of the Jotnar. They also used the term *Asmoði*, the mod of the Æsir, to describe the powerful force that the Æsir bring to bear against Jotunmoði. Thor is described as being capable of both, and in fact I'm not sure what the difference between them is, if any, except in how this powerful state is applied in action. This kind of mod sounds to me very much like wode when it refers to battle-wode, berserker-wode (not poetic / inspirational wode). The difference between wode and mod as states-of-being, as I see it, is a subtle one, and has to do with which soul the power is flowing through. (See Chapter 5 in Book I for more about wode.)

Exploring Mod

Wode, in my understanding, flows through our Ghost, while mod flows through our Mod soul. Wode empowers Ghost to transcend the physical, to operate beyond the body's limitations. Thus we see the berserker phenomena of fearlessness and absolute lack of caution, also of delayed or suspended reaction to wounds and bleeding. The wode-trance allows people to walk barefoot over burning coals, to ignore severe wounds and suppress bleeding until the trance has abated, and even to heal or to create physical wounds, marks or other changes in its Lichama through spiritual power, as happens in some types of religious ecstasies and shamanic trances.

What happens here is that Ghost temporarily takes over the body and uses it as though physical limitations do not exist (which is Ghost's normal attitude, anyway!). But except when it is in a super-high state of wode, Ghost is not able to convince our strong Lich-Hama to view things the same way...fortunately for us, for the sake of maintaining our normal physical life and safety, our awareness that physical limitations do exist, and that they do matter while we are physically alive!

Just as wode can flow into us as a gentle stream of inspiration, or pick up steam and grip us in a powerful state of creativity that *must* be expressed, or in rare cases explode through us in an uncontrollable ecstatic state, so mod-energy can act through similar, graduated expressions. Our everyday level of mod-energy sustains us in our daily activities, and if it is diminished we suffer from depression, fatigue, lethargy, lack of motivation, and are more easily subject to illnesses. A stronger upwelling of mod-energy and Mod-will can spur us to achieve mighty deeds of various different kinds, when properly controlled through upright character and well-honed Will. If our character is weak or flawed, then higher mod-energy may express itself as anger and bad temper, selfishness, moodiness, and overall unpleasantness. When the higher level of beneficial mod is steadily sustained, we are able to maintain a level of achievement and character that shapes a truly admirable and productive life.

When very high levels of mod-energy are present but are not controlled by a well-developed character and Will, then we have people who are characterized by rage, savagery, cruelty, abusiveness, hyper-aggression, sociopathy, uncontrolled passions in general. In contrast, people with a well-directed Will can sometimes access the highest levels of mod-energy during times of great challenge (for example, during marathons, Iron-Man or Olympic competitions), or during life-threatening situations (e.g. defending against an attacker, fire-fighting, or dealing with a storm while sailing), and use the power and determination they gain thereby to achieve deeds of almost supernatural strength and prowess.

Exercise 9-2: Do you squash your Mod-force?

In the previous exercise, you explored your sense of strength and will in your core, and how that strength and will naturally wants to express itself. I used the example of myself wanting to jump up and take some kind of action. There are, of course, instances in our life when this is not a wise move, like musing over our grievances and then wanting to jump up and beat the stuffing out of whoever we are mad at.

But I think it's fair to say that we often have a situation where our Mod does want to jump up enthusiastically and get going with some kind of worthwhile action, physical or mental, and we find all sorts of reasons for not doing it. The main reasons are often inertia, stagnation, negative self-talk, lack of confidence, distraction, and the like. We end up simply ignoring or brushing off Mod's enthusiasm, often accompanied by a sense of guilt about doing this. The semi-conscious uneasiness that results from this process leads us to avoid even thinking about the action that Mod wants to take.

This is very discouraging to our Mod, especially when it becomes a life-pattern that continues for years. *Courage is a major characteristic of Mod, and dis-couraging Mod by dismissing its courage and energy is injurious to its potency and its fulfilment during our Midgard life.* When Mod is frequently squashed like this, we find that when we really need Mod's courage, strength, determination and Will, it may not rise within us as it should. We may also, usually unintentionally, do the same thing to other people: our children, spouse, family, friends, and people with whom we work.

For this exercise, keep the awareness of your Mod in the back of your mind as you go through your daily life, and especially when you may be 'wasting time' or engaging in avoidance activities. (True restfulness, relaxation, and refreshment are not 'wasting time'; they are essential to our well-being, but not all of the activities that we claim fit into those categories actually work that way. Not being able to shut down the screen when it's time to do other things like go to sleep or make a good dinner is an example of avoidance activity: something with little benefit that we persist in doing so we have an excuse not to do something else that is more worthwhile, but takes more effort.)

Exploring Mod

So, keep your Mod in the back of your awareness, and notice when Mod perks up with enthusiasm or energy, wanting to do something, even something small, quick, or trivial. Take a moment to notice this and consider what it is that Mod wants to do, what this spark of enthusiasm, urge or drive is pushing you toward. Then examine your reaction to it. Do you automatically deny it, squash it down, throw cold water over it? Do you sigh in long-suffering or resentment, and 'punish' your Mod / yourself for having such ideas? Consider, as you are pursuing this, whether you are doing the same thing to other people, intentionally or unintentionally.

It's true that some of Mod's urges can be unwise to indulge in, so the pause to consider, before taking action, is a good idea. It isn't so good, though, when that pause for consideration fills up with excuses, dis-couragement, self-doubt, negative attitudes, etc., when Mod just gets brushed aside and disrespected no matter how worthwhile its urge to act really was. Years of this kind of behavior end up weakening our Mod and / or turning its activity into very negative forms.

Mod *needs* to take action and express itself in our life, and we need to be aware of this and cooperate in a wise and well-balanced way. With this exercise, you become more aware of how you are treating your Mod and its needs, and how this is impacting your life and affecting the many qualities and strengths that Mod can contribute when it is encouraged to do so.

Study participant experiences

<u>Anonymous participant</u>: These exercises were easy in themselves, but deeply engaging with mod and oneself has been difficult and

foreign to me in ways that I never feel with the other souls/soul-parts. This is going to be the lesson that has extra credit, the one that gets too personal for my own comfort. And that's good – these lessons force us to actually deal with our shit. But after we go through the lessons, I'll share a personal essay on Mod-sickness. ...

... Let me tell you. Nothing and no one ever made me feel persecuted the way that being cancelled did. I've been Mod-sick ever since. I'm terrified to talk to people, to make reasonable boundaries, to do anything that makes someone think I'm a "bad person," to the point where my anxiety over making decisions prevents me from making one at all. I'm so afraid of making ethical errors that I just isolate myself entirely.

I don't know y'all. It's wild to come of age in this kind of world, it's just wild. I don't know how to properly balance my obligations to others with those to myself.

Well, I guess we're just in that same cognitive dissonance issue addressed earlier. But it's also not going to be something I can fix overnight, which isn't even expected, so I've been and will continue to try not to hold myself to that. I'm only 24 and I've already got brow wrinkles, for gods' sake. I'm not where I want to be, and I won't be until I die, so what's the rush?

<u>My response</u>: *Writing this post is a deep-thinking and courageous deed, and I salute you for it. And note that both deep thought and courage are characteristics of your Mod! (And Hugr.) So really I am saluting your Mod for this deed of cathartic communication.*

A challenge for you now is finding enough common ground between your life path and activity, and the expectations of the communities you want to be a part of, while still remaining true to yourself, your souls. This is an essential soul-struggle for all of us who want to be true to our Self and to our communities and the life we want to live within those communities. And we each have to shape our own path through that tangle. This seems to be the challenge now for your Mod soul, in particular, and very much for your Modsefa as well, the common ground between your Mod and your Sefa souls.

"I'm not where I want to be, and I won't be until I die, so what's the rush?" This sentence of yours is the quintessential definition of "personal growth", I would say, associated with many growing pains, and in a state of constant flux. Our modern culture and economy are founded upon the illusion that life is supposed to be easy, fun, and free; that we are owed everything we want, and something is seriously wrong if we don't get it.

If we imagine there will ever be a state that we will arrive at, where we have gotten everything we want, or have reached some point of unchanging stability, any honest evaluation will show us that "there is no There, there." This is a lot of what happens during a person's midlife crisis. Many people feel terribly disillusioned when they discover this, and are tempted to give up.

The Heathen understanding that life is an Ordeal--an ongoing challenge laid down for us by ørlög and by the nature of life in Midgard--offers courage, guidance, and moral support to us on this strenuous but worthy path. There is no free ride, and no such thing as a stopping place on our path of life. There is only growth and striving, only the struggle to walk toward an ever-evolving vision of....something....that shines at the farthest horizon of Being. Walking this path *is* our life; this is what life really is—not the achievement of some static, idealized state, or piles of possessions and status symbols, but the striving itself toward our own ever-evolving vision.

Exploring Mod

The Thorlings

The kind of courageous, driving, powerful energy that we're discussing here was often called 'mod', but also called 'mægen' in the ancient Germanic languages, and very often these terms were used together, to give a complete picture of a powerful form of energy that can be directed by our Mod-soul. These two terms come together perfectly in the names of Thor's and Jarnsaxa's sons, Magni (main, megin, mægen) and Moði (mod-y, filled with mod), and are further enhanced by the name of Thor's and Sif's daughter Thruðr or 'strength'. Thor himself, of course, is the embodiment of Mod and mægen, as well.

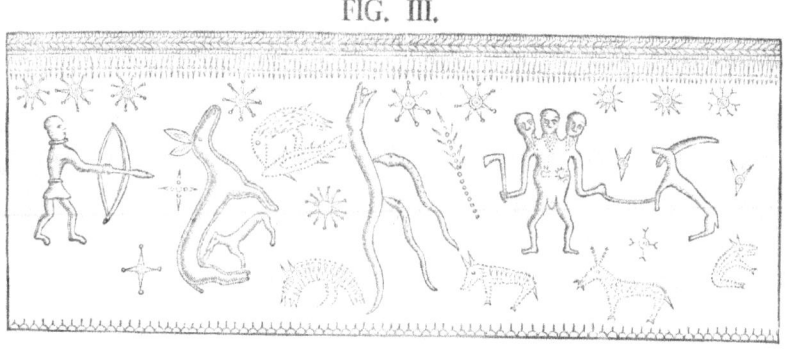

FIG. III.

There is a strange figure of a three-headed man shown on one of the Danish Gallehus horns (dated to the early 5th century CE). This is generally thought to be Thor. He is holding a long-handled implement, an axe or a hammer, and with the other hand holds a rope tied to a horned and bearded animal, probably a goat.

Here are my own thoughts about this figure. I also think it is Thor, and that the heads on either side of the

Exploring Mod

central one represent his sons, Magni and Móði, with their powers which arise from his own.

I think many or all of the figures on the Gallehus horns show indications of 'mystery cults' or ritual patterns dedicated to various Deities, and that this three-headed figure represents one of those mysteries. The strange depiction of Thor with three heads, in my view, indicates both the multiplication of his mod-and-main power, and the budding of his offspring or emanations, Móði and Magni. All of these: budding or growing mod and main, sacrificing (the goat) to his need, and then bringing dead bones to life by hallowing with his Hammer, are part of Thor's mystery. There is much to ponder here, as we seek to understand the full expression of mod and mægen, sacrifice and revival into life, and the great and complex powers of Thor expressed through his mighty Hammer. (See also discussion in Waggoner, *Our Troth* vol. 1, p. 50-52.)

These mysteries of Thor are also, in my view, mysteries of the Mod soul (and of the Ferah—Thor has important connections there, as well). Meditations, devotions, magical workings, and other focused attention on Thor and his children are very fine ways to develop and shape the energy of our Mod-soul. It's my opinion that modern Heathens would do well to pay more attention to the 'Thorlings' or Thor's children, not least because they were / are / will be Ragnarök survivors and thus among the divine leaders of the next cycle of the Worlds. The idea that 'mod, mægen and strength' are focused through them and into the worlds is not a trivial consideration!

The phrase 'mod and mægen' together was how the ancient Germanic scholars translated the Latin term 'virtus' or 'virtue', specifically the kind of virtue that refers to 'special powers, outstanding potency' of things like potent medicinal herbs and magical implements. This understanding implies that the triple Thorlings, Mod-Mægen-Strength, can be called upon to imbue something with power and virtue, including our own Mod-soul, but also magical and healing items and spells, among other things.

This may have been an underlying meaning of the rune-inscription *Wigi Thonar*, 'Thor hallow', on the Nordendorf fibula: calling on Thor not only to make the inscribed item sacred or hallowed, but also to fill it with virtue and power, mod and mægen, for some special purpose. (See illustration on p. 225.) Being filled with power and focused on a purpose is what Mod-soul is all about, and the general idea of virtue in the sense of having a good character and strong, well-directed will-power is also part of what our Mod-soul is capable of.

Exercise 9-3: Your Mod-magnets

Once you've been able to recognize the main source within you of your Mod-energy or power, and become more aware of how you consciously respond to it, then it's time to think about how best to shape and direct this power. One of the ways we can build and channel mod-power in our lives is, in a sense, to work backwards. Instead of trying to grow mod-power directly, we can grow it through a process of 'suction' or 'magnetism'. We do this by deciding where we most want to use our mod-power, and allowing our focus and dedication to these areas of life to pull our Mod's energy and abilities in that direction. The importance, to us, of whatever life-areas we have chosen to focus our Mod on,

Exploring Mod

draws energy and attention from our Mod-soul like the power of suction or a magnet.

Once this power / energy starts flowing strongly, it helps to break up energy blocks and pinch-points that our life experiences and circumstances have created, which hamper our access to our own mod-power. There is no concern about running out of mod-power, because our Mod soul accesses this energy from ambient sources: solar, telluric, lunar, elemental, planetary energies, their interactions and enhancements of each other, and the surging, intertwined flows of natural life-energy all around us. Mod has its roots as an elemental being or a wight of nature in some form, and naturally has access to these energies.

Since I'm suggesting the analogy of a magnet here, let me add another point of attraction: the similarity between 'magnet' and Magni Thor's son. The word 'magnet' comes ultimately from Magnesia, a region named after one of the demigod sons of Zeus, Magnes, who was considered the founding-father of the ancient Greek tribe which settled in that region of northern Greece. Magnetic ore was found here, and was called 'the stone of Magnes.' *(Online Etymology Dictionary.)* Here we have two powerful sons of Thunder-Gods, with basically the same name, which is associated with the word for magnetic iron and thus can form a connection with Thor Thunder-God's mighty iron Hammer and its flows of power (likewise with Zeus's Thunderbolt). The title of this section, 'Mod-Magnets', combines our own two brother-Gods' names and domains of power: Móði and Magni. As you pursue this exercise for Mod, ask Móði to power-up your Mod, and attune yourself to Magni's power. Try to sense Magni's

Exploring Mod

magnetic energy, and ask him to help you find sources of such energy in your own life, to magnetize your own Mod and mægen and enhance its flow.

The idea for this exercise is to seek and clarify the 'magnets' in your life, that have the power to draw mod-energy toward them and get the flow really moving for you. Where, at this time in your life, are the best channels for these things? One thing that *doesn't* work for this exercise is to focus on what you 'should' be doing, but are not doing, or not doing well enough. Mod is all about enthusiasm and eagerness, and those things fall flat as soon as we start talking about 'should'!

Yes, there are plenty of things we 'should' be doing in life, whether we want to or not, and we'll talk more about that soon, in the context of building character. Once the flows of mod and mægen are running powerfully through us, they can light up those areas of life as well, helping us find ways to approach them with positive power and right attitude. But the 'shoulds' of life will not serve as a technique to maximize the flow of mod and mægen through our Mod soul; they are not 'mod-magnets.'

For this exercise, use meditation, self-observation, and input from others who know you well (including Deities and ancestral spirits), to find and explore some area of life that fills you with enthusiasm, that mobilizes your energy and your Will with an eager power, that magnetically attracts you. It could be anything: a hobby, your vocation or calling (whether paid or volunteer), parenting, relationships, intellectual / artistic / esoteric interests, sports and physical activities, gardening, homemaking, helping others, crafts, decorating your home, 'self-improvement' of any kind that appeals to you, playing

Exploring Mod

a musical instrument, interacting with animals tame or wild, creating a collection of some kind, whatever. It can be something that others might find 'small', 'silly', irrelevant, but you just enjoy it anyway, and feel a drive and desire to pursue it.

If you notice that these suggestions are similar to those I suggested in Chapter 4 for the Ghost, this is not a coincidence. I wrote earlier about the similarities between Ghost's wode-energy and Mod's mod-energy. In practicing Heathen soulful-living, these are both powerful and amazing soul-energies that we want to develop and direct in beneficial ways, rather than having their negative expressions take over and impact our own lives and the lives of those around us. Working to align and coordinate our wode and mod energies is well worthwhile, not only during life, but after life, as well.

I discuss, in Chapter 8 of Book I, my idea that after death our Mod-soul joins our Ghost-soul as a partner in the God-realms. As this takes place, I see a melding of their wode- and mod-energies to power their afterlife activities with the Deities. There is every good reason to begin aligning these powerful energies, here and now in Midgard, by coordinating the urges and enthusiasms of our Mod and Ghost souls through the activities we prioritize in our life.

Mod's nature

So, here is our Mod soul at its best: filled with courage, strength, power, striving, character, will, purpose, determination, intelligence, capability, potency, virtue in all its highest and strongest senses. It's easy to see how having this daemon-soul as a member of our soul-household or *hiwship* can potentially serve humans and humankind extremely well. However, we can't forget that Mod definitely has another side, with potentially serious flaws of character and will.

I think that some of these 'flaws' are in fact characteristics of Mod's origins as a non-human, elemental nature spirit, unconnected with and uninfluenced by human values. Mod has evolved along with humans; it retains its daemon or elemental characteristics, but its association with humans over many generations has given it the capacity to become more aligned with, and supportive of, human values and human ways of seeing and doing things. However, this does not happen automatically. The Mod soul (and the Hugr) within each person needs to be trained, needs to develop and mature, to learn from experience, including learning from the hard knocks of life. In Chapter 12 of Book I, I discuss how Mod is 'humanized' by interfacing with our Sefa soul to form our Modsefa.

All the ways, within the family and within society, that we use to teach and train children about ethics, responsibility, civility, citizenship, education, aspirations, goals, work ethic, relationships, self-expression and self-fulfillment, how to handle life in general...all of these are actually directed toward educating children's Mod, Hugr, and other souls. And as we can easily see, sometimes the results are excellent, other times the results are dismal failures, and many lie somewhere in between. It seems to me that the better we understand our, and other people's, Mod, Hugr, and other souls, their natures and their needs, the more effectively we can teach and guide children to develop their souls in beneficial rather than harmful ways.

I emphasize Mod and Hugr especially here, because these two, along with Sefa, are our most Midgard-oriented souls, the ones who are most often reflected in our everyday character, behavior, choices and deeds, for good or for ill. They are also souls that, in my understanding, are not shaped or influenced on our behalf by the Deities; rather, they are souls which arise from and act within the Midgard realm, with all its urgent and conflicting needs and pressures.

Building character

Mod and Hugr can express themselves in very positive ways, and in negative ways, as well. Our discussion here applies to the issue of things we 'should' do in our lives, that we were deliberately staying away from in the previous section about Mod-magnets. This is a different dimension of Mod. Instead of exploring a magnetic *force*, a force of attraction to start our mod and mægen flowing strongly, as we did earlier, here we're looking at growing a stable *form* to shape our Mod into solid strength and goodness of character. Force and form need to work together to shape substance.

What does it mean to 'build character'? Think about this in the context of yourself. For me, it means to clarify my values and important goals in life, envision the person I want to be, and try to live up to this, day by day in my life. This is an ongoing process with several stages, all of them involving Mod as one who is acting, and Mod as one who is acted upon. (As an analogy, think of our muscles when we exercise: we're using our muscles to exercise, and at the same time, our muscles are being changed and improved by our exercise. Muscles are both 'actors' and 'acted upon' when we exercise.) Mod is a strategic thinker and a primal motivator, very good at identifying goals, figuring out how to achieve them, and motivating us to do so.

Unfortunately, Mod is also very good at getting in our way when we try to do these things. It can draw us into 'moods' where we might not want, nor feel up to, doing what needs to be done; where we argue, complain, make excuses, become irritated and impatient, feel tired and fed up, and toss the whole project out, at least temporarily! Every time this happens, it strengthens the negative associations of what we're trying to do, and makes it more difficult to get back on track.

What's happening here is Mod being its own complex, contradictory self. It's got a lot of strengths of character, and a lot of character flaws as well; this is true for each one of us, and it's part of the nature of Mod (and Hugr) as a Midgard-oriented, human-oriented soul. Midgard, and life in Midgard, is a complex and contradictory place to be! We are subject to many competing needs, forces, goals, desires, that all tend to get in each other's way. To be able to work constructively with Mod's fundamental nature, we need to go back to the deep root of Mod and really understand it.

Mod as Will

I find it useful to understand Mod, at its deepest, most primal level, as Will itself, sheer Will-Power, that is capable of barreling through everything in its path. The thing is, at this level Will has little that is shaping and directing it. It's very primitive and 'just wants to BE': just wants to express itself 'because it's there', 'because it can'. This is what the Norse viewed as a characteristic of the giants, and called it *Jotunmoði*, an overwhelmingly powerful but primitive determination to take what one wants and do what one wants, to crush all obstacles, and to Hel with the consequences! This is pure Power, and like other forms of power such as electrical and nuclear power, it can be devastatingly destructive when it is not appropriately directed and controlled.

Modern esoteric workers talk about our 'true will.' This is an important and valid concept, but it's wise to understand that if we, as a living human, follow our Will down deeply enough, we'll encounter this powerful, single-minded Mod-Will within us. This is when the would-be wizard can get side-tracked onto a destructive path of self-referencing, selfish aims and outlooks, and begin to misuse their power, as one can see all too often when looking at the life-history of famous esotericists. Only by being aware of this Mod-Will within us, and learning how to work with it, can we avoid such problems and harness it constructively.

Now let's follow this deep, inner Mod-Will up a few levels. Here we're getting into physical life in Midgard, and this life has its own necessary requirements. We need food, shelter, safety, the opportunity to reproduce. Our Will is a useful driver to motivate us to do whatever we need to do to obtain these things. One of the essential ways humans obtain them is through social networks and social interaction, and we have essential needs relating to these social interactions as well. But things begin to get very complicated here, as we move on up the chain-of-being from primitive, elemental Will to complex human life.

Our Will is pulled in different directions all the time. Primitive Will says it's fine to steal food from your tribe-members, and maybe injure or kill them in the process. You need food, right? And you're going to get it. But then that destroys or distorts your access to social needs and social goods, and your Will is frustrated when you can't get those. So then, you 'behave nicely' by whatever standards your tribe has, and gain some social goods, but have to suppress parts of yourself that your Will wants to express, and give up or delay some things you may want.

More frustration, more complexity, and it continues to build, the more complex human society and human life becomes. Eventually our primitive Mod-Will, deep within ourselves, hunkers down and sulks and feels resentful, and breaks out through whatever gaps and cracks it can in our life to mess things up, just when we feel we have everything under control. Does this sound familiar?

Study participant experiences

Leif Höglund: *The challenge comes with Mod. My Mod and the rest of my souls have a... functional relationship. Mostly. Mod is my deepest challenge and frustrating. I adore Thor, I am allied to Thor, and he is one of the closest deities of my hearth cult. But there's some kind of fundamental difference in our dispositions that leads to some kind of spiritual miscommunication with us.*

Exercise 9-4: Shaping character and will.

Your character and your will are very personal to you, shaped by your experiences, environment, family, genes, education—all the factors of your life. How much of your character and the direction of your will has been shaped by these things, and how much have they been shaped by your deliberate intent?

This is the kind of question that is good to ask ourselves periodically, to undertake an evaluation and an inner housecleaning, so to speak. How much of Mod's power of character and will, or lack of such power, in your life is shaped by external factors (for example, advertising, 'influencers', peer pressure, etc.)? These things can creep in and influence us a great deal. They are not necessarily bad or wrong: we are social beings, and we all need to adapt in some ways to as to maintain the social fabric of family, friends and community, and healthy social ties. But these influences and adaptations should be a conscious choice on our part—choosing traits of character and exercises of will that we agree are good and desirable based on our own criteria that we develop with all our souls together.

For this exercise, spend some time honestly evaluating your character traits and the ways you enact your will in your daily activities and interactions. For example, how about your temper? Is it too hot, too cold, too pushy? Do you have a tendency to fudge the facts in your favor, or do you regularly tell the truth? Do you accept your responsibilities with goodwill, or do you tend to shirk them? And so forth….this is a lot of work, of course! But you can pick one or two traits of character that, upon examination, you are not really satisfied with, and work on making changes that will enhance your self-respect and self-confidence.

Roots, trunk, and branches

I've mentioned two aspects of Mod here: Character and Will. Will is the taproot, it sucks up ambient energy to power it; it is Mod's base of power. Let's think of Mod as a tree here, where the roots suck up ambient mod-and-maegen energy and shape it into Will. This energy is then channeled up through the trunk of the tree. This is a really important phase of action, because here is where the wild Will-energy is shaped and contained within a strong, stable structure: the tree-trunk. The trunk can be seen as our Mod-character; people even use the expression of someone having an 'upright character' like a tree trunk.

If we grow in right ways, our tree-trunk grows stronger and taller year by year throughout our life, and sends forth many stout boughs and branches above it. These leafy branches symbolize our actions and deeds: energized by Mod's Will and supported and directed by Mod's Character, they reach out in all directions, supporting and branching off from one another, to make a huge canopy above. This is our own World-Tree, our Tree of Deeds!

....And then the seeds

Finally, there are the fruits and seeds, that the tree lets go of, and sends out to carry its essence far into the world. The fruits and seeds symbolize the influence that Mod can have, that goes beyond its own place and time. This influence can take many forms; it is our own legacy, the outcome of our deeds in the world.

I propose that this is also where new human Mod-souls come from: the Mod within a living human sends out a pod or a seed of itself, which floats around and attaches to an infant human as part of the infant's new soular-system. If this is true, that makes it even more important to grow our own Mod-tree well, so that the pods it sends out to the new generation are grown from worthy roots and branches, and carry with them the essence of what our Mod-soul achieves in this life.

How does this work?

This all sounds very good, but how do we get Mod to work this way? Mod is obstreperous and ornery in many ways. How do we get it to grow like a tree instead of like kudzu, growing and twining and taking over our life with its tangled, willful energy? Based on my experience, I'd say this is not something that happens once and for all. It's a matter of daily actions and choices, like the Norns patting layers of clay each day on the trunk of the World Tree, nourishing and supporting it. Our daily actions and choices need to take into account what our Mod is like, what it wants and needs, what satisfies it, or we just end up fighting and struggling with it all the time.

Here is a key insight: *Mod wants to take action.* Mod is *mody:* it's brave, energetic, up-front, determined, strong-willed, eager, striving. It needs to act, and if you don't give it opportunities to take action and achieve as it's capable of, then it will sabotage you right, left and center. It's like a strong animal or an unruly kid who is just not getting enough exercise and freedom, and acts up in all kinds of ways as a result.

There are numerous ways to satisfy Mod's need for action, and they'll vary from person to person, and will vary throughout a person's lifetime as they grow, mature, and age. 'Action' can very much include mental as well as physical activity, social as well as individual activity. But there are key components that need to be present for an action to satisfy Mod, whatever form it takes. These components include: *striving,* expending energy in some form. Having a *meaningful goal, purpose or intention,* and directing your actions toward that. *Solving problems,* especially knotty, difficult problems that are really challenging and also meaningful and important to you. Reaching toward *excellence*, whatever it is that you're doing.

Mod does not care about wimpy, half-hearted actions; it wants something it can throw itself into and excel at, and the more challenging it is, the better. Whether it's an intricate knitting project, learning a new language, figuring out a better household routine, sorting out a relationship problem, improving your fitness or your job performance, or running for mayor of your city, Mod wants to achieve something it can be proud of and satisfied with.

What Mod hates is being surrounded by challenges, opportunities, problems that need fixing, and being held back from doing anything about them. That's when it will start acting up and make things even worse than they already are, especially by kick-starting your own bad habits, attitudes and moods into a downward spiral. Mod is determined to act, and if it isn't enabled and directed to act in positive ways, then by Thor it's going to act in negative ones!

Exercise 9-5: The power of the gut

This one is totally mundane and gut-level, but it's important, too! I've written, in Chapter 8 of Book I, that I think a primary physical foothold of our Mod-soul within our body is our microbiome, and particularly our gut-microbiome. When someone is 'mody', is tuned into their mod-power, people say this person 'has guts!' We have a gut-feeling about something. When we go through an experience of awful emotional shock, it feels like we've been kicked in the gut.

Exploring Mod

These expressions are meaningful, and they relate to our Mod's abilities of courage, character, knowingness, emotional power. The primary locus of Mod's power-core within our body is in our solar plexus and abdomen, where there are major nerve-centers, and also where our gut-microbiome resides.

I wrote, in Chapter 8 of Book I, about how the condition and activity of our gut-microbiome can affect our moods and attitudes, our mental abilities, our physical health and well-being. If you are not already doing this, take some time to learn more about the gut-microbiome, what it does, how it is affected by diet, stress, sleep-wake cycles, physical activity, intolerances, and other lifestyle factors.

Recent research is showing how the condition of the microbiome (of ourselves, and even of our parents) may play a role in many neurological problems like depression, anxiety, autism-spectrum, Parkinson's, dementia, schizophrenia, behavioral problems, and others. Dr. Verny points out that the gastrointestinal tract, including the microbiome, is now understood to have a very strong influence on our motivational and emotional states (p. 81). These are all situations that affect and are affected by our Mod and its mental / emotional / physical power, or lack thereof. There is much more to be learned here, I believe, that is of great importance for our health on all levels—both our personal health, and the health of our society as a whole.

Keep in mind that Mod's nature of powerfully 'wanting and willing' reflects in part the effect that our gut-microbiome exerts on our diet and other lifestyle choices. A gut overrun by yeast or microbial overgrowth, for example, can cause us to crave the desired food of these organisms, which is sugar, thus throwing us into a vicious cycle of unhealthy eating and related unhealthy lifestyle patterns. These things exert more control over us than we may realize.

Focusing on our gut seems so mundane, but it truly is a significant source of our Mod's strength and balance. If you want to develop and fine-tune your Mod and mægen to a high level, you need to keep your gut-microbiome healthy and functioning as optimally as you can. And to do this, you need to learn by experience about the 'care and feeding' of your own microbiome, including figuring out what is harmful to it, and act on that knowledge.

I recommend not getting too caught up in expensive supplements and treatments, but rather figuring out the kind of diet and lifestyle that best nurtures your own unique microbiome, which varies from person to person, and varies from one stage and condition of life to another. There is no one-size-fits-all approach, which is why you need to depend on your own observations and experiences.

You can tell how you are progressing in this effort, by observing your moods, energy levels, mental alertness, sleep quality, and overall sense of wellness. I can say, based on years of positive and negative personal experiences, that this is an important area of knowledge and action for us as holistic soul-body life-practitioners. Your Lichama, Aldr and Ferah will thank you for this, as well as your Mod!

Exercise 9-6: Where is courage?

If someone asks the question, "What is courage?" there are some fairly standard answers. "Courage is when you keep going even when you're afraid or exhausted." "Courage is facing things instead of running away." And the like. These statements are certainly true, but do they always touch us where they need to? When we say these things to ourselves during times of difficulty, do they really help us then? Maybe sometimes they do, but maybe not so much, especially during extreme circumstances.

Let's try a different approach. In this course of study we're paying a lot of attention to our inner feelings and sensations, and even to parts of our body and its functions where particular souls are rooted or most express themselves. So let's explore this question: not "*what* is courage," but "*where* is courage?" Where, within my total being, can the motive energy of courage be found? The tougher a situation is, the less helpful are intellectual ideas like "courage is…(whatever)". Instead, we need something at the gut-level, something instinctual that we can tap into whenever we need it.

Like all our exercises, this is not something with a prescribed answer that you're supposed to guess at; it's something unique to each of us, that we each need to find for ourselves. Courage lives within you; it is part of the life-force that expresses itself through you, and every other being. Now the task is to find where it pools and collects within yourself, where it takes root within you and feeds your Mod-tree that we talked about earlier.

First, sit quietly and clear your mind. Explore in your feelings, sensations, and imagination: what does courage really *feel* like? Not a definition of "what is it?", but "how does it feel?" It is unlikely to feel like 'fearlessness' or lack of fear. Fear is always there inside us; it is an important instinct that, in its healthy forms, helps us protect life, safety, and wellbeing for ourselves and those we care for. If

Exploring Mod

courage really erased fear within us, it would deprive us of this important source of information that we cannot afford to ignore. Courage helps us not be blinded, handicapped or defeated by fear, but it does not *erase* fear, nor should it.

Sit quietly and ask yourself "where is my courage concentrated within me? What does it feel like?" Let your responses arise within you, focusing more on feelings, images, sensations, than on verbal answers. After exploring this for awhile, then ask "how does it feel when I can't find my courage, when it seems like it's not there?" Remember instances in your life when your courage was low, versus when you were able to respond with courage, and compare how those experiences felt in your body-sensations and analog-senses. Use both these sensations—the presence of courage and its apparent absence—to refine your perception of where your courage is rooted within you, and what it feels like when it is active.

Absorb news, documentaries, history, movies, books and stories old and new, to see examples of people who deal with their circumstances with courage, and people who fail to do so. How do these examples make you feel and react? Can you recognize the root of your own courage within you, as you share in these other people's experiences and their responses?

When you've made progress with that, then work in your imagination and memory, to figure out what makes your courage grow and be accessible to you, versus what makes it shrink and be hard to find when you need it. Again, focus on sensation in your Lichama, your Mod, Ferah, Hugr, and other souls. Keeping yourself as healthy and well-nourished as you are able, on all levels, is likely to be supportive of your courage, though it is true that people

Exploring Mod

who deal well with serious health problems are among the most courageous of all. Exercise of your courage in daily situations, and growing your positive experiences of courage, day by day, helps a lot. But these are just words, generalizations; you need to discover and practice what works for you.

This exercise may require many repetitions, and is likely to be uncomfortable, at least to start with! *You're trying to find your 'courage-muscles' and figure out how to strengthen and train them,* and this is probably an unfamiliar approach to the questions "what is courage? How do I get more of it?" I hope this exercise will support you on your way to finding and growing your own deepest levels of courage.

Exercise 9-7: Partnering with Mod

You've gone through a number of Mod-exercises now, to learn to sense who your Mod is, what its power is like, how it behaves, what it wants. Now it's time to begin consciously partnering with it, to harness its energy in your life, and work to ensure that this energy doesn't backfire into negative expressions. Take it for granted that Mod wants to take action in your everyday life. Now, look for opportunities to tune in and ask your Mod how it wants to handle things. The previous two exercises, focused on understanding the connection between your Mod, your courage, and your gut, are among the many ways to begin partnering with your Mod to enhance Mod's power and improve your access to it. Here are some more suggestions.

When you first wake up in the morning, before you get out of bed, tune into your power-cores, sense your Mod and ask it where and how it wants to take action during the day in front of you. Agree that you will work with it, allow it to take action. Whenever you're facing a challenge, issue, choice, or problem during the day, tune into your Mod again. Show it some trust, ask it to step forward and use its strength, skill and will to address the issue.

A primary way to communicate between your conscious mind and your Mod is through *trust:* trust that this deep, instinctual, powerful soul within you has a great deal to offer, that it needs to offer it, needs to learn and gain experience and fulfill itself by acting in the world.

Use what you've learned about how and where you feel your Mod-strength and Will, to conduct these 'conversations', or really, 'sensation-conversations' within you, to figure out what Mod wants to do. And here is a clue to tell you whether you have actually accessed your Mod: *check your level of enthusiasm.* Mod's energy expresses itself very frequently as enthusiasm, the positive flip-side of its characteristic negative expression of rage.

Look for that sense of rising energy in your core, that get-up-and-go, as you ask your Mod about what it wants to do and how it wants to handle things that need doing. You may be quite amazed by how much your enthusiasm increases, even for things you need to do but would rather not be doing, once you let Mod step forward and take action. The more you practice this, the more it will become second nature for you. Try consciously letting Mod step in on small, insignificant events of life first, for practice and to build trust between your conscious mind, other souls, and your Mod. As trust and skill grow, you can extend this practice into more important and far-reaching actions in your life.

Exploring Mod

It's also useful to practice this in your imagination. Imagine a situation in your life, then seek your Mod-center and its energy, feel it flowing out toward the situation, and follow that flow of energy with your attention. Stand back and observe, in your imagination, how Mod would deal with the situation. (Of course, Mod is dealing through you; you are taking action yourself, but guided now by your Mod-soul.) Then afterwards, review your Mod's actions and see how well it worked, whether there are ways your Mod needs to improve its approach, etc. Mod learns by experience; it needs experience to shape and grow its power.

Mod has a great deal of power, and also has the potential for really going wrong, but the response to this knowledge should not be to just suppress your Mod. It should be, as I've said here, an increasing awareness of your Mod on your part, ongoing practice for your Mod to handle itself, through you, in real-life situations, and ever-increasing trust and reliance on this powerful soul of yours.

Also allow your Mod to choose some leisure activities for you to engage in: hobbies, sports, games, music, cooking, activities with family and friends, with the emphasis on mental / physical / social *activity*, not on passive 'consumption' of whatever input! Mod wants to have fun, and for Mod, that means activity of some kind: physical, mental, social ways of actively using your skills. I don't mean to suggest that rest time is unimportant, of course it is necessary and beneficial too. It's a matter of striking a healthy balance.

If you remember the study and exercises for the other souls so far, you'll notice that there's lots of overlap

Exploring Mod

between what satisfies Mod, and what fulfills other souls, too. Thank goodness, or you'd never have time for it all!

Mod and Ferah can go hiking and exploring in the woods or other wild lands together, go bird-watching or fishing, work at landscaping your garden, or engage in enthusiastic devotions and worship.

Mod and Ghost can enjoy intellectual and creative hobbies and interests together. Mod can express itself through the many skills and abilities of the Lich-Hama.

Mod can definitely work with Aldr's ability to feed nourishing energy into our body and souls, to support our health (including microbiome) and extend our life-span.

Mod and Hugr have so much in common that when you're working with one, the other is likely to be deeply involved as well. Mod really wants to 'do stuff', and is quite happy to do stuff that other souls want, too! This is one way that a jumble of souls can shape themselves into a supportive and interactive soul-household.

Study participant experiences

<u>Leif Höglund</u>: *I think I often equate "power" with "focus" or "attention." I have a lot of ideas, but often struggle with execution of those ideas, which feels a lot like a lack of power to me. This is, I think, an oversimplification on my part. "Power" is really more akin to the concept of potential energy in physics, insofar as power is latent until it is expressed through particular channels that are contingent on the circumstances, and the wielder of the power. Power is simply the amount of energy released in a given time; in essence, I am confusing "energy" with "focus." Unsurprising — ADHD is treated with stimulants after all.*

I feel it's important to note that power can remain "potential energy" and still be power. Power held by certain groups of people, for example, can act passively, without thought or even much action. The power is the default – the potential energy is enough to maintain the power without further action. It is a latent power for me to walk down the street in a bad neighborhood at night without a second thought – I don't have to use my power, but its potential energy, its capacity to do work, is very much present.

Perhaps then, power is the potential itself, to some degree. Those who have more power tend to be able to conserve their energy from less desirable tasks to apply that energy elsewhere. This would create a positive reinforcement cycle of power.

<u>My response</u>: *Your discussion of power and energy is excellent, offering very useful insights! Here are some thoughts that follow on from yours. We can see our own souls as reservoirs of latent energy within us. We may be aware, or unaware, of their power, their presence, of how to tune into them and channel them into our outer life. When we are completely unaware, that energy is mostly latent, but can burst or pop out unexpectedly and complicate and confuse our life. As we become more aware of the souls, that latency turns to potential energy; we are aware of it and know we can use it when it is needed, use it in a useful rather than a negative way. That gives us a lot of confidence, a solid foundation to draw on as the circumstances of our life call for various powers and actions. This study of soul lore that we are pursuing helps the process to move from latent, to potential, and then to actualized energy or 'work', and back again to potential energy, in ways that we consciously intend and want to do.*

Exercise 9-8: Who or what do you admire?

This exercise builds on the work you did in Exercise 9-4: Shaping character and will. One of the things that helps to shape Mod-energy is admiration and emulation. Just like a healthy youngster looks up to admired adults and wants to be like them, Mod is motivated by admiration, whether it's for a person, or for ideals or achievements. Mod wants to 'be like that', or 'do that thing, as well as, or better than, others are doing it.' By choosing what to admire, we can help shape our Mod into something admirable.

Think about this for yourself. Are there people or ideals that you especially admire? Are there, perhaps, even better people or ideals that you could set your admiring sights on? You won't know that until you find out about them, which you'll do by gaining more knowledge, whether it's through history, biography, literature, news, getting to know more people, learning more about your own ancestors, or however it might be. This is another activity for your Mod!

Pursue what is admirable and honorable, and encourage your Mod to shape itself in accordance with the best examples and ideals that you can conceive, rather than letting it run wild and landing you in trouble!

Help from the Holy Ones

In closing, let's turn to Thor and his children again. I suggest that you call upon them as you work through all the material on the Mod-soul. Moði represents our Mod and its power. Magni represents the magnetic force that can pull out mighty flows of mod-power in a direction that we choose. Thruðr, 'Strength', represents strength of character and Will.

Móði represents the *substance* of Mod, Magni the *force* that flows through this substance and seeks expression, and Thruðr the *form* that shapes the expression of the substance and the force. Thor himself ties all of them together: a God not only of might and main, but also a God of trustworthy character, of right and beneficial action, and a God whose actions are powerful and effective.

All of them can add might and main to our efforts to grow and shape our Mod-soul, and serve as guides and role models, once we come to know them and their mysteries more fully. One resource for building a connection with Thor is Baer's *Hammer, Oak and Lightning: A Thor Devotional*.

Exploring Mod

The large Rune Fibula of Nordendorf I. (A fibula is a clasp for clothing, like a safety-pin, but a lot fancier!) Found in 1843 in an Alemannic grave field of mid 6th to late 6th century A.D. near Nordendorf, Bavaria, Germany.

The fibula bears a runic inscription on the back side of its head plate: (first line) logaþore wodan wigiþonar *(second line)* awa (l)eubwini. *Photographed at the Römisches Museum, Augsburg, Germany.*

Exploring Mod

An example of Mod and Hugr in action:

The Battle of Maldon

Hugrs shall the harder be,
Hearts the keener,
Mod shall grow greater
As our mægen lessens.
Here lies our Ealdor,
All hewn about,
Good man on the ground.
Ever will regret
He who from this war-play
Thinks to wend forth.
I have broad wisdom,
I will not leave,
But by the side of my lord,
By so dear a man,
Think to lay myself down.

These are lines from a long Anglo-Saxon poem from the early 900s CE. The old warrior Byrhtwold speaks these words as he gazes at their fallen leader, Bryhtnoth. They have been fighting for a long time, and have lost many comrades. Some of the warriors have deserted the battle, and others are debating doing the same. Byrhtwold is committing himself to fight to the death, and encourages the others to do so as well, by calling on their soul-powers to compensate for their waning strength, their fear, discouragement and exhaustion. (My translation.)

Chapter 10

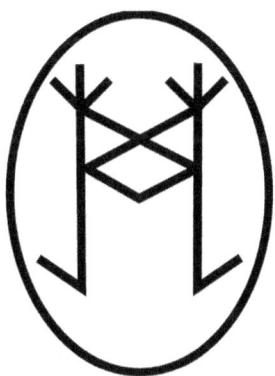

10. Exploring your Hugr

{Primary runes in the bind-rune above: Mannaz, Eihwaz, Algiz, Ansuz, Ingwaz, Dagaz, Kenaz.}

Background reading: Chapters 9, 10, 11 of Book I. Alternatively, the web articles "Hunting the Wild Hugr," "Who is Hugr?," and "The Occult Activities of the Hugr, Parts 1 and 2."

A framework of thought

I wrote in Chapter 2 of this book about how our sensations have to go through a process of interpretation before we can make sense of them as meaningful perceptions about the world around us, whether the outer physical world, or the inner world of the imagination that bridges to the Otherworlds. Our physical sensations are picked up through our sensory organs, transferred through our

Exploring Hugr

nervous system and into our brain (and other parts of our body too), and are there interpreted based on instinctive, rational, and cultural cues and imbedded information. Our imaginative perception system works in analogous ways. I discussed the role of our souls in both of these processes.

These systems are our 'perceptual framework'. It is partially instinctive and built into our body systems, and partially learned and conditioned by our life experiences and by what we are taught, and how we are taught, about the world around us.

Our 'framework of thought' works in similar ways. Part of it is instinctive: we have an instinctive ability to learn language, for example, and to use it for communication along with body language. Much of our framework is constructed through our responses to our life experiences, to what we have been taught and learned, and through social conditioning. There is additional, mostly subconscious material coming in through Hugr's connection with ancestral and past-life Hugrs, which adds subtle dimensions to our framework. Though I'm calling it a framework of 'thought', emotion is intertwined with these thoughts as well. This whole instinctive / conditioned / reasoned / subliminal amalgam of complex mental and emotional action and reaction is the core of our Hugr soul, though other souls such as Mod are involved, as well.

As we perceive this amalgam in ourselves and others, it may at times seem to be a shapeless, churning mass of many strands tangled together. But at its core, it is not: it is an exquisitely detailed framework that our Hugr constructs and maintains throughout our lifetime. Hugr latches onto our instinctive mental and emotional capacities during the earliest period of our life to begin building and operating through this framework of thought, and continues for as long as our Lichama is able to sustain mental functioning. All of our thoughts, experiences, reactions are material for Hugr to use, to construct and modify our own framework of thought. This framework shapes the way we think and reason, the way we react and desire, and our perceptions, attitudes and judgements about everything around us.

Study participant experiences

Here is an interesting comment about the effect that writing a novel and entering into the mindset of different characters can have on the Hugr of the writer.

<u>Leif Höglund:</u> *I am frequently driven by curiosity rather than by easily executable goals. I follow the trails of my mind's thoughts ...my writing process happens organically. This writing process is also starting to be...strange.*

To try to fully embrace the inner monologue of many perspective characters is to spend time projecting your Hugr, molding your Hugr, shaping your Hugr, into some kind of precisely balanced yoga pose. It requires stretching, and practice; however, it can still be an intense process. It is the author's version of method acting, and it means spending less time with the Hugr as one's own self. It grants insights beyond – but it comes with tradeoffs, as anything else.

In a nutshell, here is how the framework operates. We use all of our perceptions, our thoughts and ideas, our desires and longings, our reactions and judgements, to build a picture of the world around us, and of our place and role within it, which seems coherent and logical to us (though we may not like it, nor feel we have chosen it ourself). Each experience and each thing we learn either strengthens and confirms this framework of understanding, or it helps to fill in missing parts and weak spots, or it challenges part or all of the framework because it is so different and does not fit in with what we have already constructed.

Along with this process come emotional reactions: defensiveness, curiosity, enlightenment, anger, rejection, resentment, fear, avoidance, rationalization, excitement, acceptance, and many more. We take in experiences and ideas, and we send out thoughts, ideas, reactions, attitudes, words and deeds. In the center of the framework lie our desires and longings, the deep roots of Hugr, shaping everything that passes through. Everything, as it comes in and as it goes out, is shaped into coherence for us as it passes through our framework of thought, built up over our lifetime, and past lives of our Hugr, as well.

Depending on the associated emotions, we may be open to re-tuning our framework in the light of new understanding and information, or we may hunker down in our framework-bunker and defend it for all we are worth. If we are too open to influence and change, our thought-structure becomes shaky, confused, garbled; its foundations are insufficient to support the large but flimsy superstructure of new, unexamined and untested ideas, thoughts and desires that are shoved into it at every opportunity. If we are not open enough, our structure becomes a stagnated fortress, unable to expand, adjust, evolve; increasingly maladapted to an ever-changing environment. It handicaps our ability to interact with others in constructive ways.

Hlutro Hugiu: Clarifying the Hugr

In Chapter 10 of Book I, I talk a bit about the process of clarifying the Hugr, creating a *hlutro hugiu,* a clear or clarified Hugi / Hugr. When we understand the role that Hugr's hama, our framework of thought, plays in our life, our thoughts, our actions, we can see the importance of this clarification of our Hugr-soul. If our whole perception of the social / mental / emotional world around us, and our sole basis for action and reaction in that world, is a muddy, clouded, tangled, stuck-together mess of bits and pieces, our own actions are going to be ineffective and counterproductive for ourselves and others. There will be mismatches galore between our perceptions and actions, and the actual situations, thoughts and emotions of others around us, all working at cross-purposes.

The clarification of our Hugr is a process of self-examination, of honesty and objectivity about ourselves, our thoughts, actions and choices in our lives. We need to re-examine our perceptions and assumptions about the world, by trying to honestly match our subjective opinions and assumptions with an objective assessment of 'what is really out there', to the best of our ability.

This requires a lot of life-experience; it is an ongoing process of clarification. We can think of it as a quality-control process to ensure that as our framework of thought continues to build, day by day, the things we select to build into it, and the way it is built, are worthy and meaningful, true to our highest ethical standards, and bear as much relation to 'reality' as we are able to perceive. And we can work our way through what has already been built, our current way of seeing and interpreting our human, social world, to see what components and structures might need restructuring, based on a more objective and ethical perception of the world around us.

Emotions as fuel for Hugr

A clarified Hugr is sensitive and aware of emotions as they arise within us, and is able to judge when action needs to be taken, based on these emotions. Our emotions are like signals and responses that go on all day and night, responding to our inner and outer environment, building on each other and powering our actions, thoughts and attitudes. Hugr can read and interpret these emotional signals; as it says in the Havamal (verse 95): "Hugr alone knows what lies near the heart; Hugr alone knows Sefa." (See Chapter 11 about our Sefa, the place where we hold what is closest to us, what matters most to us.)

Hugr knows and feels our emotions—it participates in them, is alert to them, and will use them as 'fuel' for its thinking and actions. Then the question becomes: do we want our Hugr to use our emotions to act in negative ways, such as powerful envy and greed, manipulation, deception, vengefulness, and so forth, to gain its own selfish ends? Or do we want our Hugr to take a different path, to use its powers in different ways? As we pursue the process of clarifying our Hugr, we become aware that Hugr accesses all our emotions, positive and negative, and that we can choose how those emotions will power Hugr's actions in our life.

The role of awareness

Clarifying the Hugr involves—not necessarily the *separation* of thought from emotion—but the *awareness* of how our emotions are involved in our thoughts. Once we achieve that awareness, we can choose how we want to proceed from there. Are the emotions involved in our thoughts supportive of our thought processes? Do they help us achieve what we want to achieve by our thinking? Or do they distort our thoughts and sidetrack or coopt our purposes for thinking?

Here's an example using the emotion of fear or worry, which often colors our thinking. Let's say that we are worried about our financial situation, and fear the consequences of it continuing. That worry and fear may overwhelm us, to the point where it is hard to think clearly and act rationally to work on the problem. We may use the tactic of avoidance and excuses because of our painful emotional reactions, or even fall into a state of subdued panic, so that we try not to even think about the problem in the illogical hope that it will 'just go away.' Here, strong negative emotions are seriously blocking our thought processes, preventing us from actually pursuing rational approaches to the problem.

When we have learned to clarify our Hugr, this cooptation of our thought processes by strong emotions can be nipped in the bud, if we choose. Instead, the emotion can be used to *motivate* clear thought, instead of to block and confuse it.

Courage and clarity

A primary characteristic of a strong Hugr (and Mod) is courage, an attitude that should never be undervalued, but should be brought into play whenever we are faced with a problem or situation. This needs to be super-emphasized: *courage is a fundamental characteristic of Hugr and Mod*. Life is full of challenges, great and small: personal challenges, and challenges that are part of our membership in larger circles of family, community, nation, world. I believe that one of the main reasons for the integration of Mod and Hugr into our soular system is their quality of courage that allows us to survive and thrive in the face of all the challenges of life. At a very basic level, courage is what keeps us alive and able to act in this world, and it is the gift of Hugr and Mod, our Midgard-oriented souls.

So, back to our example of worrying about our finances. Fear can paralyze rational thought, and prevent us from finding workable approaches to our problem. Or else, the emotion of fear or worry, when it first begins to arise within us, can trigger our clarified Hugr to sit up and take notice, and realize that courage and clarity of thought are needed. Then, the fear or worry can serve as a spur, a motivator, for clear-thinking, analytical Hugr and courageous, strategic Mod to step up and focus all their powers to find the best course of action for our situation, and pursue it.

The same process can be applied for other emotions, such as anger, indignation, impulsiveness, discouragement, etc. It also applies to situations where we are not trying to solve a personal problem, but are trying to understand something clearly, which has strong emotional overtones. We are daily faced with obvious examples of this: social conflict, climate change, pandemic, resource scarcity, and on and on. These are major issues that are saturated with emotional overtones as well as factual components. We need a clear and courageous Hugr, with a clarified framework of thought and perspective, to be able to pursue deeper understanding of these vital and complex matters, and form a clear perspective that allows us to respond in the best way we can. Fear, anger, outrage, can overwhelm clear thought about these matters and drive destructive responses, or they can energize our thinking and our desire to seek rational, workable solutions, depending on how our Hugr handles things.

The value of clarity

Having a clarified Hugr does not mean we have removed emotion from our thinking. It means we recognize the dynamics in operation among our emotions and our thoughts, and are able to use these dynamics strategically rather than becoming overwhelmed by emotion which is blocking our rational thought processes.

Here we return again to the matter of 'building character', as I discussed in the previous chapter about Mod. A person of good and strong character still has negative and weak emotions and impulses, just like everyone does. But such a person's Hugr and Mod have the skills to handle such emotions and impulses. They may turn their energy into alternate forms, for example, turning rage *against* something like injustice into enthusiasm *for* its opposite, the pursuit of more just procedures in society, as a remedy. Or they may simply choose not to use that particular emotional energy, without trying to beat it down or beat themselves up for having such emotions. Being aware of what lies within us means that we can choose how to respond to it. Being unaware means that we are driven by subconscious impulses that can lead to disruption and harm in our lives and actions.

The role of desire or wish

Hugr's deepest roots lie, not in thought itself, but in desire, longing, yearning: the inner part of ourselves that reaches out into the world for what we truly want, with all our heart and soul. Thought, courage, character, behavior, all the traits and strengths of the Hugr soul, both positive and negative, are capacities that Hugr develops in order to pursue and achieve its deepest desires. This is where we need to begin, in order to gradually and progressively clarify our Hugr.

Tightly wound with desire and yearning are other deep emotions. We fear that we will fail to attain our desire, or that we will lose it, if we do attain it. We are envious of others who have what we desire. We become angry and defensive when we compete and contest with others who we perceive are taking or threatening what we desire. When Hugr is focused upon these threats to its desires, it develops subtle and intelligent, but exploitative and selfish ways of thinking and acting. It develops a framework of thought that interprets the world around it as being hostile and threatening, ripe for exploitation and manipulation, and considers that its task in life is to react accordingly.

I think that if we look within and around ourselves today, in every direction, we can see this happening within our sociopolitical world. I think that the current social / political / economic problems we are all struggling with are a massive manifestation of collective Hugr and Mod reactivity, felt across the political and social spectrum. This illustrates how powerful these souls can be, and how difficult it is to handle the situation when they switch into their negative modes. On all sides of the issues, deep drivers of people's actions are fear of losing or failing to achieve what they desire, envy of others who have what they want, and angry defensiveness against whatever stands in the way of achieving their desires. These are all natural urges of our Hugrs.

When I say this, I do not at all mean to imply that people's deepest desires themselves are 'wrong', neither our own, nor anyone else's. The 'wrong' comes when those desires are pursued in selfish, violent or exploitative ways, rather than pursued as a collective and cooperative venture where others' desires and needs are respected, as well as one's own. Whatever way one goes about this, our Hugr and Mod souls are deeply involved, and hence the need to clarify our Hugr and direct our Mod's Will appropriately.

Study participant experiences

Sara Axtell (regarding Ferah and Hugr interaction): I can really feel what you are saying, Winifred, about the Ferah and hypervigilance and reactivity. How it feels to me is that these patterns of reactivity can influence our other souls. In particular, I think it can lead to the Hugr engaging in dysfunctional patterns of action and reaction.

My response: I think you're right, Sara, about a hyper vigilant Ferah triggering the Hugr into reactions and actions we may not want, and the same goes for the Mod. One of Hugr's main roles is to serve as warder of our inner being, so Ferah's sense that "there is something threatening out there," whether true or not, would trigger Hugr to pick up its defenses. Mod, also, would be triggered into its angry or outraged phase.

If we look at our current societal phenomena and challenges in this light, I suggest that this 'feeling in the air' of something going wrong is picked up by our Ferah, who senses both nature-based and social cues. There's certainly plenty there for it to pick up! Then Hugr steps in, and things get interesting, because Hugr wants to explain and understand things, and it uses its framework of thought to do this. Depending on how the framework is constructed, the person may or may not see things clearly, may perceive what is not there, or fail to perceive what really is there. The framework is further reinforced by selective information and staying in one's bubble. Then Mod steps in with its easily triggered outrage and tendency toward acting out, and we're off and running! ...I do think that Heathen soul lore can offer useful insights into both personal psychology, and societal phenomena.

Our Hugr constructs and maintains our framework of thought, and expresses itself through it as we live in this world of Midgard. We can see the framework as one of Hugr's *hamas*, a soul-skin that it creates during Midgard life. When we look at it in this way, we can see a linkage between Hugr's thought-framework hama, and Aldr's Werold-hama (see Chapter 7, Book I). Aldr's Werold-hama is a fabric made of our life-experiences, woven on the loom of Time and ørlög. Hugr's framework of thought is the way it operates in human social space in Midgard; its loom is the society, the mental and emotional context, within which we live and take action, both inner action and outer action. Our Werold *records* our life-experiences, while our Hugr's framework of thought *shapes* our life-experiences, our perceptions of them, and the way we take action in response to those perceptions.

Our Hugr can learn to observe our conscious self, and others around us, with clear eyes and an unblocked heart, a heart and mind full of courage and wisdom, to deal with the human world-outside-us as it is, and not as we fear it is, or wish it were, or are determined to force it to be. This does require a great deal of courage, insight and wisdom, strength of character, honest understanding and compassion toward ourself and toward others. This is a life-long process of inner learning and development: it is the path of clear-sighted wisdom and stout-heartedness that is Hugr's true nature and destiny, that it will carry forward into lives yet to come.

Exercise 10-1: Your deepest longings

Disclaimer: Read through this exercise first, and decide how safe it is for you to pursue it. I realize that it could be overwhelming. Yet, to make progress in healing our souls and our lives, it's important to reach the point where we can do this kind of exercise. If the exercise appears overwhelming or unsafe, consider whether there is some way you could slowly 'tiptoe' into the experience, and / or create a safe space for yourself that would hold and protect you while you pursue the exercise.

Become still, and sink your awareness deep into your Heart. Use your physical senses to sense your heartbeat and the flow of your life-blood in and out, and how your breath and the movement of your lungs work with it. Feel your heartbeat, and sink into that sensation.

Use your other-senses to tune in to what is there, at the root of your heart: your deepest longings, yearnings, wishes, desires. What do you truly, truly want, more than anything else in the world? What longing lies at the very root of yourself?

Tears may flow as you do this; you may feel a 'wallowing' or churning sensation in your breast, a roiling of emotion, a desire to shout, sob, growl, howl or roar, or experience an unexpected bursting-out of galdor. The energy may want to follow its natural flow from your heart into your throat and voice that express what is in your heart, or that block this expression. Let this energy flow, let it churn and stir things up within your breast: this is your deep-Hugr waking up and coming into your awareness. It's uncomfortable and unsettling, disturbing, but necessary for your deep-Hugr to rise into your awareness like this.

Write about this experience in your Daybook; you may or may not wish to share it with others. Often, this feels very intimate and private, and sometimes it is emotionally clear, but difficult to express in words and rational description. Often, when we put our deepest desires into words, they may just seem like trite platitudes. For example, the sentiment 'I wish we could all just get along with each other' is often expressed, and may often be quite a superficial feeling. But not in all cases; people who are in conflict-ridden situations, and people who empathize and sympathize with them, do mean this sentiment with all the desperation of their hearts.

The very process of 'wording' or verbalizing these deep feelings may rob them of much of their power, so don't force them into words unless that feels natural. Often art is a better way to express these longings: through music, poetry, painting, dance, etc., and this can be done in the imagination as well as in the physical world.

Exploring Hugr

As you work through this exercise, one time or multiple times, discover some kind of symbol, token or key to these deep longings of yours, that you can use as a shorthand for focusing your awareness. It could be anything: perhaps a bindrune, a color, a piece of music, an image, a few words or a poem, the memory of an experience, or a sensation within your breast.

Exercise 10-2: Attuning actions with longings

As you go about your daily life, keep a part of your awareness on the token that symbolizes your deepest longings. During the day, and at the end of the day as you go to sleep, evaluate how well your actions and thoughts are attuned to your deepest longings, and how they serve either to bring you closer, or cause you to drift away and be distracted from the heart of your Hugr. Gradually, guide this awareness and attunement between your deep-Hugr, and the daily actions of your surface-Hugr, into becoming a habitual frame of mind and basis for daily action.

This is the first step in clarifying your Hugr: becoming aware of the deep-Hugr's longings, and beginning to see how well, or how poorly, your daily thoughts and actions match up with those longings, and move you toward achieving them.

Here is a personal example. One of my own deepest longings, as well as I can express it verbally, is for a stable condition of inner peace and tranquility, that I can maintain as a refuge and as a wellspring of pure, nourishing spiritual energy, amidst all the turmoil of daily life. Anything that goes on in my thoughts, feelings, and in the world around me, can and often does disturb, roil and muddy that beautiful and tranquil wellspring, the token of my longing. I hold the image of this wellspring in my mind, imagining it located in my breast, heart and throat, and try to attune my thoughts, emotions, words and actions in such a way that they feed clear water into the spring, rather than disturbing it, polluting it, or cutting off its flow. The more I am able to keep this up, the stronger and more stable this wellspring of peace feels within me.

Exercise 10-3: Making friends with Hugr

As I wrote about in Chapter 10 of Book I, Hugr (and Sefa) is the soul where we feel the emotions of love and friendship. Hugr longs for trusted relationships, for networks of social interaction and mutual support, and all the emotional richness and complexity involved with this. Hugr's powers of thought are designed to support our participation within complex networks of human activities and interactions. And equally so, for our relationships and activities with non-physical beings such as spirits and Deities.

Friendship, trust, understanding, knowledge, loyalty: these things are highly valued by Hugr, and it is the Hugr within us that urges us to pursue and maintain these things with others. Likewise, it is the Hugr who feels wistful, envious, or vengeful, when these gifts of human interaction are not working the way Hugr wants them to. So, among the first things to do as we work with our Hugr, is to make friends with it ourself, and promote its friendship with our other souls. I find it a bit difficult to 'prescribe' how to do this, since each of us has our own ways of pursuing friendship. But there are certain things we may all agree on, as being good ways to begin the pursuit of a friendship.

Very often, one of the main things that appeals to us about our closest friends is that we 'like the way they think'. When we say this about a person, 'the way they think' certainly includes emotional factors as well as intellectual ones. Emotions as well as thoughts are major components of friendship. Here, we are firmly within Hugr's domain: thoughts enriched by emotions, emotions clarified and expressed by thoughts, all serving as the medium within which a rich and satisfying relationship can grow.

So, here's the challenge for this exercise: make friends with your Hugr. Get to know and understand your Hugr, using the approaches I've outlined here and in Chapter 8: understanding Hugr's deepest desires and longings, understanding what motivates it, how it responds to positive and negative situations, what its reactions are like, beginning to understand the framework of thought it has been constructing during your whole lifetime, and observing how it thinks about things. Approach this as you would a new friendship with another person you think you will like, not by being critical and controlling toward yourself and your own behavior.

This is obviously not something that will be done in a couple of meditation sessions! Just like building a friendship, it begins tentatively and grows with time, as you get to know yourself and each other better. Any friend you make is not going to be a 'perfect person', and part of building friendship and trust is learning how to deal with our own and our friend's imperfections. Same with Hugr: approach Hugr as an 'inner person' with its own strengths and weaknesses, its own ability to learn, change and grow, its own needs and motivations, its own patterns of thought and behavior.

I know it's confusing, because all these things relating to Hugr are our own Hugr-soul, our own thoughts, feelings, motives, so it's hard to understand how to do this as though we are dealing with two different people. Try to identify, within yourself, the 'observer' who can stand back and see things about yourself objectively. The one who says: "*I* am feeling frustrated, *I* am feeling relaxed, *I* am thinking about what I should do, etc." How do you know these things about yourself, know what you (and your various souls) are thinking, feeling, doing? You can only know them by observing yourself, which means there is something within you capable of stepping back from the 'actor', the one who is doing / feeling / thinking these things, and is able to make these kinds of observations.

This observer-self should observe your / Hugr's thoughts and behavior with a friendly, interested attitude, an attitude that says: "I know you're not perfect, but you're very interesting and intriguing, very deep and strong. I think we've got a lot in common and I'd like to get to know you better." (To further add to the confusion, Hugr is also an observer of our self, as I am suggesting here that our self can observe our Hugr. It's sort of like standing between two mirrors, and watching the multiple reflections. Just do the best you can here!)

Something to keep in mind: when we make friends, or have any other kind of relationship with another person, positive or negative, it is largely the other person's Hugr (and Sefa) that we are forming that relationship with. Humans interact 'Hugr to Hugr', though of course other souls are much involved as well. Human activities,

Exploring Hugr

including relating to each other, involve all our souls, but the souls that are primarily responsible for building and maintaining relationships of any kind are Hugr and Sefa, working through our Lich-Hama. In learning to create the most healthy relationships with others, it also behooves us to create a true and trusting friendship with our own clarified Hugr.

Note: For discussion and exercises relating to Hugr's warding and guiding functions, refer to Chapter 12: Sefa, Hugr and Modsefa.

Exploring Hugr

Friendship Song

Frith and friendship fail not while faring
 Boldly along the byways of Worlds.
 Bare is back without brother behind it:
 Frith makes friend the fairest of kin.

Always while young alone I traveled;
 Ever and again I wandered from my way.
 I knew myself wealthy when I found a friend:
 Man is the joy, the joy of man!

No need to give away great gifts always,
 Small things are very often enough.
 Half a loaf and a lifted horn
 Oft and again have found me a friend.

Now, an untrusty friend lives too far away,
 Even though their path lies right upon your road.
 But it's no distance to one who is dear,
 Though you fare far over mile after mile.

Always be faithful, always keep troth,
 Never be the first to fail in friendship.
 Grief grips the Hugr that must ever be wary,
 Keeping itself always hidden away.

True bonds are formed when folk keep faith,
 Hiding not their Hugrs from one another.
 Anything's better than breach of friendship:
 A true friend will say what you'd rather not hear!

If you have faith in a friend of yours,
 Fare you to find them again and again.
 Brushwood and grass will soon grow high,
 Covering the path no wayfarer walks.

I wrote the first verse, and adapted the others from the Hávamál.

Chapter 11

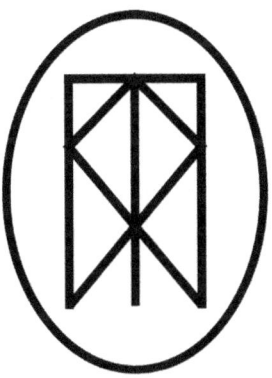

11. Will and Wish: The Dynamism of Mod and Hugr

{Primary runes in the bindrune above: Uruz, Wunjo, Raidho, Othala, Nauthiz, Kenaz.}

Background reading: Chapters 8, 9, 10, 11 in Book I, or the articles on my website titled "Dances with Daemons: The Mod Soul;" "Hunting the Wild Hugr;" "Who is Hugr?," and "The Occult Activities of the Hugr."

Will and Wish are the two fundamental reaching-out forces of Mod and Hugr, the magnetic lines which connect these souls with domains of action in the Worlds. These concepts are so powerful in the older Germanic languages that we can find them as personifications. Odin's brother's name, Vili or Wiljon, means "Will". In Grimm's *Teutonic*

Mythology (p. 144ff) there are several long pages of examples from German poetry and aphorisms of the 12th and 13th centuries, showing Wish as a powerful, creative, godlike being. One of Odin's bynames in Norse is Oski or 'wish'. Both of these words, will and wish, had broader and deeper meanings in the old German languages.

Will and Wish are powers inherent in each of us, rooted in our souls, that can be developed, trained and directed to shape our actions and our life as a whole. Among other things, this is the aim of many esoteric, magical and mystical paths. When Will and Wish exist in us as subconscious, entirely self-focused, repressed or distorted forces, they can wreck our life and the lives of those whom we touch.

Here I will focus on the will and wish powers of Mod and Hugr, as they are such fundamental aspects of these two souls. Keep these two points in mind, though. One is that most of our other souls also have wills of their own, often going off in quite different directions. The other is that the wills and wishes of Mod and Hugr are not singular—they are complex, contradictory and tangled. In the discussion and exercises here, I've treated them as though they were simple and straightforward, because we have to start somewhere! I'm only discussing the ideas and the basic approaches here, which you can use as a basis for deeper exploration if you wish.

Will

In the old German languages, *willio* or *willo* meant 'will, intention, purpose, mentality, disposition, character, way of thinking, viewpoint, opinion.' It was also used in the sense of 'goodwill': it meant graciousness, benevolence, kindness, patronage, favor / favorable attitude. (Becker p. 22.) "Before Christianization, *Willio* must have been an important word that was full of life and rich with meaning" (Becker p. 166). (The reason he refers to pre-Christianization is that after Christianization, the focus in the writings of that time was to direct the will toward their God, and away from 'sinful', but lively and important, worldly matters and daily affairs.)

All of these things are among the characteristics of our Mod soul, and overlap strongly with Hugr as well. In the old German writings, the expression "Mod's will" and combinations like *muat-willo* were frequently used.

Let's look at the God Wiljon or Vili for a moment. He and his brothers Odin / Wodanaz and Ve / Wihaz are the sons of Bor (*Edda* p. 11) and were the ones who brought the trees or logs to life as the first humans, Ask and Embla (*Edda* p. 13). Odin's name comes from Oðr or Wode, which we explored in Chapter 5, meaning breath / spirit / inspiration / ecstatic states of various kinds. Ve's name comes from the word for 'sacred', *ve* or *wih*. Bringing humans into being and filling them with spirit was a sacred act, indeed, but we can see that a motive force was necessary to bring such a deed about. Vili supplied that motive force, that Will, in both necessary ways: his was the power of will that directed this creative action, and in the process, his own power of will took root in the new human couple. This power urged the humans to take a firm grip on their gifts of life, body, souls, and made them determined to survive and thrive in this challenging world of Midgard.

Wish

Grimm defines the old meaning of Wish (German *Wunsch*) as "the sum total of well-being and blessedness, the fulness of all graces". It is probably derived from *wunja*, related to German *Wonne* = bliss, to the rune-name Wunjo, and to older words *wunisc, wunsc,* meaning Perfection or the Ideal. Here's a quotation from Grimm: *"der Wunsch was an ir garwe."* He translates it as "the wish was in her complete," but I would give it slightly differently. The word *garwe* meant clothing (garb), but is also related to 'gear' or equipment. I would give the meaning as "Wish, in her, was fully equipped (with everything that could be wished for)." In other words, she was considered a perfect representation of everything that one could wish for. *"In dem wunsche sweben"* means literally "to dream within (the) Wish", a state of bliss. A magic wand was called a *wunschiligerta* or 'wishing-rod.' Grimm interprets the name Oski as "he who makes men partakers of Wish, of the highest gift." (All in Grimm p. 138.) "With Wish's might the old man blessed her" (p. 142).

It's notable that the old meaning of Wish focuses on a state of achievement, of 'perfection' in the sense of 'completion': first something was longed-for, then it was achieved or obtained: the wish was completed and perfected. Wish was a Being, and also a state-of-being that came about through contact with, or action by, the Wish-being or Wish-power. *Wish itself is power,* in this view.

Nowadays, there's a subtle but important difference in the meaning of 'wish': it implies a longing for something that we are unlikely to get, although it is remotely possible: "I wish I could win the lottery;" "I wish everyone could just get along," etc. Beginning a sentence with the words "I wish..." is, if you think about it, an expression of powerlessness and possibly even of hopelessness. I 'wish' for something because I don't know what else to do about the situation or the longing that I have. There is no real action implied here. There is none of the creative power to make things happen, that the old words *wusc, wunisc,* etc., implied, and that powerful beings called Wish, *wusc-frea* (wish-lord), or Oski could bring about.

Love as Wish fulfilled

There is a close connection between the old meaning of Wish, and the things that bring the greatest happiness to Hugr. I wrote in Chapter 10, Book I, about how closely Hugr is connected to the heart and to the Sefa soul, and how it is involved in the experience of love. While Sefa's expressions of love, affection, compassion, are spread broadly across all kinds of relationships and interactions, Hugr's love and attraction are more focused on the most intimate forms: romantic love, sexual desire, and also the heart-to-heart intimacy of our closest friendships. Keep in mind that our closest friendships may, if we are fortunate, include those with our family members such as siblings, cousins, or parents and adult children, who are close heart-friends and have a lifetime of shared experiences and family culture to draw on.

It is of the greatest importance for Hugr to be able share its deepest thoughts and feelings with a few true and trusted loved ones. When we are fortunate enough to have such relationships, this provides the completion, the fullness, the satisfaction of our yearnings and longings that we spoke of earlier. This is Wish in its wholeness, comprised of both the longing, and the satisfaction of the longing: the 'wish come true.' If we succeed in achieving such relationships, it is thanks to our own efforts to make the wish come true, the dedication of our Hugr and Sefa to nurturing and treasuring such relationships. There is little that is more powerful in human life than this; here we can begin to grasp the profounder meanings of the old conception of Wish.

Dynamic Tension of Will and Wish

I view Will and Wish as closely related, but not identical forms of energy or power. The primary difference I see is that Will or determination is a 'push' coming forth from inside ourself, while Wish or longing is a 'pull' toward something outside ourself. This difference may not matter if we are looking at these meanings in an intellectual or generalized way. They do matter, however, when we try to sense how their energies are embodied within our own being, our soul-body complex, which is how I am trying to guide much of our practical soul work here. When we combine these energies of push and pull together, going in the same direction, the sum total of the two is of course more powerful than either acting alone. If they are working at cross purposes from each other, they subtract from each others' power, or fail to amplify it.

Exercise 11-1: Finding Will within you

In Exercise 9-6, I asked you to find the location, within your soul-body complex, where your courage is located, and asked you to explore how courage *feels* as it rises and sinks

Will and Wish

within you. Now let's extend that exercise into the domain of Will, closely related to courage.

First, seek within you for the core energy and the sensation of Will. I suggest that you may find it around the same location as your wellspring of courage, though it may extend even farther throughout your soul-body complex. In many ways, Will is located within every cell in our body—this is what motivates them to take all the actions that are natural to them, thus supporting our life here in Midgard. During healing and protective work, exploring this more expanded locus of Will is important.

Now, however, let's focus on the overlapping centers of Will and courage within. This is likely to be in your *megingjörð* area, that corresponds to the area of Thor's body encompassed by his broad belt of power. Different bodies, including the bodies of different genders, shapes, and ages, will have this area in slightly different places. Note that in Traditional Chinese Medicine, the kidney-adrenals are responsible for generating courage and will. They are within the same broad horizontal band of the body as our solar plexus, covered by our imagined *megingjörð* or belt of power.

However, it's important for you to find your own center of Will, and not just take it for granted that it's in a given location. There's a lot of courage and will in our Heart, as well, where Hugr hangs out! Our will-center may also move around, depending on the focus of our will in specific instances. One obvious example is when our will is focused on sexual activity to the exclusion of all else.

For this exercise, in your imagination (or memory) develop a scenario that involves the utmost determination and will within you. Perhaps it's standing your ground for

Will and Wish

something you believe in, to the utmost. Perhaps it's defending or rescuing someone you love with all your heart, especially a child or a beloved but frail elder, someone toward whom you feel tender and protective. It could be an animal, too, a pet or wild animal you are trying to save from death, danger or abuse. Perhaps it's something you want to do or to achieve, more than anything else, in spite of all obstacles. Be aware of the strength that gathers in your body as you imagine this great Will building within you.

Now feel your Will as it gathers in your Will-center in response to the imagined challenge. How does it feel? Like a solid boulder, a volcano, a tidal wave, a star or sun? Is it rooted or surging, hot or cold, dense or expansive, heavy or rising-up? Imagine different kinds of scenarios, situations, intentions of will, and explore whether your will-sensation, and perhaps its location, change accordingly.

Then, explore how your Will exits yourself, pushing out toward the situation you're facing in your imagination. Does it feel explosive, or slow and steady but inexorable? Does it take over the whole space around you, or send out a focused ray of power? Are there progressive ripples of Will extending out from you, or one big surge? Does it have color, sound, texture, shape? Do these characteristics vary, as your scenario varies? Or, does your Will-force fail to push out from you, or not exit far enough? Focus your awareness to fully understand the characteristics of your Will.

Once you've got a sense of what your Will-expressions are like, you can start thinking, and imagining, how these expressions might be improved. Are your

Will and Wish

expressions of will sometimes too strong and explosive, or too set in place and stubborn, for the situation you want to resolve? Are they too weak and peter out before your Will is accomplished? Does your Will need to be better focused—is it confused and all over the place? Is there anything that blocks or distorts its expression, preventing it from pushing out, or misshaping it against your conscious intention?

Can your Will be shaped so that it attracts cooperation and collaboration in appropriate circumstances, instead of running over people in pursuit of your goal? This has to do with the charisma (or the 'luck', in some traditional views) of our Will, a complex topic that I won't pursue at this level of soul lore. But keep in mind that our Will and Wish both have potentially strong charisma that can attract other people to collaborate and cooperate; in some cases even to the point of them becoming our followers in some way. Such power carries opportunities for principled leadership, and for severe abuse. (If you'd like to see an analysis of the roles that the 'luck' and will of certain leaders played during the conversion era, you could read my article "Webs of Luck and Wyrd: Interplays and Impacts on Events," on my website.)

It is also possible for Will and Wish to have negative charisma or bad luck, and repel others away, or else attract them for negative and harmful reasons. The latter is one of the factors underlying the subconscious behavioral dynamics between long-term, habitual abuser / victim pairs who are in denial. Clarifying and understanding these dynamics of Will and Wish can help to free one from such negative connections.

As we develop our souls through this soul lore study and practice, we always need to be aware of how all the powers of our souls are affecting other people and the world around us, and take responsibility for appropriate actions in response to our insights. As our souls become more powerful, more focused, more self-aware, our power to cause good or harm grows greater as well. So does our awareness of the more subtle patterns of our behaviors and the behaviors of those around us, and their impacts on the past, the present, and influence on the future. We become more aware of wyrd and ørlög, and of the close connections between personal power and personal responsibility.

Returning to our exercise here, there are likely to be many possibilities for fine-tuning the expressions of your Will, once you become more familiar with these expressions. And it is much more fun to explore your will's nature and the improvements you might make, in the imaginative and energetic ways I describe here, than it is to be lectured or to lecture yourself about these matters! Turn this effort toward self-understanding and self-improvement into a challenging and unique game, using your inner senses and imagination as I have described here, rather than engaging in yet another session of self-scolding, frustration and defeat!

Personal example

When I first began working on this exercise, it did not go as smoothly as I may have implied, as I tried to describe the process above. It's kind of like being in an anatomy class in school, where you're supposed to dissect something. There are all these nice tidy images in the book or on the screen, showing the different parts and organs clearly. Then you begin the dissection, and everything is just a mess in there! What is that purple blob, anyway? I'm sure it's not in the book....

This is kind of how I felt. I could feel a strong will located in the spine of my neck and upper back, extending into my brainstem; that's what I felt first. I could feel another strong will in my solar plexus, another in my sacroiliac, and for goodness' sake, also in the soles of my feet...they really want to go barefoot all the time, as a way of connecting to the world around me and absorbing mod-energy. This foot-will is frustrated a lot of the time in the physical world, but I depend on barefoot-senses and energy when exploring other Worlds in quasi-physical form.

None of these areas of Will seemed to be connected to each other; no fortifying or feeding into each other, which explained a lot to me. They are also areas that have various health or pain issues, perhaps not coincidentally. If I can connect these various different will-centers, will my body and my energy improve, as well as the exercise of my overall Will? And then, what about coordinating with the Wills of other souls as well? Are some of these will-locations within me really the expressions of other souls' Wills? (The answer turns out to be 'yes'.)

I'm gradually working my way through these questions and indicators, with interesting results. The more we discover in soul lore, the more there is to explore!

Exercise 11-2: Working with Wish

In Exercise 10-1, I asked you to enter your Heart and Hugr, and explore your deepest longings. This exercise follows on that one. Choose one of your deepest longings, identified in your previous exercise, and explore this question: What would it take, for this longing within me to reach a sense of completion, of wholeness and fulfillment?

This is truly a profound exercise, because our deepest longing may be for something that is not possible to fully achieve in this World of Midgard. Perhaps it is, perhaps it isn't.

If it is achievable, here are my suggestions. Work with a Deity, or other spirit such as an ancestor or landwight, who can embody the power of this Wish for you, the power of bringing your longing to a state of fulfillment. Swell and grow your own Hugr as a Wish-Being, a Will-Wind, who has the power to reach your goal, perhaps by using magic or other esoteric practices. (For more background about these Hugr-powers, refer to Chapters 9, 10, 11 in Book I of this series, or the articles about Hugr on my website.)

Work with your own Will, and with all your souls, focused on the fulfillment of your longing. If you have to make some adjustments to the details of your longed-for situation, in order to make it realistically achievable, accept that with a good heart and goodwill, and proceed accordingly. There is no room for pettiness, fretting, and false, picky perfectionism in this endeavor. This is a work of true Heart and Spirit, a work that will shape who you are from here on out, as you work to give shape to the longings of your Hugr and your Heart. Be patient, committed, flexible, keep your eyes on the goal, stay attuned to your Hugr and Mod and their true powers within you, and stay attuned to any spirit-beings, the embodiments of Wish, who may be guiding and helping you.

Dealing with the unachievable Wish

Your deepest longing may, however, be something that really is not achievable even with some adjustments, but still remains within you as a powerful longing. For example, your longing may be for something like a world, or even a small part of the world, where environmental harms are healed, where people all accept one another peacefully, where social justice and personal freedom both prevail, where no one goes hungry or homeless, where species and cultures do not go untimely extinct, where sacred places and sacred ways are respected by all. Or something more personal: for someone you love to be healed or brought back from the edge of death, for example, when this really does not seem likely to happen. Another example is deeply wishing to change something about yourself or a loved one, that is not physically possible to change.

Of course, on one level you can work to do what you realistically can, to create a pocket of better circumstances according to your desire. But the deeper desire may remain unfulfilled within you, the desire for complete fulfillment or perfection of the longed-for situation. How do we put Wish to work, in this case? How do we keep Hugr's Wish-power alive and vital, ready and willing to act where it can, in spite of unachievable longings?

Clearly, there is no real answer to this, in the sense of magically being able to achieve something that is not realistically achievable. There are various ways that people can sanely deal with this dilemma. One is to express your wish symbolically, with art in all its forms (including things like architecture, dance, music, books) being a primary form of this expression. Achieve this wish in your imagination, and express that image through artistic or other symbolic channels. This is the dynamic that has driven most of the great artistic creations of this world.

A related tactic, when your wish is not achievable for yourself, but may be achievable for someone else, is to generously work to promote the achievement of your wish for those others. Here, instead of expressing the achievement of your wish through a symbolic artistic form, you are expressing it through a human form, but not your own. Both ways are exercises in soul-deep creativity.

Another time-honored way to deal with a real inability to achieve your great wish, is to develop a deep, serene acceptance of the situation. This can take years of struggle, as part of your process of spiritual maturation, and has been the focus of spiritual striving in many religions and philosophical paths of life throughout the human span of existence.

It's the way I've chosen, for some of my deepest unachievable longings, and I want to note this about it: acceptance of what cannot be changed may not be an endpoint, so much as an ongoing process in life. At least, that is how it is so far, with me. I cannot forget, put aside, ignore these deep wishes; there are always reminders, situations, lived consequences, that bring them back to mind again. When that happens, the exercise of active acceptance is again needed, though I will say that this becomes easier with time and practice. And it does build a type of very worthwhile spiritual strength, which is a particular blessing as we age, and realize more and more clearly that there are some wishes we will not achieve in this lifetime.

Will and Wish

Do not forget this important point: Hugr is the soul who reincarnates. There may be ways that your Hugr can train and prepare itself during this life, that will place it in a better position for achieving its wishes in the next one. This is another tactic that I rely on for myself, and it gives me comfort and courage with which to counteract life's disappointments. I will share a true Wish of my heart here: I think of my soul lore and other Heathen writings as seeds that I sow out into the world, with the hope that my Hugr in the next life will encounter them and be able to pick up from wherever I leave off in this life, instead of having to start all over again from scratch!

Another way to deal with the unachievable wish is to truly and honestly transform it into something that is achievable. This is not as straightforward as it might seem. It is easy to *think* we have transformed our wish, and to set to work achieving our transformed wish. But if we are not careful, we may then fall into the pit of being dissatisfied when we achieve the new wish, just because it isn't the original wish, after all. This is very easy to do, and causes great feelings of resentment over all the effort we put into this achievement, and all the various costs to ourself and perhaps to others, all for something that is ultimately disappointing.

If we choose this path of wish-transformation, it has to be done with self-knowledge and soul-deep honesty about our motives, desires and goals. We need to make a bargain between our present-Hugr and our future-Hugr, that our future-Hugr will accept the decision and the efforts of our present-Hugr with goodwill and appreciation, and make the most of it. This effort takes place in the context of our Hugr's framework of thought, and requires that we make changes in this framework to accommodate the transformation of our desires.

Exercise 11-3: Examining your difficult wishes

Take a look at your own deepest longings that you earlier identified. Are there any that are probably unachievable? If so, how are you dealing with the potential disappointment and frustration that may arise from this situation? Does this approach work well for you, or might you want to consider other approaches?

In closing

Will and Wish are enormously powerful forces that shape both our inner world, and the outer world we live in. They are profound expressions of our souls, and it is vital to understand, shape and direct them appropriately, for our own benefit and for the benefit of those around us.

Will and Wish

Wodan in his broad hat.
(Arthur Rackham)

Odin combines in himself both Hugr and Mod, Wish and Will. He is an exemplar of a broad, powerful Hugr, but he also embodies Mod. In a lovely medieval German riddle, Odin or Wodan is himself called 'Mod.' Here is the riddle:

> *Mod in his broad hat*
> *Has more guests*
> *Than the Fir-Wood has branches.*

The answer to this riddle is 'the Stars'. The stars are considered to be souls or Ghosts, the 'guests' of Wodan in the sky with his broad hat, and there are more of them than there are branches in the great woods. (Meyer p. 38.)

Odin and Sleipnir, by John Bauer.

Hugr and Mod, Wish and Will, drive this great God and his eight-legged horse powerfully through Time and Worlds. The etheric wake that Odin and Sleipnir leave behind them, as they surge through other-space, stirs the tides of time and events in our own World.

Sometimes, we can sense their Ghosts streaming by on the night wind: the wind of Odin's Will, the Hugr-wind of the God's passing, as they pursue and snatch up strands of Odin's wishes across the worlds.

Chapter 12

12. Sefa, Hugr and Modsefa

{Primary runes in the bind-rune above: Wunjo, Othala, Jera, Gebo, Algiz, Tiw, Nauthiz, Raidho, Kenaz.}

Background reading: Chapters 8, 10 and 12 of Book I, or the web articles "Dances with Daemons: The Mod Soul;" "Who is Hugr?," and "Sefa: The Soul of Relationship."

Sefa

Sefa is a soul deeply rooted in our heart, our emotions, emotional perceptions and sensitivities. It is the 'soul who cares' within us, the soul who wants to relate to other beings and to situations through the process of perceiving, understanding and caring about them. This caring nature of Sefa is vulnerable to harm through mistreatment by other humans, and by ill-intentioned spirits as well. If Sefa

Sefa, Hugr and Modsefa

suffers great harm to its caring nature, it can become grim and even savage in response; it covers, hardens, even denies its potential for caring behavior and relationships as a way of self-defense. Sefa is also vulnerable to worry, anxiety, sorrow, grief, even obsession, when it perceives or fears that the things it cares about and relates to are being threatened, harmed or lost.

Sefa is intimately related to our Hugr and Mod souls. As I wrote about in Chapters 8, 9, and 10 of Book I, I see these latter two souls as 'daemon-souls', souls which can exist independently of us. I understand the original Mod-entities to have a non-human origin as elemental spirits, and the proto-Hugr-souls to originate as images and wisps of longing from the wetlands of Hel. Both Mod and Hugr can be fierce, self-centered, grasping, laser-focused on what they want. I understand Sefa to be a humanizing influence on Mod and Hugr, potentially infusing them with compassion, empathy, caring, perceptiveness, all leading to deep and meaningful relationships with others.

Sefa's desire for love, friendship and relationship flows out into the world through our Hugr soul, with its own longing for love and friendship. Sefa and Mod create their own common ground in our Modsefa, where ideally Sefa's caring and commitment combine with Mod's strength, courage and desire to act and to achieve in the world.

When these souls have been distorted, their fears, anger, grimness, envy, self-centeredness build upon each other as force-multipliers. Modsefa can change from the soul-space which blends all the best qualities of Mod and Sefa, to a space where anger, grimness, hatred and obsessions prevail. These soul-interrelationships, whatever form they may take, shape our character, temperament and behavior as these souls interact and express themselves in our life, and are in turn shaped by our life experiences and how we make use of those experiences.

The selfish, grim, or savage Sefa

Each of our souls possesses its own sense of selfhood and can be consumed with pursuing its own self-interests; this is especially true of Mod, Hugr, and Ghost. Mod wants action, Hugr pursues its desires, Ghost focuses on its own disembodied interests. All of them can run roughshod over our other souls and our Lichama, over other people, and ignore or counteract the many concerns and responsibilities related to living in a community and in a healthy natural environment.

Sefa, too, can pursue a path of selfishness. The 'relationship' nature of Sefa can turn inward rather than outward, and care only for how other people treat us, unconcerned with how we treat other people. This leads to the 'queen bee' or 'king of the heap' phenomenon, where a person wants all the focus of attention on themselves, and fails to offer caring interactions toward others. This can also lead to a person being consumed by grievances and resentments, believing that others owe them everything, and they owe others nothing.

A perfect example of this is the 'incel' or 'involuntary celibates' belief, where certain resentful men feel entitled to get whatever they want from women, and become filled with anger, hatred and abuse when they don't get it. It never seems to occur to them that it is impossible to create a healthy relationship with a person holding this super-selfish attitude, and that any sensible woman would avoid

Sefa, Hugr and Modsefa

this situation like the plague. Of course, people of any gender can fall into such counterproductive selfishness; this is just one example.

In the old poetry, the Sefas of warriors, nobles and rulers are sometimes described as 'grim', and even 'savage.' It's easy to see how their Sefas could take on these traits, especially in warriors, who are focused on killing others instead of on relating to them in any constructive way. The only way a healthy Sefa could take on such a focus is for self-defense and especially for the defense of others. It is easy for leaders to present any conflict in such terms: 'defending the homeland, way of life, etc.', whether that is literally true or not, and whether better solutions to the problem exist, or not.

This is how people overcome the natural tendency of the Sefa-soul to care about others: by telling themselves that by their actions they really are caring for others, but only for others who 'matter'. There are all kinds of justifications for strife and violence toward other people, and sometimes these justifications may be supported by facts, with both sides taking violent action against each other, and thus being forced to defend themselves.

People whose life and focus are rooted in these kinds of situations, whether they choose this or whether it is forced upon them, may well develop a grim, and even a savage Sefa in response. Their Sefa is desperately wounded and distorted, and we see the results in people returning from a war zone, being released from prison or captivity, or stepping back from some other type of violent or abusive situation. Even though they may long for healthy relationships and a 'normal' life, it is difficult and time-consuming for them to heal their Sefa sufficiently to be able to achieve this.

All of their souls need to participate in this healing. Their Hugr needs to be especially involved by making its own changes in its framework of thought, its attitudes and behavior, so that it can support these changes in the Sefa.

Hugr as Sefa's warder

In Chapter 10 of Book I, I discussed the threefold nature of our Hugr soul. It is an 'inner self', where our desires and longings are rooted, where our thoughts and feelings work away like yeast within ourselves and establish our framework of thought. Along with Mod and others of our souls, Hugr establishes our character, our persona and ego. Secondly, Hugr is an inner warder, a soul-being who stands on the boundary between our inner and outer worlds, offering warnings, cautions, rede and wisdom, foresight, and insight into knowledge that is hidden from our conscious mind. Hugr also has many skills and abilities for human social interaction, both positive and negative. Thirdly, in some circumstances Hugr can roam as an independent soul-entity, away from our body and sometimes even from our conscious awareness, to take its own actions in Midgard or in other worlds (see Chapter 11 of Book I for more).

In the previous chapters, I discussed Hugr's roles within our inner self, as well as the role of our Mod soul which overlaps in many ways with Hugr. Here I will focus on Hugr's warding role: the soul which stands between our innermost self and all the beings and influences of the outer world of Midgard, and worlds of spirit-beings, as well.

Sefa, Hugr and Modsefa

This 'innermost self' which needs Hugr's warding is our Sefa. In an ideal and kindly world, Sefa would not need warding, and could reach out and relate as it wishes to everyone and everything. People from various different religions, professions and paths of life who treasure and pursue the path of compassion develop their Sefas very strongly. They have learned to courageously withstand the threats to their Sefa without Sefa burrowing into a hole to escape them, and have trained their Mod and Hugr to support Sefa's standing-forth and action in the world. (Of course, they would not use these specific soul-concepts to describe what they do; this is my Heathen analysis of what is going on.)

Nevertheless, it happens all too often that people on the path of compassion become over-extended, burned-out, exhausted, suffer compassion-fatigue. They may be forced to withdraw from their efforts, temporarily or permanently, and sometimes may become cynical as a way to ward themselves from continued burnout. There are exceptions, in particular for very spiritual people who can access spiritual strength that can carry them beyond ordinary human levels of achievement and endurance. These people are often seen as 'saints', however their culture or religion defines that.

My understanding of Sefa is that it is not naturally strong in the abilities of judgment, strategic action, decision-making, analysis, and the like. Sefa is loving, impulsive, enthusiastic, eager, emotionally insightful and perceptive, but tends to be naïve in the ways of the world. It may not be cautious enough when it comes to acting on those caring impulses. This makes Sefa very vulnerable to exploitation and manipulation, and seduction of many

Sefa, Hugr and Modsefa

kinds: sexual and relationship seduction, for example seduced into becoming an 'enabler' or a co-dependent of someone else's harmful behavior in the mistaken assumption that one is helping them. Likewise, Sefa can be seduced into harmful beliefs and principles, and into unhealthy and unprincipled paths of relationships, associations and actions. All of these situations are driven by the desire for relationship and connection, but they are pursued unwisely and without sufficient care for one's overall well-being and safety, including one's moral and mental health.

Sefa is also easily subject to worry and anxiety, things that inevitably develop whenever we care greatly about anything, including ourself. A Sefa unwarded by Hugr and not strengthened by Mod can go further, into panic attacks, obsessive-compulsive or overly-controlling behavior. This is even more likely, if the person's Ferah-soul has been damaged by life-circumstances, leading to oversensitivity, hyper-reactiveness, fearfulness, phobias, and the like. Sefa and Ferah then interact in their worries, viewing the world as an existentially threatening place filled with threatening beings, with no refuge or help to be had. Then, when unscrupulous 'helpers' appear, and / or inaccurate ideas and beliefs that seem to resolve everything are presented to Sefa, it is all too easily led astray.

Here is where our Hugr-warder steps in. A well-developed Hugr is strong in the very areas where Sefa needs it: judgment, analysis, decisiveness, strategic thinking, boldness, clear-sightedness, firmness of purpose. Sefa and Hugr need each other. A healthy Sefa gives shape, warmth and expression to Hugr's longings and desires, infusing them with emotional perceptiveness and empathy.

Sefa, Hugr and Modsefa

A healthy Hugr protects Sefa from over-extension and from unwisely pursing Sefa's emotional impulses. As they work together over the years of our life, these two souls create the potential for deep wisdom: wisdom of the heart combined with the wisdom of the world; wisdom shaped by perceptiveness, insight, judgment, compassion, and life-experience.

Study participant experiences

Leif Höglund: *I have a lot of issues maintaining healthy boundaries for myself, or even knowing what my boundaries should be. It often feels more painful to not help than to help. This is obviously an unsustainable emotional framework, and often leads to emotional burnout. Nevertheless, knowing that a problem exists and figuring out how to solve it aren't quite the same thing. This is where I was stuck for quite a long while. This was an issue the Norns ended up forcing. My boundaries were crossed in such a ludicrous, absurd way (but certainly not the most destructive, fortunately) that my Hugr rose to defend the realm.*

Invitations to Goddesses

If you like to work with the Deities, consider inviting Sif (Sippe, Sibbe), Sjöfn, Frigg, Syn and Hlin to work with you on the following exercises, and on your work with your Sefa in general. Sif is especially concerned with kinships, Sjöfn with the love and affection of romantic relationships and close friendships, though they and Frigg help with all relationships. Frigg is a supporter of frith and community relationships, where each person takes responsibility for maintaining the behavior and commitments that allow communities of any size and kind (family, workplace, neighborhood, city, etc.) to function fairly and productively. (Maire Durkan's *Circle of Frith: A Devotional to Frigg and her Handmaidens* is a good resource for pursuing such Deity-work.)

Hlin is a Goddess of refuge and protection. Though it is best when Sefa works with our other souls to deal with challenges as they arise, there are times when we all need a restful refuge, a safe space, to recover from stresses and build our strength up. Hlin can help us find such spaces, inner and outer, and help to ward them for us.

Syn is the Goddess of denial, of closing the door, setting boundaries, drawing the line. In a larger sense, she strengthens us to develop and maintain our own self-respect and our willingness to stand up for ourselves when our healthy boundaries are threatened. I don't see her as a belligerent or confrontational Goddess; I perceive her as calm, dignified, wise and kind. But she is firm and insightful, understanding that our personal boundaries must have some flexibility and 'give', but that there is a point when we must be firm and stand up for ourselves and for others, when personal boundaries, dignity and self-respect are threatened.

Hugr is a very complex and multi-faceted soul, and its connections with Deities and their gifts and strengths are multiple. Though Hugr's and Odin's natures overlap a great deal, when it comes to Hugr's warding function, I find that Syn is a natural Deity to turn to. She knows when to open the door to our inner self, and when the door must be closed and warded. Syn's wisdom, strength and firmness are very much needed in the world today, where personal and larger boundaries are continually disrespected and invaded. Malicious Hugrs are often the culprits here, but

Hugrs aligned with Syn, and working with Mod's strength and determination, can also help to remedy such situations.

Our Hugr-soul, who wards our inner self, benefits from the power of the Goddess Syn, who wards gates and doors, and denies entry when she deems it necessary.

Exercise 12-1: Pursuing Sefa-awareness

A. Review the assigned reading about Sefa, open your Daybook, then sit quietly and clear a space within yourself. Begin examining, honestly and compassionately, the ways that you have pursued and experienced relationships in your life, and the emotions and needs that have driven your pursuit of different kinds of relationships. Evaluate how healthy and fulfilling your different relationships have

Sefa, Hugr and Modsefa

been, for yourself and for others in the relationship. What are the weak points and strong points in the ways that you relate to others? What kinds of feedback, direct or indirect, have you received from others, that would show how perceptive and responsive you are towards them? How well or poorly have others in your relationships understood and responded to you?

B. Make a list of your different kinds of relationships, such as various familial relations, love and friendship, work and neighborhood / community relationships. What qualities would you use to describe these different relations? For example: commitment, loyalty, neediness, fear, enjoyment, common values & interests, resentment, burdensome, rejuvenation, enrichment, satisfaction, necessity, etc. Do some of your relationship-types seem healthier and more rewarding than others? Are some kinds of relationships more problematic and disappointing for you?

C. What can you learn from this analysis: about yourself, about how others treat you and respond to you, about your ability to communicate your inner self / Sefa to others, and about how well you perceive the inner selves of others?

D. What about your own Sefa, in and of itself, not as it relates to other people? Refer again to Book I, Chapter 12, and look at the discussion of the rune Wynn or Wunjo at the end of the chapter. How does your Sefa feel when it is in its 'burg', in its place of safety and homeliness deep within yourself, when it can just be itself naturally? Does it feel an inner joy and sense of tranquility, a sense of being as it is meant to be? Or does it feel damaged, unhomed, unsafe to be itself? Is there work here that needs to be done, to bring your Sefa to its inner place of calm, steady happiness and loving care?

These exercises are obviously a long-term effort, likely to be emotionally and intellectually demanding and tiring, but should bear good fruit for you. Take them in bite-sized chunks, but keep notes in your Daybook so that you can perceive and analyze the broader patterns of your Sefa's nature, behavior and experiences throughout your life to date, and so you can track your progressive learning about Sefa as time goes by.

Attuning Sefa and Hugr

Exercise 12-2: Awareness of Hugr as warder

Here is something important to understand about Hugr: your Hugr may, or may not, be willing, skilled, and effective in its warding role right now. Much depends on our maturity, our life-experiences and what we have learned from them, and also on our Hugr's past-life experiences and training. The first steps in developing our Hugr as an effective warder require that we become aware of our Hugr and get to know and understand it as a soul-being. The Hugr exercises in the previous chapters should be pursued first, in preparation for this exercise. Hopefully, you will have recorded the results of these exercises in your Daybook, and can refer back to refresh your memory now.

All of the Hugr-exercises to date have focused on getting to know your Hugr as a soul-being and a major source of your character, temperament, personality. To date, we've focused on the *nature* of the Hugr; now we're

Sefa, Hugr and Modsefa

going to focus on one of Hugr's major *roles* in our life, the role of Warder.

A warder needs to have certain qualities and abilities, and these can be exercised in ways that can be useful and helpful, or conversely can sometimes be obstructive and counter-productive. A warding Hugr may shield us from unhealthy influences, but it may also block us from worthwhile experiences and relationships, out of an excess of caution, a history of bad experiences, or due to lack of understanding and wisdom. Likewise, it may fail to protect us when needed.

If our own Hugr is manipulative toward others (whether we are fully aware of this behavior or not), it may be so focused on manipulating others that it fails to pay attention to how we ourselves are being manipulated, and how our own Sefa is being exploited or suppressed. Keep in mind that sometimes we may do or say things to others 'for their own good', that are subtly manipulative even though well-intentioned. There are many semi-aware 'relationship games' and a lot of vicious circles we can fall into, when our Hugr's warding function is not operating in the best way and when its awareness is distracted or distorted.

Now let's take a look at how your own Hugr's warding function has operated in your life to date. I know that this exercise could feel threatening, if you have had severe negative experiences. Read through it and consider before proceeding farther. I would encourage you to see whether there is any way you can safely do some of this exercise, though, because the whole point is to improve your Hugr's ability to ward you from repetition of your bad experiences. If you can pursue this exercise to any extent, it will help to lessen the instances and the impact of people ill-treating you (deliberately or not) in the future.

Enter stillness and open your awareness to your Hugr, as you have begun to get to know it in the previous exercises. Settle in, and begin to mesh your awareness with your Hugr, like fitting your hand into a glove. Now go through your memory and select an instance when some interaction with another person resulted in emotional pain, distress, disappointment or harm to you. If you need to, you can select a minor instance, not very impactful, in cases where your memory is too full of major and threatening situations. When I say 'interaction', I mean that you also were involved in what happened, you made choices and took actions, or did not take action, as well as the other person.

Now, challenge your insight-memory, your Huginn-and-Muninn inner team, to try to pinpoint any inner warnings, clues, insights, instincts you might have had, while the situation was unfolding, that you failed to act upon. You may find your best clues to these memories, by remembering what you regretted after the event, things you wished you had done or not done or done differently, things you wish you had known or understood better.

If you can recall any warnings or inner promptings, gut feelings etc., this will show how your Hugr was trying to serve as your warder in the situation. If you don't recall any such things, look even harder at your post-situation regrets: these are the lessons that your Hugr was trying to learn and to bring to your attention, so that you and your Hugr are wiser the next time a similar situation comes up.

Next, look for a memory of a situation that could have gone wrong, but didn't. The time you almost said something that would have really upset or hurt someone, but you decided not to say it. Or the time when it really was important to say something risky, for your sake and / or the sake of the other person, and you did say it, and it all turned out well. Your Hugr was helping you here.

Look at some of the important choices you've made in your life, and try to remember whether there was any inner voice, gut feel, or instinct that guided you during those choices. If you do remember such situations, compare them with other instances in your life when you felt unrooted, without guidance or direction when you had choices and decisions to make. Compare the outcomes of those situations, and look for traces of your Hugr's actions, however small.

Work through a number of your memories in these kinds of ways. Are you having trouble seeing any warding or guiding activity from your Hugr? If that's the case, then you know something important now: your Hugr needs more training as a warder, and you need more awareness of your Hugr: what it is telling you, what it needs, and what it can do.

This kind of training is a lifelong endeavor, and I can't offer a lot more step by step guidance here. Working through the Hugr exercises in the previous chapters will help a lot, as well as carefully studying the chapters about the Hugr in Book I, and any other writing on the Hugr you may find, as well. If you work with Deities and / or with ancestral Hugr-spirits, seek their help in learning to be aware of your Hugr and its communications, and help in training your Hugr to ward you better. I have written an article, available on my website, that offers a method for entering your *Hugiskeft*, where your full awareness is centered in your Hugr. Though the focus of the article is on healing, the Hugiskeft exercise can be applied in many other contexts. ("Disir, Hama and Hugr as Healing Partners." Future soul lore writing will develop *Hugiskeft* training in more depth; here we are attending to the basics.)

Exercise 12-3: Tuning in to your warding Hugr

No matter how good a job Hugr is capable of, however, it's useless unless you actually listen to it! It's essential to begin making a habit of this: enter into your deeper awareness, and spend some quiet time just 'listening' or being aware of your Hugr, whenever you have an important choice or decision to make, or are considering some action, including those involving relationships and interactions with others.

With practice, you can briefly enter such a space, listen, exit the space, and right away take action that is based on Hugr's guidance. You can learn do this as you go about your daily life at home, at work, anywhere: drop in briefly to consult with your Hugr, then move on as needed. Obviously, when you are dealing with more complex, long-term decisions or issues, you will want to spend more and deeper time consulting with your Hugr.

When I say 'listen', this is metaphorical, of course. You are not likely to hear actual words, but words or ideas may just arise in your mind. You'll start getting a 'sense', a 'feel', an image or visualization, an urge or an idea, concerning the best course of action.

So, for this exercise, spend quiet time with your Hugr to focus on how it prefers to communicate with you, and how you can most easily perceive its messages. Is it a physical sensation, a sense of uneasiness, for example, that arises when you're headed toward making a mistake or taking unwise action in a social situation? Do you start to get a headache or upset stomach, or feel shaky or weepy? Restlessness, irritability, discomfort? Twitches, tics, cramps? Or is it something non-physical, perhaps an emotion like a sense of dread, aversion, exhaustion, dislike?

What about positive reinforcement from your Hugr, when you are considering a situation or action that Hugr approves of? Perhaps you get a sense of relief and inner relaxation, of warmth or brightness, quiet happiness, a sense of rightness. Rather than sensations, Hugr may send you images, phrases, ideas, hunches, urges, usually in very quick glimpses that are easy to miss if you are not tuned in, and easy to ignore if you haven't learned to trust your Hugr's advice or 'rede'.

When you've identified cues and signals that work for you and your Hugr, strengthen your ability to perceive them by going through some imaginary situations, or replays of your memories, where Hugr's guidance would be important. Play out these situations or memories, altering the memories as needed, so they become imagined success stories between you and your Hugr: success in the sense that you and your Hugr communicate clearly with each other about the situation. This creates positive reinforcement for your training. In other words, *use your imagination as a training ground for you and your Hugr to fine-tune your mutual awareness, communication, and coordinated action through dramatic, imagined scenes of challenge and success.*

Modsefa and ethical action

In Heathen Old Saxon and Anglo-Saxon culture, both Sefa and Mod were seen as our Inner Self. Sefa was primarily our 'inner Self as it relates to others', while Mod was fundamentally the inner power, drive and Will to decide what 'I' want, and to pursue it. Mod is power and will; when things go wrong for it, it becomes angry and wants action. Sefa is love and caring; when things go wrong, it worries and wants a refuge. Sefa wants safety, for itself and everything it cares about.

Modsefa is the space they make together, where power and will can support the active expression of love and caring; where love and caring can guide power and will toward ethical action. Our Modsefa is where our understanding and pursuit of ethics and ethical action is rooted. In the process, our character is shaped and developed.

Exercise 12-4: Tuning in to your Modsefa

For this exercise, spend some time exploring these themes within yourself. How do you experience your own inner power? Where and how do you focus your Will? How do you think that power and love interact and interrelate, both positively and negatively?

What about the interrelationships between Self, Will, and caring, both as inner, spiritual-emotional phenomena, and as they are expressed through actions in the world? What do all these things mean to you, how do they shape your life and your Self? As you work through these questions and develop greater clarity about the vital interrelationships between love and power, Will and caring, Self and Other, you are coming to know your own Modsefa and its potentials.

You are also exploring the roots of your own personal ethical sense, grounded in your Modsefa. Take some time to explore and clarify your own ethical principles, and how you express them in your life and actions. What do you truly believe and commit to, in terms of right action in your life? How well do you follow this in practice? Is there more work you need to do here?

Gender stereotypes

You may have noticed, reading through the chapters here and in Book I about Sefa and Mod, that many of Sefa's traits align with stereotypes of more womanly characteristics, while Mod aligns with more manly stereotypes. Everyone, wherever they may fall on the gender spectrum, has both of these souls. Many cultures tend to encourage certain attitudes and behaviors, and discourage others, based on our perceived gender alignment. This gives rise to the stereotypes, which, in fact, can prove to be supportive and offer social rewards if one happens to fit comfortably within the stereotypes. Of course, many people do not, and even more people must expand outside their 'assigned' gender roles because of their circumstances, whether they wish to or not. The whole issue of gender roles is fraught and complex.

The practice of Heathen soul lore can, I believe, heal these potential dissonances within us. I think that our Modsefa is key to this healing, because it is the meeting space, the common ground, between our own Mod and our own Sefa. This is the place where we develop our own personal balance between these soul-forces, unique to ourself, and this is also where we root our own sense of ethics and ethical behavior.

A well-developed Modsefa has access to the strengths of both Sefa and Mod, and can express them in balanced and powerful ways into the world of action and of relationships. In my view, rather than rebelling against all stereotypes of masculine and feminine behaviors, we can embrace what we find to be valuable about both of them, and turn aside from their more negative or extreme expressions. Our Modsefa can handle both modes (and other modes as well), can learn to understand when and how each one is appropriate to the circumstances, to our own nature and our ethical beliefs, and can shift back and forth as needed along a spectrum of behaviors.

I don't mean to imply that gender roles are the only important thing about Sefa, Mod, and Modsefa, however; far from it. This is only one of many aspects of life that these souls are involved with, and this particular issue may be of greater or of lesser importance to you on a personal level. Regardless of how it applies to you personally, however, I invite you to consider the social and psychological issues surrounding gender, placing them in the context of Modsefa and soul lore generally. My hope is that this will lead to a deeper understanding and appreciation for each person's unique expression of their own humanity.

Building trust between Sefa, Hugr and Mod

As you and your Hugr learn to interact wisely and strategically in social settings of all kinds, your Sefa will become more relaxed and trusting, willing to entrust its safety and wellbeing to your Hugr's skills and insights. Likewise, when Mod and Sefa work together to create their own powerful common ground, the Modsefa, both souls are empowered to be the best that they can be. When Sefa trusts that it is safe and that access to it is well and wisely warded, it will flourish and blossom into its full power of love, caring, and taking joy in these things, even when it is in challenging situations such as caring for others who are suffering.

All religions and cultures are aware and admiring of the power of love and compassion, and what this power can accomplish in the world. Sefa provides the power of love, compassion and relatedness. Mod and Hugr energize this impetus with their strength, skills, courage and intelligence, and carry it out into the world of action and interaction, thus fulfilling Sefa's greatest need and wish.

At the same time, Hugr protects this precious well-spring of loving power and joy, the well-spring of Wunjo within us, ensuring that it is not abused, strained, drained, or polluted by negativity. Mod and Sefa create together their common ground, Modsefa, which, if well developed, reinforces the positive strengths of both of them. Truly, the more people who can reach such a state of productive and healthy goodness and willingness to relate to others and the world around us, the better off our world of Midgard will be.

Sefa, Hugr and Modsefa

Souls working together

If you have friends whom you really trust,
And from whom you want what is good,
Consider matters well together:
Blend your awareness with theirs,
And merge your understandings.
Share gifts with them, and get together often.

(My own rendition of the Old Norse Hávamál verse 44, in the Poetic Edda. I have included more phrases than the original has, in order to capture the meaning more fully.)

Chapter 13

13. Sefa: The Channel of Compassion

{Primary runes in this bindrune: Wunjo, Gebo, Fehu, Ansuz, Eihwaz.}

Background reading: Chapter 12 of Book I, or "Sefa: The Soul of Relationship" on my website.

Note: This shape is similar to a Christian symbol called the Chi Rho, after the two Greek letters it is formed from. The story goes that before a decisive battle in 312 CE, the Byzantine emperor Constantine saw a vision in the sky of this symbol, and was told "In this sign, you will conquer." He placed the sign on his battle-banners and adopted it as his own, and did indeed win the battle, establishing Christianity in Byzantium. I tried many other combinations to express what I wanted in this bindrune, so it would not resemble the Chi Rho, but somehow it kept reshaping itself to this one. What made me finally decide to choose this

Sefa: The Channel of Compassion

shape, however, was the delightful idea of stealing the promise purportedly given to Constantine, and giving that promise to Compassion instead: "In this sign, Compassion will conquer!" May it be so, indeed.....

Our Sefa-soul is a song, sung into being by our other souls. It is thus intimately connected to the essences of each of our souls. Sefa is focused on relationship, on kinship and connection, social bonds and community, including the community formed by our own soular-system. Sefa is a channel through which compassion can flow toward any or all of our souls at need, either coming from Sefa itself, or coming through Sefa from outside. These outside sources can include the Deities, ancestors, and of course our own friends and loved ones. Likewise, the flow can be reversed: Sefa can gather compassionate impulses from our other souls, Deities, ancestors, well-wishers, and channel that flow toward other people or beings who need it, or use that energy to undertake compassionate action that needs to be done.

    The texts and tales passed down to us from earlier Heathen times do not offer a great many examples of compassion, although related impulses such as generosity and frith are praised. These texts were written during times of great difficulty and cultural change, and their focus was on the warrior life and warrior values—thus the poets and tale-tellers made their living. Anything relating to everyday life, parenting, elder care, care for the sick and dying, neighborliness, and other opportunities to practice compassion was given short shrift in the poems and tales, though there are brief, passing examples in the sagas and some poems.

Sefa: The Channel of Compassion

We, as modern Heathens, do not need to remain stuck in these patterns of the past. Modern Heathen ethics and community values are topics of lively discussion and exploration among us, and the need for compassion is acknowledged within our faith as well as all others. What I present in this chapter are examples of ways of seeking compassion from within and outside ourselves in a Heathen context, using that compassion to strengthen us and attune our souls to the energy of compassion, and then passing it on to others and to the world around us. Many of us are already pursuing these matters in our own ways; here I share a few additional thoughts and ideas.

It's important to note something that frequently serves to block and confuse all of us, as we seek compassion in times of need, either from other people or from the Deities. Compassion can take many forms, sometimes unexpected and even unwelcome forms, such as 'tough love' (which may be truly compassionate, or may not, depending on how it is applied). Different states of need, and different people, personalities and circumstances, may require different forms of compassion in order to best address the need.

Here is one example of godly compassion from our lore *(Gylfaginning* in the prose *Edda,* Sturlason p. 38). Thor stops overnight with a peasant family, slaughters the goats who draw his chariot, and shares their meat. Unbeknownst to him, however, the son breaks a leg-bone for the marrow. When Thor resurrects his goat the next morning and finds it limping, he falls into a Mod-fury and threatens the family in revenge. But he is not in a blind rage: when he sees the family's terror, he *sefadiz,* he shifts from the raging of his

Mod into the compassion and calm of his Sefa, and agrees to accept compensation rather than enact revenge.

The family offer their son and daughter to Thor as compensation, and from our modern perspective this does not seem like a compassionate situation. Look at it from the perspective of the society at that time, however. For peasant children to be taken into service with a great Deity would be the ultimate dream come true, an honor and benefit to the whole family. Thjalfi gained fame as a brave and trusty companion of Thor on his adventures, something he would not have achieved as a laboring peasant, no matter how hard he worked. Roskva goes with them on their next adventure, but we don't hear more of her after that. I assume she eventually joins the household of Thor's daughter Thruðr, or his wife Sif (herself an embodiment of Sefa-qualities), and gains the advantages of the ensuing higher social status. The 'compensation' Thor accepted was, in truth, a continuation of his compassion and his blessing for the family, as indeed was the original sacrifice and feast of his goats to feed a poor peasant family (as well as himself, of course!).

Sefa's role

Compassion is a form of energy, as our souls and other beings are, too. As compassion flows through a living being, physical or non-physical, it is shaped by the 'container' of that being, then shaped again as it reaches its destination within us or other beings, and begins to nourish us with its healing energy.

Our Sefa-soul, dwelling in our heart, is the channel for this compassion-energy to flow into, through, and out from ourselves in its constant circulation through the beings of the Worlds. As compassion flows through each being, including each of us, it absorbs shape, flavor and vitality from that being, thus becoming more enriched and powerful as it flows, enriching and empowering others in turn.

'Compassion' comes from the Latin words *con* and *passio*, meaning 'with' and 'feeling': we feel with others, feel what they feel, and respond in solidarity with them. (*Sympathy* means exactly the same thing, coming from Greek rather than Latin words.) This is what Sefa does with our other souls. It is formed by them, shares in their substance and energy, and through these, Sefa 'feels with' them.

Unfortunately, if any of our other souls are damaged enough, that damage tends to spread to Sefa as well, through their soul-connections, in addition to Sefa being damaged directly though harmful interactions with other people. When Sefa is harmed or damaged, compassion is the healing energy that is needed: compassion from people, from spiritual beings, often even from animals who are close to us, as well as the healing powers of nature.

Exercise 13-1: Sensing compassion-energy

As we've done with other exercises in this book, let's focus on how the energy of compassion *feels* within your whole soul-body complex, rather than trying to define it and prescribe what to do with it. One of the first things you may notice about compassion from this perspective is that it is a *flow*, a flowing-through of energy in constant motion. Some of the other energy-feelings we've explored, such as courage, will, mod and maegen, have 'home bases' within us, where they pool and root themselves, and support us from these home-bases. Compassion-energy would stagnate and mutate into something more self-centered, if it ever held still long enough to root itself this way. It needs to keep moving, and we need to let it be free to do so.

For this exercise, spend some time sensing what compassion and its flow feel like, within you. Observe yourself when you engage in compassionate behavior, however minor—for example, spending a few minutes sincerely sympathizing with someone else's troubles, and offering encouragement, as you go about your day. Or sharing their joy or relief when something good has happened. This includes members of your family as well as others.

This is one exercise that I find difficult to do in the imagination, because there needs to be a real receiver of your flow of compassion, if you want to see how that flow feels. It's like the other person or being draws the energy of compassion forth from you, and it's hard to create that flow in a vacuum consisting of one person (you) alone, trying to do it in your imagination. The best way to do this in your imagination is through deep prayer on behalf of another person, where your prayer flows forth as a wave of compassion-energy even when the person is not there.

Next, sense how it feels when compassion flows into you, from people, Deities, ancestral spirits. You may even feel it from pet animals or from some interaction with nature. The way you would sense it from these sources—animals or nature, would be through feelings, and possibly from actions like licking or friendly contact from animals, or a ray of sunshine breaking through the clouds. Instances of human compassion can even be tiny flashes, like meeting the gaze of a stranger who is momentarily sharing your feelings in some situation that creates humor, or pity, or outrage, or admiration, or calls for strained patience as you deal with it.

Remember: compassion is 'feeling with, sharing feelings.' It does not always have to be feelings of pain and suffering that are shared, but any feelings. The sharing of any kind of feelings creates an energetic bond, short-term or long-term depending on circumstances. These energetic bonds add up, over time, to create and sustain all kinds of relationships, frith, and community connections. You can see the involvement of the Sefa soul, here, who focuses so heavily on relationships.

(As a reminder, severely negative feelings, such as enjoyment of others' suffering, bullying, exploitation of others, violence, cruelty, etc., can also create sick bonds between people who enjoy causing those negative feelings in their victims. This is clearly not the kind of community and fellow-feeling that we are seeking here, and we need to reject any effort to draw us into such negative bonds with others (physical or spiritual). This can happen more easily than we may be aware of: enjoyment of cruel or exploitative scenes in movies and games, for example, can set us on such a path before we realize it.)

The nature of compassion-energy

It is true that compassion can strain and exhaust us at times. The aperture in our Sefa-heart may start out rather narrow, and become frayed and bruised when the flow of compassion through it becomes too great for our capacity. Even when we enlarge our capacity and stamina for compassion, we can still reach our limit in tough situations. A good example of this is the plight of health care workers during the Covid pandemic, whose compassion and strenuous work lead them to the point of collapse.

I want to make a subtle point about this situation here. There is a difference, at the energetic level, between running out of physical and mental energy and stamina, versus running out of compassion-energy itself. They are different kinds of energy, and the difference can be important on a spiritual level, even when they are overlapping on the physical level.

It is easiest to see this in examples of compassionate saints from various religions. I will use the example of Mother Teresa of Calcutta, whose compassionate deeds and life are honored by people of all religions, and of none. Her life was a constant outpouring of compassion under circumstances where the need was dire and never-ending, dealing daily with an endless stream of destitute and dying people, with limited material resources to do so. She was a physically strong woman in her youth, but no amount of physical strength could sustain such activity over a lifetime. She suffered from bouts of emotional exhaustion and illness, as anyone would in such circumstances, but it never prevented her work. After her death, it became clear from her letters and journals that she also suffered from spiritual deprivation: she had a great sense of absence in the inner place where she expected and hoped to feel the presence and love of her God. This emptiness was the case for most of her working life, including the end of it. In spite of this, her dedication to her faith, work and vows was unwavering.

So where did her compassion-energy come from and how was it sustained? The demands on her were too great for physical and emotional energy alone. Spiritual consolation, and the energy and support it gives, she felt was withheld from her, though she never failed to give credit for all her work and accomplishments to Jesus as the 'master of the house' in which she worked.

I find this question an interesting conundrum: where, indeed, did her enormous compassion-energy come from, and how was it sustained, when there was an apparent insufficiency of physical, emotional, *and* spiritual energetic input over a long lifetime, compared to the heavy demands of her work? My own thought is that it was her emptiness itself, that allowed the free passage of a steady torrent of compassion-energy—a torrent that was far greater and more powerful than most humans could handle over the course of a lifetime of work. There was nothing blocking its way; her heart and her Sefa opened up, with no reservations or demands or qualifications, and compassion poured through unimpeded and powered her work.

The mystery of compassion

I am not suggesting this as a path for everyone, of course, though we can all honor Mother Teresa's greatness. Much of her situation was wrapped up in the mysteries and dynamics of her own religion, toward which we, as Heathens, must stand as respectful outsiders. The reason I bring it up at all, is that it illustrates the genuine difference between compassion-energy and other forms of personal energy. Personal energy alone could never have sustained the enormous amount of compassionate work that she demonstrated over a long lifetime.

Here is the lesson that I draw from this, in terms of regulating our own compassion-energy. And let me say that this lesson is not that we all can or should be like

Sefa: The Channel of Compassion

Mother Teresa! Where I'm going with this, is how to keep our Sefa true to its own compassionate, relational nature, even when the strains and stresses and demands of life tempt us to become cynical, withdrawn, indifferent, snarky, etc., as a way to protect our vulnerable Sefa from exploitation and exhaustion.

It's natural for us, when we see our resources of any kind running low, to hold on more tightly to what we have left, and limit its use. That is sensible when it comes to finite resources, including the amount of personal energy we might have available at any given point in time.

Compassion-energy, however, is different: it is a *stream flowing through us,* not a finite resource that we own. It circulates around among the worlds and beings of the worlds, picking up enhancements from each of us as it flows on its way. When we share feelings, share the energy of compassion, what is really happening is compassion-energy interacting with itself. The compassion-energy flowing through each of us reaches out to the same energy flowing through others around us; it contacts those energies and blends together as we 'share feelings' or 'share together in compassion-energy.'

We may reach the point where we cannot physically, mentally or emotionally sustain the practical demands of compassion, as in the example I gave of pandemic-era health care workers. The demands may be so great that we are injured by them, as health care workers are now suffering from PTSD, depression, anxiety, and so forth. Though it may feel natural, at such a time, to shut down our feelings of compassion in self-defense, this is actually the wrong time to do that.

Sefa: The Channel of Compassion

The reason is, again, that *compassion is a flow,* and we ourselves desperately need compassion at this very time when we are tempted to shut it down. When we shut down the outflow, the inflow may well be shut down or minimized as well. We can see this happening, using our example again, when health care workers feel a sense of guilt and failure when they try to step back or give up their responsibilities because they cannot manage any more. They may block the inflow of compassion that others are sending toward them, including from spiritual sources, feeling that they 'don't deserve it' since they are not giving compassion out, anymore. They may imagine they are 'failures', bad people who have let others down, and 'deserve to suffer.'

This is a terribly painful state to be in, and may eventually lead to what I mentioned earlier: the shutting-down of all compassion, including compassion toward ourself and our own needs. Then we end up with damaged Sefas: cynical, hardened, depressed, detached, neglectful of our own wellbeing and uncaring about everyone else. Next may come addictions and other dysfunctional coping behaviors, and it's a downward slope from there.

All of these awful experiences come about, I believe, through the root cause of trying to block the proper flow of compassion. This effort at self-protection is totally understandable, but based on a lack of understanding of the true mystery of compassion. And this mystery is simple but profound: *compassion must keep flowing.* It must not be blocked, even though the *expression* of compassion through physical and emotional activity may have to take a break from time to time, due to exhaustion and the need for self-care.

Sefa: The Channel of Compassion

Our Hugr as Warder, and the Goddesses Syn (the doorkeeper) and Hlin (the provider of safe refuge) can help us manage such needs and processes of healthy withdrawal and rest. Our Mod and Modsefa can help us maintain higher levels of strength and energy to support a compassionate lifestyle. But regardless of our state of rest or of activity, the flow of compassion must continue.

Keeping compassion flowing

You may ask "how is this compassion supposed to continue, when I am too tired and burned out to do anything? I don't want to talk or listen to anyone, or do anything for anyone that I don't absolutely have to. I've got to shut it down." But you mustn't shut it down: now you need it flowing *into* you, just as much as you were letting it flow *out* of you when you were actively expressing it. The mistake here is thinking that compassion always has to be active, which can indeed be exhausting.

Let's look at another example in our imaginations, now, as an example of the power of passive, rather than active compassion: the compassion of Being rather than of Doing. Maybe you've known someone like this; if not, imagine it. Here is an elderly and frail person, able to do very little at this stage of life. This person is a grandparent, and during their younger years, was actively involved with the lives of their children and grandchildren, their other relatives, neighbors and friends. People felt that this grandparent could really see them, know them and care about them; just being near them, saying hello on their way to school or work, was a little lift in their day. I was lucky to have grandparents like that; during WWII, they wrote regular letters to all the young men and women they knew about from their small town who were serving in the war, especially to those whose own families were not so faithful.

Now this person is very old and can't do much at all. They sit in a chair and spend most of their days in quietude. They may not be as mentally sharp as they used to be. But are they cut off from the compassion they practiced throughout their life, because they can no longer be active? No way. They have spent their life being a channel for compassion, and compassion is now flowing steadily through them with power and beauty. It waters their souls, and spreads out from them like scent from blossoms, filling the air around them. Its ripples spread outward like soundwaves through the ether. Their heart is still working just fine as a channel for compassion, even if their mental and physical powers are fading.

You may think I am being sentimentally poetic, but I have known people like this, and not only old people. I've known people whom others just want to be around, because they are quiet but spiritually strong and peaceful people who spread happiness just by their presence. Such people are rare, but they don't need to be. This is something we can all aspire to, no matter our state of strength or health, work or wealth, culture or religion, opportunity or lack of it. Such quiet saints have spread peace in concentration camps and on desperate migrations: such is their power. This kind of power is passive; it is not expressed through direct action. Rather, this energy disperses out from the compassionate person, and is absorbed through osmosis by others around them.

Hindus have a practice called *darshan*, where pilgrims simply sit quietly in the presence of persons recognized as holy people, perhaps speaking with them, perhaps not. The verb used to describe this is 'beholding' a holy person, or the sacred image representing a Deity. This is considered a valuable spiritual practice, offering peace, hope, blessing to those who are beholding holiness, even though, outwardly, nothing much happens. They are sharing in the flow of compassion.

Animals are often very attracted to people who are adept at this flow of peaceful compassion, and many people have felt a response from natural entities like trees when engaging in this activity in natural surroundings. Spiritual beings like landwights and housewights appreciate being in this kind of environment. They hate it, and tend to desert the area, when people in their environment are quarrelsome, disruptive and disrespectful, as is told in many tales of folklore.

These examples all show powerful expressions of compassion, and they are flows whose expression can be accepted by each recipient in the way best suited to them. There are often times when acts of intended compassion are actually not that well-suited to their recipients, and sometimes ulterior motives can be masked by apparent acts of compassion. All of these leave a bad taste behind them, and unfortunately they commonly occur. The flows from the heart that I am talking about here can never go wrong, because this quiet compassion shapes itself to each person's need as it flows through them.

The mystery of compassionate flow can take on many shapes and expressions, suited not only to the recipients, but to the giver's abilities as well, which will vary over time depending on their circumstances. When we cannot perform physical acts of compassion, we can still keep the beautiful, soul-nourishing flow moving vigorously through ourself and through the world around us, through a passive form of dispersion and osmosis.

Exercise 13-2: Fine-tuning your flow of compassion

Summary: compassion is a flow of energy. This energy can express itself in active or passive ways, and both are of great value. The energy needs to flow through us constantly. It flows into us from other people, Deities, spiritual beings and beings of nature. Within us, it nourishes, energizes and heals us, and it takes on something of our own 'shape and flavor.' Then it flows out from us to be shared with other beings, through physical, emotional, mental, spiritual activities, and through passive but powerful processes like dispersion and osmosis.

With this in mind, evaluate your own practice of compassion. Consider whether the flow is well-balanced: are you striving for a lot of active compassion-output, without attending to the necessary input? If so, what is this doing to you physically and psychologically? Are you a compassion-seeker, wanting a lot for yourself but reluctant to offer it to others? How might you expand and balance your practice of compassion in ways that would nourish rather than exhaust you, and others around you?

Sometimes we are so close to our immediate family and closest friends, that we simply don't notice or think about the ways we might share compassion with them. If they don't overtly demand or expect compassion from us, we might overlook their need for it, and if they do demand it, we may resent that. Evaluate how you 'share feeling' with those closest to you, not just in serious, 'heavy' ways, but in all kinds of shared emotion and activity: humor, frustrations, hopes and dreams, gentle soothing, everything.

In closing

Our Sefa, the soul of relationship, is the channel for compassion to flow through us. Compassion is feeling what others feel, and responding in appropriate and needed ways. We are part of the Whole, we feel with the Whole, and the Whole feels with us. We all share in the vital passions and energies of Life and Being. Our Sefa soul is the repository of this knowledge, this passion, this healing and life-giving energy, which flows through us as vigorously as we allow it to. As our physical and mental abilities become less, our heart and Sefa can still maintain the flows of compassion that we have attuned them to, throughout our life.

Chapter 14

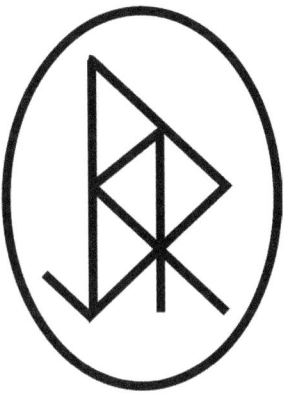

14. Saiwalo-Dwimor and the Sea of Images

{Primary runes in the bind-rune above: Hagalaz, Othala, Eihwaz, Sowilo, Ingwaz, Berkano, Kenaz.}

Background reading: Book I, Chapters 13, 14, 15, 16. Alternatively, the following articles on my website: "Hel-Dweller;" "The Soul and the Sea;" and "The Alchemy of Hel" (a six-part series).

Summary of Saiwalo

Here is a brief summary of the previous Saiwalo chapters in Book I (13, 14, 15, 16), describing my understanding of this soul. Saiwalo is an afterlife soul, little involved in Midgard life. It is rooted in Hel, and forms a phantom from itself, a Dwimor, which it projects into the Midgard plane. The

Saiwalo-Dwimor

Dwimor serves as an alchemical matrix which attracts and holds together our other souls and their energies during Midgard life. Saiwalo, through its Dwimor-matrix, holds us in life, and therefore is a life-soul whose departure means death, but it does not actively participate in our life or give us life-energy as our other souls do. Dwimor itself is not a stand-alone soul; it is a phantom image that Saiwalo projects into Midgard, which returns to its Saiwalo in Hel when physical life is over.

Saiwalo remains rooted in Hel, whether it is currently supporting a Dwimor in Midgard, or not. There, the Saiwalos form the ecosystem of Hel, which I envision (on one level) as being like a wetland which processes the spiritual waste draining down from the life-worlds above. Very slowly, through repeated cycles, the waste material is transformed into nourishing elemental Water that percolates up through the roots of the Tree and into all the Worlds.

The actual material that Saiwalos work with consists of 'images' (we could call them 'memes,' too): in esoteric terms, they are patterns imprinted within a watery matrix. Saiwalos themselves generate images and send them to Midgard through their Dwimors. In Midgard, the images / memes from all the Saiwalos enter human experience, through all the senses of our sensorium, our body's energy patterns, our emotions and thought processes. They churn together, interacting, breaking down, recombining, sparking new images.

These images are all expressed in many ways: in our experiences, in the information and ideas we exchange, stories we tell, things we see / hear about / do ourselves, in our dreams and nightmares, aspirations and ideals, fears and hopes, our stereotypes and prejudices, our triggers, imprints, fantasies and inspirations. The entire world of human thought, experience and communication is formed and stored as images.

Dwimor, during its time in Midgard, gathers the images experienced by its living person, including the other souls of their 'soular system'. This is Dwimor's treasure hoard, which it will bring back to its Saiwalo after death. Saiwalo and Dwimor do not have the capacity to evaluate these images, to judge their worthiness or harmfulness, to make choices between some images and others, to reject images according to any kind of criteria. Saiwalo-Dwimor values images for their energy-density, their intensity, rather than valuing them as positive or negative the way a living human would.

Thus, images that cause PTSD in a living person may be tightly held by the Dwimor because of their intensity, while counteractive, healing, positive images might be grasped less tightly because they are less-believed, less-attended to, less intensely felt, by the afflicted person. In addition to the physical and behavioral aspects of PTSD that make it difficult to heal, Saiwalo-Dwimor's unthinking attachment to intense image-energy can contribute to the problem as well. The same dynamic can also amplify obsessions.

I've pointed out a number of times that Saiwalo-Dwimor is a passive soul in Midgard, not participating actively in our Midgard life. To clarify: the images that Saiwalo-Dwimor generates, transmits, absorbs, and transforms do strongly influence us during our Midgard life, so it might seem that this soul is an active one in Midgard. This is not how I understand it. Saiwalo is active in Hel, doing its own thing. It is not, itself, actively participating in the character, thoughts, emotions, temperament, decisions, actions, motivations that define our Midgard life. Saiwalo-Dwimor, through its activities in Hel, churns images that flow back and forth through the Worlds, while our full soul-household in Midgard actively deals with those images and their influences on our life.

When our Midgard life is at an end, Dwimor heads back to its Saiwalo in Hel, bearing its hoard of image-treasures with it. Saiwalo, along with all the Dwimors it has generated, sent out, and received back over time, uses the ingathered images to populate its environment. Thus, depending on the nature of the images, Saiwalo's environment may be filled with treasures of knowledge, power, beauty and meaningfulness; or with images of fear, suffering, ugliness, hatred, degradation, chaos; or may simply be a dull, boring, meaningless landscape. Underneath this level of image-appearances, the alchemical-ecological wetland nature of Hel and its Saiwalos slowly works away, fermenting, distilling, regenerating, transforming the images into new ones with the potential for renewing and nourishing the imaginal energies of the Worlds.

The impacts of cultural beliefs

Images are conceptual containers for beliefs, and the whole jumble of cultural beliefs about 'Hel, hell, Underworld, pit of entropy, death, guilt, sin, punishment, evil, despair' and so on is a massive attractor and generator of powerful and terrible images. These images have a huge impact on us all, even when we think we don't accept or believe them. Even when we don't follow the religions that teach versions of those beliefs, or follow any religion at all, the beliefs easily bleed over into our value systems and personal beliefs.

For example, ideas about 'virtue, sin, punishment, reward' motivate all kinds of contemporary behavior such as dieting, personal habits, parenting, political positions, matters relating to law and judicial systems, etc. These attitudes can lead to vindictiveness, victimization, sado-masochism, and many other distortions of character and beliefs. The many people suffering in situations of apparent hopelessness—addiction, homelessness, hunger, unemployability, incarceration, exploitation, oppression, unending strife—often feel like they are 'living in hell'. There is plenty of cultural material to feed the perpetuation of overwhelmingly negative imagery about 'hell', on both conscious and unconscious levels.

The impact of these beliefs and images on our Saiwalo-Dwimors is hard and heavy. Even just writing about it makes me feel heavy and overburdened, ready to crawl into a hole and give up! I won't go into any more detail about the negativity here, because all of us can do this very well for ourselves. My reason for bringing it up, however, is to lead into an understanding of its impact on our Dwimors, Saiwalos, and on the shaping of Hel itself.

Dwimor grips image-energy

Dwimor picks up images as a form of energy, and the stronger the energy of the image, the more tightly Dwimor holds onto it. This isn't because Dwimor necessarily 'likes' the image, but because Dwimor's nature is a salty, alchemical matrix designed to grasp and hold. That is its life-serving function in Midgard: to form the core which grasps and holds all our souls, body, and life-energies together as a functioning whole.

Of course Dwimor is going to hold most strongly to the strongest energies: our souls and all the energies that they generate and draw into our being. But next in line for Dwimor are the images that come into our consciousness, from whatever source, and which we shape and nurture with our own imagination-functions. The images that have the strongest grip on our awareness, our emotions and attention, are the ones that Dwimor will hang onto most firmly, even if we wish, on a conscious level, that we could get rid of them.

Gradually, over our lifetime, Dwimor builds its soul-hoard, its treasure-trove, of powerful, gripping images that have occupied our attention, thoughts and emotions during our life. This is what it brings back to Saiwalo and Hel, and this is what shapes the Hel-environment around it until Hel's alchemical-ecological wetland functions gradually process and reshape these energies.

But this is not the end of the story: Hel and the Saiwalos are not as sequestered, as closed-off, as they might seem. Hel is permeable, and the Saiwalos are connected to the Dwimors in Midgard, while the Dwimors are connected to the other souls in our 'soular-system'. The image-energies brought down by Dwimor are not fixed in place, but continue to seep back and forth between Midgard and Hel, mixing and combining in unpredictable ways, before they are transformed through many iterations of Hel's alchemical processes.

Exercise 14-1: Growing your awareness of images

Whether we realize it and intend it, or not, our lifetime inner activity of imaging is actually a matter of world-building: our personal world / Werold and framework of thought, Midgard-world, and Hel-world are all shaped by human imaging. Imaging guides and shapes our material creations and physical activities. Our mental use and interpretation of images shapes our emotions, reactions, attitudes and behavior. The impacts of these activities continue, even after our Midgard life is over. When we are wielding this kind of power that affects us and all around us, it is vital to be aware of what we are doing, why we are doing it, and whether this is really how we want to be doing it.

This is a gradual exercise, a focusing of your awareness on the images you carry within you, and the images 'out there' which influence others and the world around you. One way that this is often done, is to examine and be aware of the stories you tell yourself: about yourself and your motives and reactions, about the people you interact with, about the larger world we hear about in the news, from books and films, etc. As an example, a hot topic right now is the image of "the police". What is your image of them? Hostile, dangerous, helpful, brutal, protective, corrupt, 'on my side', 'against me', 'my guys', necessary evil, misunderstood, mixed bag, total confusion, all of the above? What do you picture, what do you feel, when you say the word 'police'? All of this: pictures, feelings, reactions, opinions, emotions, thoughts, all together are your 'image' of the police.

How about your image of yourself? What are the words you call yourself? How do you regard your looks, behavior, abilities, activities? What images motivate you? Are they largely positive and inspired, or negative, hostile, fearful of consequences if you fail to do whatever? Who would you most like to be like, whether in looks, achievements, position, possessions, opportunities, whatever? Who are you most afraid to be like? What are your images of 'success' or 'failure' in areas that matter to you?

What are your hopes, longings, fears—what images do all these questions I've listed here trigger in you? What about just individual words or names: many are loaded with imagery, terms like "vacation, money, enemy, home, work, trap, sweet, love, hate." Or how about relationship-words: "Daughter, son, mother, father, grandparent, spouse, boyfriend, girlfriend, baby," etc. Look at the images you have of your family members, boss and coworkers, neighbors. Say all these trigger-words I've mentioned here to yourself, and note what springs to mind: visual images, emotional reactions, triggers, gut feelings. All these images are the way we shape our perceptions, reactions and motivations, but they are imperfect tools, and we need to learn to see the flaws in the images we shape about ourself and everyone else.

As you can see, this could go on forever, for a lifetime. For now, just pick a few areas to examine. One point of this is to become aware of how we shape ourself and the world around us through imaging. The other point is to examine where these images come from: your own personal experience? The media? Things other people tell you? Things you absorbed from your environment as a child? Out of the blue, you don't know where? Move into the realization that *we exist in a surging sea of images, and it's a challenge to navigate through them, consciously and with clear intent.*

Saiwalo and Sowilo

The similarity between these two words, the Saiwalo-soul and the Sowilo-rune, is intriguing. Though I haven't (yet) found a linguistic connection between them, their similarity forms a useful basis for meditation and intuitive work. The Sowilo rune represents the Sun, victory, life-energy, light. The Anglo-Saxon Rune Poem, using the Anglo-Saxon form of Sowilo, *Sigel*, says that *"Sigel is ever the hope of seamen as they fare over the fishes' bath, until they bring the sea-stallion to land."* The sea-stallion or wave-stallion is a poetic image for a boat or ship, bucking and tossing over the waves.

Here, we see that the Sun is the guide, encouragement and hope for those navigating a tiny craft over wide, unknown waters. We've explored the connection between Saiwalo and the sea (Book I, chapter 14), and the sea is also an image or metaphor for the human 'unconscious', all the deep, unrecognized, unknown parts of ourselves. To enrich the imagery of this runic verse, I like to pick up on the sound-similarity between 'sigel' and 'seagull', and point out that seagulls' habitat is relatively close to land, not far out at sea. Seeing gulls around your boat is a sign that land is near.

Exercise 14-2: Navigating the sea of images

Now let's take this runic imagery and apply it to what I wrote earlier: We exist in a surging sea of images, and it's a challenge to navigate through them, consciously and with clear intent. For this exercise, I offer the following meditation imagery.

We're a small crew in a small boat, tossing on the trackless sea, on a cloudy night. All directions seem the same to us. We feel overwhelmed, unable to decide which way to go. Then, as light seeps over the horizon, a dawn wind picks up and blows away the clouds. Sun springs into the eastern sky, and we are able to orient ourselves. After some discussion among the crew, we now know which direction to aim toward, and hope rises in us with the sun. As we sail toward the island that is our goal, we see in the distance flocks of white birds. Soon, their cries surround us, telling us that land is near. Filled with energy and courage, the gifts of the Sun, we approach our home-island with a sense of victory and achievement.

Saiwalo-Dwimor

In this meditation, the sea represents Saiwalo's deep, mysterious, unknown nature, and the surging waves represent all the images that our Saiwalo-Dwimor and everyone else's toss up and mix around in the Midgard-plane. The dark, cloudy night is a state of unknowing, a state without guide-points or direction as we float there on the sea of images. Our boat contains our crew, our soul-household, and may be sturdy and well-built, or flimsy and leaky. The Sun gives us our sense of direction, and courage and energy to follow that direction toward victory over all obstacles that are hindering us. The island is our goal that we want to reach, a place of stability, nourished and influenced by the Sea, but providing us with the other resources our soul-household needs for a stable life.

I want to emphasize again: what we are navigating across and through is a Sea of Images, the tossing sea of our own Saiwalo and everyone else's, that churns the subliminal realms of our imagination and influences all the expressions of our consciousness.

In this exercise, I encourage you to explore the personal nature of the images I've offered. What is the boat of yourself like, and what condition is it in? How do your crew-members / souls relate to and respond to the Sea of Images? With interest, respect, wanting to explore; with fear or terror? What are your personal gifts from the Sea, treasured images that the waves have brought to you? What is your Sun, that offers you a way to choose a direction among the surging sea of images that surrounds you? Are you swept away toward a different direction by every wind that blows, or do you know the land you are heading toward, and how to use the currents of images, the winds and the waves, to bring you closer to it? Do you hear the seagulls crying, calling you toward your landing? And what is the landing you are heading toward, the island that holds your hope, your chance for a stable life with all the inner resources you need to live well? And perhaps most importantly, how do each of your souls react and respond to this imagery? The response is likely to be different, for your different souls.

Give these meditations plenty of time; let all these images gently and naturally arise and play out in your mind, explore them in your Daybook. You may well find that they change over time, and that your understanding deepens as they change.

Feeding the images

Now let's work on some of Saiwalo-Dwimor's dynamics. If you've worked on Exercise 14-1, you've probably had strong reactions to some of the images, and it may be hard to turn them off, or if you do, they may keep popping up again. These can be positive or negative images: ones you enjoy dwelling on and don't want to turn off, or ones that are upsetting, angering, fearful, and grab your attention because you unconsciously feel you can't afford to turn your back on them, you need to stay alert.

In Book I, Chapter 13 *(Hel-Dweller)* I talked about the fascination that stories and images can exert on us, which can be pleasant or unpleasant forms of fascination. Either way, for different reasons, we find it hard to let go. Fascination is a form of strong soul-energy, and any of our souls may be caught up in it; each soul has things they are fascinated by. The energy of fascination acts as a lure to our Dwimor, who recognizes the image as an energy-treasure and grabs onto it for its hoard.

Fascination, attention, fixation, mental and emotional energy, repetition, obsession, whether in positive or negative forms: these things feed our images the way warm oceans feed hurricanes. They control which images Dwimor collects for its hoard, and takes back to Saiwalo and Hel. In one way, this works out well: Dwimor can haul off the powerful negative imagery to Hel's wetland and get it processed and reshaped. But this is a slow, and even random process, and in the meantime the negative stuff has more chance to circulate and influence people and events.

Image-winnowing

It makes sense for us to play an active role in the process of winnowing, sorting and shaping the images that Dwimor grasps onto, while we are here in Midgard, with all our souls working together. 'Winnowing' is the process of separating the useful from the useless, like separating plump grains from husks and chaff. It is up to each of us, to decide what 'useful' and 'useless', 'positive' and 'negative' images consist of, and to proceed accordingly.

Negative images may well be useful ones, if they are used as lessons, warnings, examples of what to steer away from, or what the consequences of certain choices may be. Negative imagery can also offer *catharsis,* a cleansing of the emotions and the spirit after great trauma and trials, as many dramas and stories, ancient and modern, seek to offer. Imagery of trials and tribulations, sadness and sorrows, mourning and regret, can be turned into beauty and power, can bring relief, wisdom, inspiration to overcome, acceptance of ørlög and wyrd. Imagery of threats, injustice and danger can inspire bravery and action to overcome the threats.

The problems begin when negative imagery declines into sheer awfulness, degradation, evil, cruelty, horror, despair, and sticks there immovably, with no redeeming purpose or function other than the dregs of addictive fascination. Negativity in the form of worthlessness, meaninglessness, powerlessness, a wasteland where nothing matters and no change is possible, is equally devastating.

Then there are the endless, petty, churning negativities of our everyday lives: images of resentments and grievances, emotional pains, discouragement and disappointments, selfishness of ourselves and others, neglect, scorn, guilt and blame, fears and anger, vengefulness, misunderstandings and all the rest. So much of our energy tends to get tied up, going over and over these petty negative images, reinforcing and amplifying them.

Are these the things we want to save up, to shape the imagery of our Saiwalo's domain in Hel? (Not to mention our day to day experience during life.) Do we want to carry hell with us, down to Hel, and plant it there?? Too many people have already done that, and it has consequences in the living world as well as in the afterworld.

Exercise 14-3: Clarifying Dwimor's hoard

Again, this is going to be a life-long process, but we can make a start here. Be observant of your habitual thoughts, attitudes and beliefs, and the images that represent them. Be aware of images that are coming into your consciousness, every day, through many avenues of attention. What is worth keeping and strengthening? What needs to be put aside to fade away? What do you want your Dwimor to keep in its hoard, either because it is something worth keeping, or because you want it to be brought to Hel for transformation?

For images you want to keep, enhance their energy by investing your attention, thoughts and positive emotions in them. Bring the images to mind often, and represent them around you with photographs, art, music, decorations, ceremonies, celebrations, activities, sharing with family and friends. Go to sleep with the images in mind, wake up and turn to them first thing. Bring those images to life and nurture them. Link them with other good images, create image-communities, create a landscape filled with your greatest images of aspirations and longings.

There is a lot in common here, with how modern Heathens and others build relationships with Deities: we focus attention, communication, devotion, share goals and aspirations, with the profound experience-images of our Deities whom we hold in our hearts. (I am not suggesting that the Deities are simply images; they are not. But we create images of them based on our experiences, and interact with them through those images as conceptual interfaces between us and the mysteries of the Deities.)

I wrote in Book I, Chapter 16 Part 3, about the *eidolon*, the Greek word that is the root of our word 'idol', and which also refers to our Dwimor or spirit-form. The word 'idol' has negative connotations because of Christian interpretations, but it was not originally negative. It simply meant an image that was invested with sacred meaning, and venerated as such. That's the kind of energy, the investment of attention, that we can bring to bear, to empower our positive images and make them attractive to our Dwimor.

For our negative images that we want to get rid of, we do the opposite: gradually starve them. Don't pay attention to them; when they come to mind, step back, step away, turn toward something else, not because you are afraid of them, in denial, or want to avoid them, but because you don't want to invest your precious life-energy into them. Don't criticize or blame yourself or other people for the images, because that increases their energy. If you feel you need to understand them more deeply before you let go, work on that for a little while, but don't get sucked into a perpetual whirlpool of analysis that isn't going anywhere. Recognize when it's time to let go. Shrug the weight of this negativity off your shoulders and be free.

If there are negative images that you believe are important to keep for a good reason, then work on reshaping them to fit this purpose. If it is to learn a lesson or offer a warning, weave imagery of the lesson / warning *and* of the desired outcome into the original imagery, don't just focus on the hard part. Perhaps you wish to honor some tragedy or sacrifice or loss, by keeping its image in a hallowed space. If you do, be careful to be clear about your reasons for this, keep your emotions relating to it clear and healthy, not going into a negative spiral. Shape the image into the outcome that you are learning, memorializing, accepting, rather than dwelling on the pain, tragedy, negativity that led up to it.

On the next page is a painting by Dale Wood, that illustrates the possibilities of reshaping images. The forest scene, representing an image or memory in our mind, is blurred out of its original shape. We can imagine this as our image-memory being washed by tears. We can choose to transform this blurred and tear-washed image, by actively using our imagination, into a new scene that holds reshaped meaning for us, which can empower us and be treasured by our Dwimor. As an exercise, think: how would you re-paint this image for yourself? How would you use the blurred area as a background for something new? What does this new image mean to you?

As you live each day, be aware of the images crowding into your consciousness, from inside and outside yourself. Take an active role in deciding which ones to accept into your Dwimor's matrix, and which ones to let glide by, not sticking to you and gumming up your works. Be aware that all images require energy in order to 'live', to persist and have power within us. The more attention they grab from us, the more energy they consume. Decide which ones are worth your life-energy, and which are not.

There's lots of important and impactful stuff going on in the world, everywhere and every day, supplying us with an endless stream of images. But we can't even try to carry images of all of this around inside us without making ourselves physically, emotionally and spiritually ill and overextended. Make your own choices about which images you allow to live within you, so you can respond to them and take action in ways that are meaningful and right for you.

Images as prayers and magical intentions

The last thing we'll focus on here is this: we can carry images, even heavy, burdensome, negative ones, as a prayer, an offering, and / or as a magical intention. Again, the art of shaping the image is of the utmost importance here. Carrying a big, heavily negative image as a prayer can easily fall into a state of blaming the Deity we're praying to about the problem, or telling the Deity what to do about it, or collapsing into desperate helplessness and pleading, and being angry with the Deity if nothing is happening. None of this is really going to help.

I use a particular image to engage in this kind of prayer, and maybe it will give you some ideas for your own approach. I envision all of my souls and self-awareness, as energy-forms, sitting together in council along with whichever Deities I am calling in prayer about the matter (plus whichever other ones may decide to show up, as often happens). An 'oversoul' or over-awareness rises above us all, generated by the power of our hearts and minds, drawing us together and uniting our focus.

In the midst of us is the image I am praying about, presented as an offering for our attention. I plant this focused image of our prayerful council in my Saiwalo-Dwimor, and return my awareness to it as often as I can, throughout the days and nights as I work on the issue. (To add more punch to the imagery, I like to call this council a *Witangemot* or 'gathering of the wise' in Anglo-Saxon. The Deities are wise, of course, and this word inspires me to reach toward wisdom, myself!)

The council of the souls. This image is symbolic of the process of our souls and our closest Deities interacting to form a spiritual council, and also symbolic of the idea that we are comprised of a household of souls, a Hiwscipe or Hiwship. ("The Alchemical Sisters.")

Sometimes, as I pursue this prayer, an image arises that shows me some action I can take. Sometimes I gradually realize that I have misunderstood, and things are not as I thought they were. Sometimes, I simply gain a deeper understanding of the matter, and realize I must come to terms with it, at least in regards to anything I can do about it at this time. Sometimes, it feels like I've added some energy and goodwill to efforts the Deities are undertaking about the matter.

Whatever the outcome, this is a worthy way to handle the burden of negative imagery, because it brings together my soul-household and our Deities in an exercise of trust, goodwill, and mutual support. This action in itself becomes an image-treasure for my Dwimor's hoard, and helps to replace the worst of the burden that the original negative image held for me.

This is an example of the 'reshaping' or transformation of negative imagery that I'm talking about: the focus turns away from negativity and helplessness, and turns instead into a sense of upholding, solidarity, facing things together, clear sight, courage, even if things do not change outwardly and the problem is not actually 'fixed.'

(And of course, sometimes it is fixed.) Either way, the image of my Witangemot that remains with my Dwimor after doing this exercise has been reshaped from the negativity it was before, into something worth keeping and growing instead of something I want to escape from.

The same type of approach can be taken for applying magical intent toward a negative image that is concerning us. Here, it is essential to re-frame the negativity into a positivity. If we focus our energy and attention on images of what we *don't* want, what we fear will happen or fear about what is happening, then the energy goes into maintaining precisely those negative images that we are trying to draw energy away from (see J. M. Greer's excellent discussion of this in *The Druid Magic Handbook,* pp. 21-2).

We need to form a new image of what we *want* to happen, focus our attention and intent, and push energy in that direction, using whatever magical techniques we customarily work with. We carefully avoid revisiting the negative images of the situation we are trying to change, so as not to feed them energy. As we do this, the new image we are creating gains energy and adheres within our Dwimor, replacing the original negative image.

This is an excellent approach and practice for clarifying and reshaping our Dwimor's soul-hoard. I would say that it's one of the main long-term benefits of practicing magic, overall: replacing our Dwimor's negative or useless collection of junk-images with true soul-treasures, shaped by conscious intent, that may continue to work like yeast percolating through the Worlds, whatever our own state of life or afterlife.

Saiwalo-Dwimor

Exercise 14-4: Practicing prayer and magical intent

For this exercise, choose one or both approaches, prayer and / or magical intent. Design your own scenario or method of prayer and participation in the work-process of the Deities, and apply it to images and situations that concern you. Practice directing your magical intent toward transforming a negative image and its corresponding situation in the world, using methods you already know how to use, or finding new magical methods that work well for this purpose.

Working on these practices over time will help you clear, strengthen, focus, and beautify your Dwimor's treasure-hoard, and will bring the unique transformational powers of Saiwalo-Dwimor into more prominence in your life and your Midgard concerns. The energy-connections between Hel, Midgard, and the Soul of the Earth are subtle and strange to our conscious minds, but are important for the metaphysical health of all these domains. As you learn to work more consciously with Saiwalo-Dwimor and its energies, you are also promoting healthy exchanges among the chthonic powers of these Worlds.

Saiwalo-Dwimor

Dale Wood

Odin's Ravens, Huginn and Muninn, bring him news of the Worlds and deepen his awareness of events.

Chapter 15

15. Fields of Awareness

{Primary runes in the bindrune above: Ansuz, Eihwaz, Wunjo, Tiwaz, Jera, Kenaz.}

In Book I, after going through discussions of each of the souls, I wrap them all up with a chapter about "The Arising of the Self." There I describe the Self as something that is created and sustained by the synergy of all our souls interacting during our Midgard life. I refer to the Self as a song, and the singers as our souls, singing our Self into being through interweaving harmonic vibrations.

I'm going to do the same thing here, but instead of the song of the Self, I'm using a different metaphor for us to work with: our Self as a broad energy-field of Awareness and Will, that is woven from the different forms of awareness, knowing, sensing, understanding, and willing that are characteristic of each of our souls.

Will and Awareness can be considered as the active and passive expressions of Being, of each of our souls. Awareness gathers in knowledge, sensations, perceptions; it is a passive, indrawing state. Will extends the essence of the soul outward through action. Awareness provides direction for Will, Will provides expression for Awareness.

If you've worked your way through this book and Book I, and put some time and effort into thinking about and digesting the information about souls that I've offered, you will be able to sense that our different souls have different modes and focuses of awareness, and their wills are directed in different ways. In the following sections, I summarize the features of each soul's awareness, and by implication, the focus of its will. I also note how each soul's awareness flows through or interfaces with our Lich-Hama, our soul-infused body, which is necessary whenever it interacts in Midgard.

Ferah's Awareness

What is Ferah most aware of?
Nature and the flows of energies through natural entities. The laws, patterns, and rhythms of natural life and the physical world that affect each of us as well as all other natural entities. Our connections with the beings of nature, both physical and metaphysical beings. Our connections and relationships with all the Deities, and especially with those who are most associated with Earth, sky, weather, and other powers of nature. A sense of Heathen piety and devotion is often an outgrowth of such connections.

Our membership in the Feorhcynn, the Kindred of the Living, and the strong connections and natural ethics that are outgrowths of that membership. An understanding of, and respect for, the need for fair laws, rules and norms to govern human societies and groups, and an understanding of how these human laws need to relate to natural laws and patterns.

For some people, all of these influences together cause them to be drawn to Heathen priesthood, a path which can take on many different shapes in practice. And / or they may be drawn to the role of the Heathen Lawspeaker or Thyle, who studies, discerns, interprets and recommends patterns of behavior that can best serve Heathenry, based on lore, philosophy, ethics, observation and experience.

How does Ferah sense and know this?
Through the impacts of outer stimuli on the sensitive subtle body of Ferah, coming through both physical and metaphysical sensory systems. Through the wisdom and experience that arise from Heathen devotion and practice. Through interactions and connections with humans and their societies, with the beings of nature, and with the Deities.

What purposes or functions does this awareness serve?
The abilities of the Ferah serve to attune us to the rhythms, patterns, laws, forces and powers of nature, of human groups and societies, and of the Deities and their worlds.

When, under what circumstances, does Ferah's awareness operate most strongly?
Ferah is most aware and active when we consciously allow our everyday mind to pay attention to the things that matter to Ferah. This occurs very naturally during childhood,

when children learn through attraction and experience that they are part of the Feorhcynn and of Nature, and can sense some of the patterns and rhythms that arise from that. Children are also busy with the process of learning how to interact in groups such as family, school, neighborhood, and begin to learn the rhythms, patterns and 'laws' or rules of life in a community. Many children have a natural interest in religious tales, observances and other patterning influences of religion. All of these things are ideal Ferah-influences during childhood. As adults, we benefit from reviving or recreating our awareness of these influences and patterns in our own daily lives.

Where, in what domain, is Ferah's awareness primarily focused?
In the domains of Midgard nature, at both physical and metaphysical levels. Within our physical body with its sensory and neurological systems, and their connections with our emotions and perceptions. In the social domains, with the patterns, structures, norms and laws that shape them. Ferah has access and connections to both physical and metaphysical beings of nature, as well as to the Deities, and thrives when these connections are honored and nurtured.

How does Ferah interface through Lich-Hama?
Through *La*, the life-power that runs through our Hama's blood and the warmth of our body. Through *Læti*, the Lich-Hama's power of movement and speech.

How can we improve the quality of Ferah's awareness?
By tuning in to the subtle substance of the life-force that fills our body and contains our sensation-awareness. By

connecting through our own life-force with the life-force, the forms and energies, of natural entities and phenomena. Through in-depth interactions with our Deities. Through a soul-deep understanding that we are members of the Feorhcynn, part of nature, part of the society and culture where we are embedded, that we benefit in various ways from these connections, and have a corresponding responsibility to participate in, support, and improve these collectives of which we are a part.

Ahma's Awareness

What is Ahma most aware of?
A sense of universal oneness. The flows of spirit through all levels of being. Limitlessness, being unlimited by time, space, boundaries, restrictions. Pure Being, and the incipient movements of Becoming that vibrate imperceptibly through this substrate of Being.

How does Ahma sense and know this?
It knows this because it *is* this. Ahma is the essence of Being, that arises from the cosmic wellsprings of Being and the potential to Become.

What purposes or functions does this awareness serve?
Ahma is the wellspring of the sacred breath of life: physical and metaphysical breath and life. At the level of Ahma, sacred breath, life, Beingness, and awareness are one and the same thing, but this awareness is usually not perceptible to our everyday consciousness unless we learn to access it.

When, under what circumstances, does Ahma's awareness operate most strongly?
When we are detached from daily concerns, engaging in forms of meditation, breathing, contemplation: whichever forms that work for us, that shape our own pathway into Ahma's awareness. This can sometimes involve rhythmic and repetitive physical activity that moves us into "the Zone."

Where, in what domain, is Ahma's awareness primarily focused?
At the level of cosmic-mythic phenomena, the upwelling energies of Ginnungagap, Hvergelmir, the Elivagar; the incipient formations of Worlds and Beings, including personal Deities, as they begin the transition from potential to actuality. These phenomena occur outside of time; they are always ongoing, and form the habitation of Ahma.

How does Ahma interface through Lich-Hama?
Through our breath, lungs and diaphragm, and through the vital energies we absorb from breathing.

How can we improve the quality of Ahma's awareness?
The quality of Ahma's awareness is already in a state of perfection or completion. Improvement occurs within our soular system as a whole, as we learn to attune our everyday awareness and the awareness of our other souls with Ahma: pure awareness itself.

Ghost's Awareness

What is Ghost most aware of?
Ghost bridges our Ahma and its habitat, on one end, with our Midgard body and life on the other. Ghost's awareness

Fields of Awareness

resides in our Ghost-Mind, which hovers over and interpenetrates our physical brain. It is powered by our breathing: not only physical breath, but the breath of Ahma, and by those metaphysical energies surrounding us that can be absorbed by breathing. Breathing, and the awareness of our Ghost and Ahma, are closely connected. Ghost is most aware of its own interests, perspectives, the intellectual and creative challenges that attract it. It is less aware of other aspects of our life, such as physical and social needs.

How does Ghost sense and know this?
Ghost works primarily through interfaces with our brain and its functions, and through our respiratory system and its metaphysical capacities that absorb and send out subtle energies through the atmosphere that surrounds us.

What purposes or functions does this awareness serve?
Ghost's awareness serves the vital function of linking our Midgard-oriented souls and Lich with Ahma and the cosmic powers it is connected to. It channels wode, inspiration, spiritual energy and life into us, and through us into the world of Midgard.

When, under what circumstances, does Ghost's awareness operate most strongly?
When we are engaged in deeply creative, intellectual, or spiritual activities, explorations, and expressions of Ghost's interests and powers. When we are caught up in a flow of wode, from the mildest to the wildest of wode-flows.

Where, in what domain, is Ghost's awareness primarily focused?
In the domains of the mind, the spirit, and of spiritual energies. Ghost is less focused than many of our other souls on the daily activities of Midgard life.

How does Ghost interface through Lich-Hama?
Ghost's primary interface comes through its overshadowing of our physical brain.

How can we improve the quality of Ghost's awareness?
Through practices of meditation, contemplation, breathwork, and the raising of spiritual energies. Through attuning Ghost's awareness with the awareness of our other souls, so they can work in concert rather than at cross-purposes with each other.

Hama's Awareness

What is Hama most aware of?
The appearances and expressions of ourselves, other humans, and other physical and metaphysical beings, along with all the information and interaction that can be gained by this. Facial expressions, body language, the messages communicated through clothing, hairstyles, adornment, body art, etc. Everything that is communicated through verbal and tonal forms of speech. Impressions; the ability to identify who others are, and remember them. The stereotypes we have absorbed and formed, with their associated assumptions and prejudices, both conscious and unconscious. Status symbols, in-group cues, and 'virtue signaling'. Any clues and cues that relate to social interactions with individuals and with groups.

Fields of Awareness

Hama is aware of, and cares about, our own personal appearance and the messages it sends throughout the stages of our life. The fear of aging, of 'losing our looks' and our abilities, of blemishes and disfigurements, are rooted in our Hama, whose focus is on appearances, presentation, speech, and all the messages these can convey. Hama is also intimately aware of our own physical body and how it functions, its capacities, its skills and limitations.

How does Hama sense and know this?
Hama is enmeshed with our physical body, creating our Lichama. It uses our physical senses, our brain and nervous system, and the experience it builds during our life in order to interpret what it senses, and to shape itself, its Litr and Læti, according to the needs it perceives as our circumstances constantly change and adapt.

What purposes or functions does this awareness serve?
Some of the primary functions of our Hama constellate around the need to engage in human social interactions, create social ties and interactive social systems. Hama must also sense the pitfalls and dangers associated with these interactions, with help from some of our other souls like Hugr, and take appropriate action, which often involves protective camouflage.

To do all this, Hama needs to be able to identify and remember other individuals and groups of people, and to communicate with them. Hama is in charge of how we present ourselves to others, whether this presentation is a clear representation of our inner being, or whether it is presenting camouflage, or an "ideal" persona, or a specific role we are playing, etc.

Fields of Awareness

Hama is also responsible for maintaining our physical body and its many abilities and skills. Its awareness needs to be attuned with all these functions so as to maintain them properly. All of our other souls must work through Lich-Hama in order to interact with the physical world, which means that Hama must also be aware of our other souls and have strong, shared links and channels with them.

When, under what circumstances, does Hama's awareness operate most strongly?
During interactions with other people and our presentation of our self to others. During any threats to the wellbeing and functions of our Lich, including illness, injury, and threats to our self-image, our psyche, our social standing, our physical and social functions and abilities.

Where, in what domain, is Hama's awareness primarily focused?
In the social and physical domains of Midgard.

How can we improve the quality of Hama's awareness?
Hama is concerned with our physical appearance and presentation, and with the appearance and behavior of others. These things matter, but can result in overlooking or downplaying other important factors of our whole being and the beings of others. This focus can also lead to anxiety, depression, lack of self-esteem, extreme and unhealthy efforts to change how we look, etc, whenever we feel that we are failing to meet whatever standards of appearance and behavior that we believe are important. These matters can create a great deal of unhappiness and stress in our

lives, and contribute to the same in the lives of others with whom we interact.

Hama is capable of taking quite a different functional approach. We can clarify our Hama by examining the stereotypes and assumptions about other people (and about ourselves), based on their appearance, that we have been taught by our family and society, and evaluate their true worth with regard to shaping our attitudes and behavior. We can work on clarifying the values that shape our Hama's perceptions and behavior. Hama can work with our other souls to allow their fuller perceptions of, and expression into, the physical world.

As we age and gain in life experience, the gradual fading of our outer appearance and physical abilities can make room for the inner beauty, strength, wisdom of all our souls to shine through our Lich-Hama into our world. As we do this, we learn to perceive and value what lies under the surface of other people as well, and not rely only on their surface characteristics. This opens up many new directions for worthwhile interactions with others in all domains of life.

Aldr's Awareness

What is Aldr most aware of?
Subtle energies that are present in food and drink, and in our ambient environment, which can serve to nourish, heal, and sustain our Lich and our souls. Time, and the passage of time, along with the natural and wyrded changes in our Lich and our Werold that are caused by time, ørlög, and Wyrd. Continuity in time, and the interplays and impacts that are brought about by the nexus of time, ørlög, wyrd, and forms of 'luck' as they affect us personally, and as they

interweave to form what we perceive as causality, change, evolution, history.

A recognition that specific beings, phenomena, and events come to an end in the fullness of time: an instinctive awareness of entropy. Also an awareness that entropy itself is a deep substrate out of which new waves of Being arise. This comes about through entropic inversion within Hvergelmir, the Roaring Cauldron or cosmic wellspring, where non-being forms into Being.

Aldr itself comes to an end at the wyrded time, subject to spiritual entropy as a phenomenon of time, and returns to the Norns' Well. Though it has ended, it becomes part of the Well of Wyrd, from which new Aldr-souls arise, which influence new beings and events in Time. This mirrors, on the personal level, the entropy-inversion that occurs within Hvergelmir. (There will be more discussion of this phenomenon in forthcoming writings.)

How does Aldr sense and know this?
Through its close connection with the Norns, their knowledge, and the Well of Wyrd. Through its nature as a fluid network of subtle channels that fill our Lich, which sense, gather, and channel subtle energy throughout our soul-body complex. Through its nature as our 'body in time', which can sense and perceive its time-surroundings as our Lichama and Ferah can sense and perceive their surroundings in space. All of these matters are part of Aldr's instinctive or intuitive awareness, embedded within Aldr by the Norns, rather than intellectual and rational forms of awareness.

Fields of Awareness

What purposes or functions does this awareness serve?
Aldr's awareness serves to govern our life in time, and our connections with the Norns, ørlög and wyrd. It is focused on nourishing and healing our Lich and our souls with subtle energy, extending our life-span, and weaving our Werold.

When, under what circumstances, does Aldr's awareness operate most strongly?
It operates most strongly through its connections with the Norns and their powers, with Time and changes through time, and through the impacts of ørlög and wyrd.

Where, in what domain, is Aldr's awareness primarily focused?
In the flow of Time, ørlög, mortality and causality, and of time-based events and impacts on our life, Lich and Werold. In the realm of the Norns. In the realms of subtle energies that flow through physical and metaphysical worlds, and have the potential to nourish our whole soul-body complex when channeled rightly. In the ability to grasp our life as an interconnected wholeness, and find meaning in it.

How does Aldr interface through Lich-Hama?
Through *La*, the life-giving energy flowing through our blood and warming our body. Through the biological mechanisms of time and change. Through the nourishment it feeds into our body and souls.

How can we improve the quality of Aldr's awareness?
Aldr naturally has a deep awareness of its own domains and functions. Its awareness is rather different from what we are used to from our daily experiences, however.

Fields of Awareness

Improvement can come about through gradually expanding our everyday awareness into the strange domains of Aldr's otherworldly awareness. Important directions for such expansion include: becoming aware of the subtle, nourishing energies that surround us and penetrate material life forms such as food, herbs, water and air, and becoming aware of how to respectfully obtain those energies for our nourishment and healing. Learning to understand more about the Norns, their powers and actions. Meditating, pondering, examining our Werold, our personal history of experiences and actions; learning from this, understanding its deeper meanings, and coming to truly appreciate our own unique Werold. Pondering the strange phenomena of Time and ørlög, and our relationship to them.

Mod's Awareness

What is Mod most aware of?
Opportunities, challenges, threats, problems, adventures, things that need to be 'fixed' in any way so they are better for us. The needs of everyday life. Things that it wants, especially opportunities for taking action of any kind: physical, emotional, intellectual, spiritual. Our own Mod-Will, and the Mod-Will of others that may be cooperative with, adversarial, or neutral toward our own Mod-Will.

Mod is mindful of these matters not only as they involve and affect ourself, but also as they affect the groups we are a part of: family and kindred, friendships, religious establishments, workplace, neighborhood, volunteer groups, clubs and associations, city / state / nation, culture, ethnicity: any groups toward which we feel loyalty, obligation, reciprocity, dependence, and the urge toward

Fields of Awareness

service (including leadership) to the group. In this way, Mod reaches toward Sefa and their shared space, Modsefa.

How does Mod sense and know this?
Mod works primarily through its Will. In a way, Mod's will is like a sensory organ: Mod can feel or sense the impact of outside events and actions on its own will-senses, on its own Will's urges and needs, and responds accordingly.

What purposes or functions does this awareness serve?
The Mod-soul or Mod-being wants to live and act through us. It is integrated with our Lich and its actions and awareness, and works with (or sometimes against) our other souls to pursue what it wants. It is in Mod's best interests to share its awareness with our Lich-Hama and our other souls, so as to participate fully in all the activities of our Midgard life.

When, under what circumstances, does Mod's awareness operate most strongly?
Threat, challenge, opportunity, pursuing desires shared with Hugr, Sefa, and Ghost.

Where, in what domain, is Mod's awareness primarily focused?
On Midgard life, with all its challenges and complexities.

How does Mod interface through Lich-Hama?
Through *Læti*, the physical abilities and activities of our Lichama, including speech, as well as the physical body itself, the Lich, including its power-centers. Through the powerful gaze of the eyes. Mod projects the power of its presence through our *Litr*, our soul-infused appearance and

the impression that our physical presence makes. The condition of our Mod—weak or strong, healthy or unhealthy, charismatic or withdrawn, very much influences the appearance of our Hama's Litr.

How can we improve the quality of Mod's awareness?
Mod's awareness is best improved by becoming more self-aware: entering into a state of Mod-awareness and observation, learning more about who our own Mod is, its strengths and weaknesses, and the nature and expressions of its Will. There is also great potential for improvement by pursuing better understanding between our Mod and our other souls, and between our Mod and the Mod of others—humans, animals, powerful natural phenomena and the otherworldly beings who are involved in them.

Hugr's Awareness

What is Hugr most aware of?
Communication from ancestors (conscious or unconscious), hidden knowledge (includes spaecraft, runecraft, other divination, hunches, intuition, etc), motivations of others, strategic advantage, general powers of observation and thought, framework of thought, love and desire, friendship and trust, opinions, world-view, Midgard life and activities in general.

My own Hugr wants to add this, as a general observation about Hugr-souls: "I see in the light and in the dark, dayside and nightside. I can open doors into the past, and catch glimpses of the future. I seek knowledge and insight from many sources; I'm good at interpreting it, and at reading people and situations. But if I am not clear / clarified, my interpretations may be skewed by the attitudes, moods, opinions, distractions, and desires of myself, and maybe of other souls of our Hiwship. I have longings and desires; I reach vigorously toward what I long for. Many of the intentions of our whole soul-household are mine, or come through me. I know what lies in our heart; I know and work with Sefa, and I watchfully ward Sefa."

How does Hugr sense and know this?
Hugr is a daemon-soul, a being in itself, who has the abilities of perception, thought, judgement, decision-making, reasoning, etc. Hugr is heavily involved with all the ways that we are used to learninging and knowing what goes on around us.

What purposes or functions does this awareness serve?
The many areas of Hugr's awareness are enmeshed in our everyday Midgard life, as well as the metaphysical extensions of this life. Hugr is a major player in the conduct of our Midgard life and in navigating its many complexities.

When, under what circumstances, does Hugr's awareness operate most strongly?
Pursuing self-interest, including both self-centered interests, and generous impulses due to caring about and taking an interest in others and in the functions of society. Pursuing love and friendship. Protecting us from manipulation, lies, seduction, exploitation, gaslighting, etc., by others. Discovering hidden and arcane knowledge. Using its many powers, both mundane and esoteric. Advising, counseling, foreseeing, warning us in our own

Fields of Awareness

best interests. Connection with ancestors and with past lives.

Where, in what domain, is Hugr's awareness primarily focused?
Hugr is primarily focused on both mundane and metaphysical aspects of our Midgard life, as well as the domain of the ancestors.

How does Hugr interface through Lich-Hama?
Through *Læti* and *Litr*, the activities and the appearance of our Lich-Hama and those of others.

How can we improve the quality of Hugr's awareness?
By clarifying our Hugr, and attending to the ongoing 'care and feeding' of Hugr's framework of thought. By training and practicing the skills of awareness in the domains of life that our own Hugr is most interested in, whether social life, intellectual pursuits, esoteric practices, personal relationships, genealogy and ancestral awareness, or whatever it might be.

Sefa's Awareness

What is Sefa most aware of?
A sense of 'self'. The understanding that other persons are likewise a 'self', and that common ground exists or can be created between these selves. Comfort and safety for ourselves and others we care about. Relationships of all kinds: kinship, family, romantic relationships, work relationships, friendships, community relationships, relationships with nature and natural entities, with Deities and other spiritual beings, etc.

Fields of Awareness

Sefa is also focused on our 'household' or soular-system of souls in the same way it is on other kinds of relationships. Sefa tries to promote communication and interaction among our souls, tries to resolve conflicts and get our various, sometimes contradictory souls to work in concert, or at least not to pull so hard against each other. Sefa is aware of the nature of each of our souls, their feelings, their condition and wellbeing.

How does Sefa sense and know this?
Sefa comes into being through the combined energies of all our other souls, and therefore is well able to sense things about, and through, those souls. Its very energy and nature is that of 'self' and of 'self in relation to other selves.' It knows that no self exists in a vacuum; that interdependence is the nature of life in Midgard.

What purposes or functions does this awareness serve?
Weaving and maintaining the fabric of frith at all levels of human interaction, both within us as individuals, and among us as groups. Sefa's awareness serves the essential function of coordinating anything and everything: people, souls and their abilities, activities, communities, cooperative action, frithweaving, etc. It does this through the outreaching, inclusive quality of its awareness. Sefa is our sense of self, plus our understanding that others also have this sense of self, and the relatedness that this implies. Sefa wants happiness, safety, wellbeing for itself, and realizes that others want the same. It uses this awareness to promote interactions in order to achieve what it and others want.

Fields of Awareness

When, under what circumstances, does Sefa's awareness operate most strongly?
When Sefa perceives the need for anything that it can do to promote its values and desires for frith, relationship, interaction, happiness, safety and wellbeing.

Where, in what domain, is Sefa's awareness primarily focused?
In all relationships and other interactions among people, souls, spirits, and other entities. In the realm of ideas and concepts: finding relationships, discovering interactions, making connections in domains of the intellect and of inspiration.

How does Sefa interface through Lich-Hama?
Through our Litr, all aspects of our appearance, and the messages our appearance sends: warm, inviting, stern, aloof, etc. Through Læti, our behavior, actions and speech.

How can we improve the quality of Sefa's awareness?
Sefa's awareness can be broadened by the practice of wise and sensible compassion. Sefa can also benefit from improving its objectivity and judgement, without leaving its loving nature behind. Sometimes Sefa is not able to evaluate situations or people objectively, and makes mistakes that bring discomfort, harm or disappointment to itself and others. Sefa is easily embarrassed when it makes mistakes, and this may cause it withdraw and hide itself, or become blustering and obnoxious to cover up the mistakes. Working closely with Hugr and Mod, and developing Modsefa more strongly, will help Sefa improve its abilities of objectivity and judgement, and help to avoid

misjudgments and mistakes with their undesirable consequences.

Saiwalo-Dwimor's Awareness

What is Saiwalo most aware of?
Images, with all of their overtones, nuances, symbolism, history, back-stories, and the personal energy they carry. Its habitat in Hel, the Hel-environment around it, and the images that populate it. Its own internal environment, with its own alchemical-ecological processes of transformation that mesh with those of the other Saiwalos around it, and together form the great spiritual wetlands of Hel.

How does Saiwalo sense and know this?
Saiwalo-Dwimor is attuned to these energies of imagery and transformation; it is not separate from them, but is formed from them at the cosmic level of being.

What purposes does this awareness serve?
Saiwalo is the first type of individual soul that arises from the cosmic processes of the Worlds coming into being. This formation itself involves transformation into shapes or images of Being. Cosmic energy is translated into form / images as the Worlds arise into Being, and Saiwalo itself mimics this activity on a smaller, personal scale. Saiwalo's awareness is focused on its functions in Hel, while its Dwimor's awareness is focused on gathering images with their associated energies. Dwimor's primary task is gathering and holding all the other souls and their energies within its alchemical matrix, thus keeping us in a living state in Midgard. Dwimor regards our other souls and their image-energies as the primary 'prizes' in its treasure-hoard,

and grasps them firmly for the duration of our life in Midgard.

When, under what circumstances, does Saiwalo's awareness operate most strongly?
The circumstances of Saiwalo's awareness are rooted in Hel and are unchanging. Dwimor's awareness is alerted by the personal energy contained within the images we absorb and generate, while we are waking or sleeping, interacting with others, or musing by ourselves.

Where, in what domain, is Saiwalo's awareness primarily focused?
In Hel, and in the mindscapes of our images.

How does Saiwalo-Dwimor interface through Lich-Hama?
It does so only indirectly, through the effects that its collection of imagery may have on the functioning of our Lichama. Some imagery may inspire physical actions, some may be healing, some may cause or exacerbate conditions of poor health or imbalance. Some images may influence our Litr, the appearance we choose to present to others. We might adapt our own appearance so as to look like our ideal of beauty, strength, sophistication, misery, dangerousness, or whatever kinds of images have been imprinted in our Dwimor.

How can we improve the quality of Saiwalo's and Dwimor's awareness?
I do not know of any ways to actually change the awareness of Saiwalo, other than the cumulative effects of its Dwimors over time. When it comes to Dwimor's influence on us

through the images it carries, our other souls can help us select, winnow and reshape those images so they stimulate beneficial effects on our body-soul complex.

It is, however, an interesting and worthwhile exercise to improve our own conscious awareness of this chthonic soul and its work, who is so very different from the usual entities we interact with, including our other souls. I've discussed approaches for doing this in Chapter 14 here, and Chapter 16 in Book I.

Eormensoul

Thus, within the holism of our Being, there are multiple fields of awareness that bloom forth from each of our souls, merging and blending at the margins, narrow or broad, where they overlap with our other souls. We are likely to be very much aware of some of these fields or soul-ecosystems, and may be quite unaware of others. If we seek to grow to the full stature of our Eormensoul, our Great-Soul or Oversoul, we must become more conscious of these different soul-fields of awareness, and learn to mesh them in functional ways that enhance the strength and quality of our Eormensoul.

An image I have of the Eormensoul takes the form of a great and varied landscape, comprised of different ecosystems and topographies. In this imagery, our conscious awareness and our sense of everyday life can take the form of our body and whatever gear we want to have with us, and can roam at will over this landscape. We can seek nourishment and treasures, find adventure, meet challenges, seek ways to improve ourself, search for knowledge, and meet with other beings who are associated with our souls: Deities, ancestors, wights and spirits of various kinds. There are endless ways to enrich our life and our Self by exploring and participating in the features of this great Eormensoul-landscape. (See Book I, "Interlude: The Eormensoul" for a brief discussion of the Eormensoul concept.)

Developing the Eormensoul is a demanding endeavor, and will not be covered here. It is the subject of future work, but it depends on the foundational work outlined in this and the foregoing soul lore books. However, here is an important first exercise in this direction, to get you started. Here, you can envision your souls meeting together in council, with the opportunity to learn more about each one through its participation in your soul-council.

Exercise 15-1: Experiments with your soul-council

It's a difficult but worthwhile exercise, to try consciously *removing* our awareness from one of our souls at a time, to see what kind of difference that makes in our experience of our life and our actions and thoughts. It's definitely a weird sensation to try to do this, and should only be done for brief periods of time, as an experiment. You've spent so much time and effort here, becoming *more* aware of your souls, and it does feel strange to try going backwards into ignorance again!

The point of this experiment is to make your conscious mind and all your souls more aware of the contributions and roles of each of the souls, by 'removing' them one at a time, for a brief period, from the overall awareness of your soul-household. The best (and least

Fields of Awareness

disruptive) way to do this is in your imagination. Take some quiet, private time, and get out your Daybook. Imagine a complicated situation that would benefit from the powers of all of your souls, especially the more Midgard-oriented ones, acting together.

A good example is to imagine some important, life-impacting decision that you need to make. You call all your souls into council together, and present the situation to them by writing the scenario in your Daybook. Then, ask one of your souls at a time to 'leave the room', to withdraw its awareness and powers from this group of souls who are trying to make a decision together. Using your understanding of each soul's awareness that we covered earlier, imagine how the decision would be addressed if that kind of awareness was missing from your decision-making process. In other words, you try your best to ignore the field of awareness of the temporarily 'absent' soul, as you proceed with this effort.

In your Daybook, record the decision-making process and outcome, as it happens with each soul in turn effectively missing from the action. What are these different scenarios like? Does the outcome of your decision look different, depending on which souls did, and did not, participate in making it? What can you learn from this challenging exercise?

Now that you've had a taste of how each of your souls contribute to your life-actions, consider the fundamental importance of having all your souls working together, each in their own ways, on any matters in your life that are really important. Even souls who are not intimately involved in everyday Midgard affairs may have surprisingly relevant input for you, again in their own unique fashion.

This input may include, among other things, the awareness that one or more of your souls could sabotage your efforts if you ignore it. (At the level of Saiwalo-Dwimor's beloved fairy-tale images, this is the situation of the evil fairy, angry because she was not invited, coming at the end of the child-naming ceremony and turning all the well-wishing and blessings upside-down with a curse.) This action of your uncooperative soul could be deliberate sabotage, or more likely, simply be the result of its own particular energies not meshing well with the energies of the other souls who are involved, because no effort was made to integrate it into the process.

The topic of how to actively mesh and coordinate all our souls together, to pursue all of our life's aims more effectively, is a very great one, deserving of detailed attention. I will be returning to it in my future books on Heathen soul lore. For now, I believe there is plenty to work with, getting to know each of your souls in depth, and beginning to get a sense of how their presences shape your consciousness and your life as a whole.

Let's close this chapter with some thoughts about how Frigg and Frau Holle help us pattern our souls and our lives in an orderly way, and move on from there to some suggestions about incorporating soul lore practice into daily life.

About Frigg and her spinning

My response to a query about Frigg, her spindle, and our souls:

Frigg and our souls....that's a big and beautiful area to explore, as are the connections between each of our Deities and our souls! Here are some highlights of my thoughts about her role with our souls, and you're right that a good part of this role relates to the image of the spindle.

So let's start with the spindle as an analogy or symbol of our total being. The upper end accesses Ahma, the lower end is rooted in Saiwalo / Hel. I've seen Frigg in spae-visions quite a few times as she sits or stands beside Ginnungagap and draws out the primal material, Ond or Ahma, to wrap around her distaff in preparation for spinning things into being. At this level she is the Gatherer, the one who collects primal material in preparation for shaping, and then begins to shape it by the energy and direction of her spinning. I see what she spins as the threads that are woven into so many things: our souls, the fabric of Wyrd, the material worlds.

I see the process of creation along a two-way axis. On the 'right' and 'left', so to speak, the horizontal axis, are the primal polarities of Fire and Ice. In the center between the polarities stands Frigg's spindle, its 'top' resting in Ahma, its 'bottom' resting in Saiwalo / Hel. (These directions are simply analogies so that we can envision the process.) As Frigg spins this spindle, threads of energy are drawn out from 'left and right, up and down', and wrap around the spindle. As the threads wrap the spindle, the whole mass, the spindle with its threads, becomes more material, more solid and able to hold its shape within the stresses and strains of Midgard life.

The threads represent our different souls and soul-parts, also the material of our physical body, and the wyrd-threads that shape our life. All of these threads are coming in from different directions, influenced / shaped / colored by various Deities and cosmic processes as they form. It's the energy that Frigg sets into the spindle and its spinning, that holds the whole thing together during Midgard life. Then, it's our job to make good use of all these threads, all these parts of our being, our life experiences, and inputs from Deities and Wyrd, to take this thread and weave the fabric of our lifetime in Midgard: our Werold, our tapestry of life-long experience.

All that I've written so far is very abstract and 'cosmic'! Let's take it down to the level of everyday life now. I've written an article, "All in a Day's Work", posted on my website, about Frigg's power of creating order in everyday life, and how the Goddesses associated with her participate in that.

This power to help us order and shape our lives is an earthly reflection of what I wrote above, about how Frigg takes primal energy / material and shapes it into thread wound about a spindle. As she sets into motion the 'process of who we are' with her spinning, so we continue the 'process of who we are becoming' through our deeds of daily life. And of course, all of our souls are involved in these processes of shaping and ordering who we are and what deeds we generate, as our souls express themselves and act through our whole soul-body complex during our life in Midgard.

So, I think this is one of Frigg's primary roles in the domain of our souls: this process of shaping raw soul-material into incipient soul-beings, and helping them order themselves and their actions into a whole that becomes an individual human and this human's Werold. I think that all of this is closely tied to her function of gathering raw material and spinning it into thread, and tied to her oversight of our daily activities and daily lives that shape, day by day, the person we become and the life that we live.

"Frigg Spinning" by John Charles Dollman

In terms of Frigg's connection with specific souls: she and each of our other Deities may have ties to any of our souls, and we can ask her for help and insight regarding our work with any of the souls and their roles in our life. Frigg does have a special connection to our Mod soul, in its aspect as a wise and knowing soul, a soul who strives for excellence of mind, of character, and of deeds and achievements. Queens, counselors, wise-folk and elders were praised in ancient poetry for their Mod, their excellent mind, wise rede and good character, and Frigg stands as a model and a support for us to follow their example.

Frigg and her fellow-Goddesses are clearly involved with our Sefa soul and its concern with relationships and social ties. I also see a close connection between Frigg and Ahma, through Frigg's power of Awareness that she expresses through the Goddess Vor, whom I see as Frigg's 'daughter' or as an extension of Frigg herself.

We can see a lot of overlap between Frigg and the Goddess Frau Holle, also a spinning Goddess and also deeply involved with all aspects of our daily life. But there are important differences as well. I don't see them as being the same Goddess, but I do think we can understand each of them to be involved in similar ways with the processes of coming-into-being that we symbolize using the spindle. Feel free to work with the one you feel closest to, the one who draws you to herself, if you are attracted to these images of world-spinning!

I've listed some books and articles about Frigg and Frau Holle in the Book-Hoard (Bibliography), if you'd like to learn more about working with them, and you can find others elsewhere.

Finding the Time

Chapter 16

Our house-wight Elmindreda tackles her daily work with gusto! by Winifred Hodge Rose.

16. Finding the Time: A Guide for Daily Soul-Work

This is always the challenge: finding time! Our lives are full of tasks and responsibilities, especially when we have a young family, or elders to care for, in addition to all our other daily work. We need time to relax and rest, time with our loved ones and friends, time to spend on personal things and perhaps on volunteer work as well. So, where to find time for soul-work, on top of all this?

I have some suggestions for you to consider. All of them build on the skills of awareness, soul-communication, and imagination, that we've been emphasizing all along here. These are suggestions for integrating Heathen soul-learning into daily life, for you to pick through and apply if they are helpful, and ignore if they are not.

Fitting practices into your day

<u>Selecting a soul to work with.</u> There is no need for you to work with the specific order of souls that I've laid out in this book, if you are drawn to a different order. Read through all of the material, and notice which souls seem to call to you the most strongly as you read. Then go back, read about and think about them some more, and decide where you want to start.

<u>Soul-Work during your day / active time.</u> Once you've selected a soul to start working with, begin considering the relevant exercises. You might find it helpful to copy or print out that soul's exercises from my website (Soul Lore Study Guides on HeathenSoulLore.net, which has the same exercises as in this book) and keep them in a handy place so it's easy to find and review them. One convenient option is to use a 3-ring binder as your Daybook, and put copies of the study exercises, plus the pages you write as you journal, into the binder, one section per soul, so you have everything together. Alternatively, you could copy the exercises into an e-file, and write your responses below each exercise.

Finding the Time

Either option allows you to expand and rearrange your material as you begin to discern your own soul-patterns and connections.

It's handy to write <u>reminder-notes</u> about the specific exercise you're working on right now, on your phone or tablet, or an index card that you post somewhere you will notice it often. If you find any quiet moments during the day, you can use these notes to refresh your mind about what you are trying to keep in your awareness that day. You may also be able to carry a small reminder-token in pocket or purse, either associated with a specific exercise you are doing, or as a general reminder to briefly return your focus to whatever soul-exercise you are working on, whenever you touch the token.

If you have some control over your time while you are working, you can set a <u>reminder-signal</u> on your phone or wristwatch, reminding you at certain times to refresh your memory and awareness of the soul-work you're currently doing.

<u>Liminal time.</u> Try to extend, even by just a few minutes, the time you spend awake in bed, in the dark, not doing anything. The time as you are heading into sleep at night, and the time when you are waking up in the morning, can be among the most valuable of your soul-practice opportunities, if you use them rightly.

Allow yourself 10 minutes or so, before you have to get up in the morning, to review your dreams and your mood as you awaken, listen to your body, make space for thoughts and insights to arise. I realize these may not always be pleasant, but we can always learn from paying attention to our various states of being, instead of trying to ignore or fight them. The way to change something we don't like is to understand it clearly, then work with our soul-strengths to make needed changes based on that understanding.

As you awaken, open your awareness to the soul you are currently working with, and tune in to its perceptions, needs, and wishes for the day that lies ahead. Before you fall asleep at night, gently go over the events and experiences of your day, and perceive how the soul you were working with was involved and impacted. I say 'gently' because this isn't the time to get worked up over things or engage your analytical mind too deeply; then you'll find it hard to sleep. Instead, just *open your awareness to the soul you're working with, and enter into a quiet perception of what the day was like for that soul, without judgement or analysis. As you head into sleep, maintain that gentle awareness of your soul, a sense of quiet, undemanding companionship.*

Falling asleep and awakening are valuable times for quiet, non-judgmental awareness and attunement with our souls; I hope you make the most of it! I might also note that the same procedure and attitude of gentle awareness and sharing is a lovely way to close the day with your children at bedtime, and with your spouse or partner, or anyone you are caring for, such as an elderly or ill person.

<u>Writing in your Daybook.</u> If you're not into essay-type writing, or don't have time, try just jotting notes, phrases, keywords to help you remember your insights. You can also write poems, draw pictures or graphics, or note the

name of a song, music, poem, story, or film that is evocative of what you are learning about your soul.

Another shorthand when you are exploring how the soul has expressed itself during your life, is to note and refer to phases in your life, like your grade in school or year in college, the year you got married, the time you held that job you hated. If you have these cues to the mood and state you were in at that time, you won't need to write and analyze all the details, you can just use the time-period or the significant event as a shorthand, as you consider the role of your soul in these events. All of these ideas will help you keep track of your insights, without too much writing, so that you can build on this knowledge as you proceed with getting to know your souls.

These are all ideas for general practices. Following are suggestions for two specific practices, Awareness and Communication, that combine soul-awareness with daily activities that you would be doing in any case, so as to maximize your opportunities for soul-work during your busy days.

Awareness

We'll start with awareness of time, and how your own awareness fills your time. Spend some time, however many days you need, becoming more aware of how your inner thoughts, emotions, self-talk, etc., fill your time and your inner space all day long, and even your dreams. If you're like most of us, there's a running stream of inner chatter constantly going on, filling up your thought-space. There tends to be lots of repetition in these thoughts, and they're often not all that valuable or worthwhile, in comparison to

Finding the Time

other possibilities. This mental activity is also a lot more energy-intensive and tiring than we may realize, and the payoff for that degree of energy outlay tends to be pretty low.

Once you become aware of yourself doing this, consider shifting some of this time and inner-space over to soul-work. Any time you are working on auto-pilot, like vacuuming, washing dishes, folding laundry, going for a walk or jog, waiting in line or in slow traffic, riding the bus, taking a shower, falling asleep or waking up, keeping an eye on the kids playing, you can shift some of your awareness over to soul-working instead of the usual mental chatter (or scanning your phone and picking up other people's mental chatter!). You can't do deep, emotional pondering like this, but you can maintain simple awareness and communication with whichever soul you are currently working on. In a number of the exercises in the preceding chapters, I suggested you seek some kind of symbol or token to use as a cue and shorthand for a specific awareness exercise. This is the time for you to make use of that awareness-key.

Here is an example of what I mean. Most of my awareness-keys are inner sensations, ways that my body, parts of my body, my senses, or soul-bodies feel when I am tuning in to a specific soul. I often feel a pleasant, relaxed heaviness, rootedness, and warmth or coolness when I am tuned in; my inner senses become more alert and also more appreciative of what I am sensing. The inner space I am experiencing expands and brightens, and there is a feeling of pleasant anticipation.

So, when I get a chance I call up these keys, starting with the initial sensation-key and then expanding into the

Finding the Time

fuller experience. The result is my everyday awareness expanding into and welcoming the soul I am working with. I like to envision this awareness-activity like a flower, that opens into a full blossom of awareness and experience when the opportunity arises, and closes into a bud of potential when I need my full attention for my Midgard activities. I have a soul-garden full of these blossoms and buds, and it gives me great joy to be in this garden!

Having worked on this for years, I'm able to reach this state very quickly, and able to do so while having part of my awareness still on the outer-world activity or situation that I am auto-piloting. I don't do any heavy-duty soul-working in this state, since I need to keep connected with the outer world and ready to return to it at a moment's notice. I just spend time and feeling on attuning to the soul I'm working with, getting to know it better in a non-verbal, holistic-sensing way. I'm learning to feel at home with it and within it, enjoying our shared space.

This kind of activity is very worth our time and energy, even though we may only spend a few minutes at a time on it, slipping into and out of this tuned-in state as opportunities arise in our daily life. It's also excellent training and foundation for more intense soul-work, when we are able to place our full attention on that; we need less time and effort to enter into the right state of awareness, and can get straight to work. And thirdly, this is a fine relaxation exercise, any time you want to take a little while to relax and refresh.

This soul-awareness requires some practice at first, but I find that it is something we learn very rapidly, perhaps because it is so rewarding and enjoyable. There is a great return on investment of only small amounts of time and energy; time that otherwise would pretty much go to waste.

So, this is my suggestion related to awareness: *be aware of your constant stream of consciousness and inner chatter (and outer chatter like TV), and look for opportunities where you can interrupt that stream and slip into and out of soul-awareness,* even when you need to keep some of your attention on auto-pilot in the outer world. Use a cue or key, whatever works for you: a rune, a tune, a feeling, a line of poetry, a token you carry in your pocket, a mental image, that you associate with the soul you want to attune to.

This awareness activity is so enjoyable and rewarding, such a worthwhile expenditure of your life-energy, that it's not hard to turn it, first, into a habit, and then into an important part of your life and spiritual practice. And the only time you need for this, is time snatched from the constant, not very useful, repetitive ruminations and churning of your surface mind! Ideally, as time goes on, you spend less and less of your precious life-time on mental chatter, and more time on soul-attunement.

Soulful communication

Here, we're thinking about souls and getting to know our souls, about the responsibilities and the needs of our daily life, and about how to find time for it all. If we try to do everything we need or want to do as single-purpose activities, we'll never find time or energy for it all. Ideally, we want to meet several different needs with one activity, during one period of time, that satisfies multiple purposes. We can do this with soul-work, applying the abilities of our souls to our daily activities in ways that both use and grow our soul-power, and at the same time enhance the usefulness and success of our activities. Here, I'm going to focus on one important example: communication, not only with our own souls, but with the souls of other people close to us, as well.

All of our relationships require communication; it is the primary basis for any relationship. All of the exercises in this book promote communication between our conscious mind and our souls. They do require time and effort, so let's see whether the exercises can be combined with things we need and want to do in our everyday life, as well.

Communication is a major element of our outer life as well as our inner life, and the quality of our communication matters a great deal. When we become aware of how our souls and other people's souls are involved when we communicate with each other, our interactions deepen and become more satisfying, more clear and effective, and produce fewer misunderstandings and misfires.

When you want to work with a soul lore exercise, consider how you could use that work as a basis for quality time with those who are close to you, including children and grandchildren, parents and grandparents, as well as spouse, other family members and close friends. There's no need at all to get into Heathenry and technical soul lore for this, no need for complicated explanations and introductions. People like to talk about what is meaningful to them, and especially they like to be sincerely listened-to. All we need to do, to start the ball rolling, is lead into the topic and devise a question or two, relating to the exercise we're doing in an appropriate way for the person we're talking to.

Finding the Time

Here's an example. Exercise 8-1 for Mod and Hugr as motivating forces involves looking for threads that run through our Werold, our lifetime, to see how those threads have influenced our actions and choices. A personal example I used for this exercise was my longing for a home of my own, and how that influenced many decisions and directions in my life. Once you've noticed one of these threads of influence in your life, one that you feel comfortable sharing with people close to you, you can bring it up in conversation: "I've been noticing lately how much influence {this thing} has had in my life, that I didn't completely realize until now. {Give some examples.} Have you ever noticed anything like that?" This type of question is often especially interesting to explore with siblings, if you have a good relationship with them, because of the early-life roots and family culture you share.

As you get further into the conversation, you can exercise your soul-lore muscles by keeping part of your awareness on perceiving how your and the other person's souls are involved, both with the interactions between you, and with the topic and the underlying meanings of the conversation. This requires empathy and mindfulness, really tuning into the presences taking part in the conversation: all the interacting souls. It is an excellent activity, both for growing your awareness of your own souls, and for enhancing and deepening your relationship with the other person and their souls. This definitely counts as quality time, for all concerned!

Here's another example. Exercises relating to Ghost and Mod ask you to explore things you really love to do, things that motivate you and get your energy moving. This is another good conversation-starter, including with children. The leading questions for the conversation include things like: "What's your very favorite thing to do? What do you especially like about that thing? How does it make you feel: excited, calm, powerful, intrigued, etc.;" and other leading questions. Give examples of your own; build the energy of the conversation by bringing your own Ghost and Mod to the fore of your awareness, and picking up on the energies of the Ghost and Mod of the other person or people.

Another example, also great to do with children or adults: "If you could go to, or create, the perfect place for you to live, what would it be like? What things would be there, such as friends, animals, otherworldly beings, favorite objects, vehicles, clothing, objects of beauty, food, whatever?" They don't need the explanation that they're talking about 'soul habitat', unless you think they'd be interested in that idea. But you can stretch your awareness to try to understand which of their souls is talking about its 'dream-space', thus learning more about souls in general, and about the person you're talking to, specifically. And as you take part in the conversation, describing a favorite soul-habitat of your own, you're working on the soul lore exercises, too.

Another idea relates to the exercises exploring your Hama-covering, discussed in Chapter 6 of this book. Kids and adults can have fun and gain insights as they discuss how they'd like to 'dress up' in different creative ways, or how they've always felt there was a part of themselves that felt like an animal, or some historical figure like a knight, or other Hama-related explorations of their self-image, images they have of others, and feelings about these images.

Finding the Time

The overall idea here is to *meet two purposes at once: (1) increase your awareness of your souls and other people's souls, and how they work in our lives, and (2) enhance quality time and relationship connections with people whom you are close to*—something you would want to do anyway, soul lore aside. Not to mention, this tends to improve the conversational, listening, and imaginative skills of everyone involved, also a worthwhile outcome! These conversations might not take very much time, maybe just a few minutes, but the 'return on investment' of a little time for a large benefit is very high. You can bring up such conversations while riding together in the car, over the dinner-table, hanging out with the kids, whenever. And of course, these are great conversation-starters with Heathen friends, as well.

Daily experiences

After you've spent some time on the preceding activities and built up your awareness skills, you can make it a habit to keep an ongoing part of your awareness on the souls of yourself and the people you are interacting with. There's a lot you can learn about Hugr and Mod in your workplace; about Hugr and Sefa at a family reunion or an anniversary night out. How do people think, form opinions, express themselves, make choices and decisions? Which souls are at work there? Getting to know, on a deeper level, the souls of your children, parents, spouse, siblings, grandparents, friends, is profoundly meaningful and enriches your life together. Understanding how souls interact with each other in public spaces, work spaces, neighborhoods, school, etc. teaches us a great deal, and enables us and our own souls to navigate these complex social spaces in more effective ways. As we proceed with this, we can teach and set a good example for our children, grandchildren, and others whom we influence.

What we're doing here is integrating soul lore with daily life, with our Werold that we weave, day by day. It does take effort to start the ball rolling, but it can be done, and done in a time-efficient way. Channel the enthusiasm and energies of your souls, to help you find additional creative ways to learn about souls, ways that fit into your own life-circumstances, your own relationships and responsibilities, your own wishes for a well-shaped life. As we do this, we are benefiting not only ourselves, but those around us as well. Life is better for us all, when we have awareness and respect for the nature and powers of our own souls, and for the souls of those around us.

Finding the Time

*Our house-wight Elmindreda tends a soul-garden with care.
by Winifred Hodge Rose.*

Chapter 17

Pursuing Heathen soul lore is an ongoing challenge for us to rise to the greatest heights of insight, understanding and achievement.

17. Walking a Soul-Path

This seems like a good point to ask yourself what you'd like to do with the soul lore you're learning. Are you satisfied with how it's going now, or is there more that you'd like to do with it? Here, I'll share some suggestions about a few of the potential paths or directions you could consider, if you want to take Heathen soul lore farther.

The Path of Relationships among your souls

This is the foundation of Heathen soul lore, and it's what we've been working on so far, with the first two soul lore books. Book I is like an introduction and a meet-and-greet with your souls. This is where you began opening conversations with your souls, along the lines of: "You seem like a really interesting person! Tell me more about yourself." And you began discovering that—surprise—you have a lot in common with them!

So then, in Book II that you've just worked through, you began pursuing more in-depth friendships with your souls. This is where you got to know them at a deeper level, below the intriguing surface chit-chat. You come to realize that you've been through a lot together, over the course of your whole life. You've grown up together and worked through challenging situations, shared the ups and downs of life. You've started to understand how your everyday self and all your souls rely on one another, and all participate together in all aspects of your life. Your wounds are their wounds, your triumphs are theirs, your dreams and aspirations are theirs, your relationships with others depend on them. Your souls are not, now, just interesting new people you've met. They're now heart-friends, soul-friends. You can see the outlines of rock-solid, fully conscious, vital relationships coming into being among all of you.

This is an amazing accomplishment, and you may find that further growth along this path of personal relationships among your souls is entirely satisfying on its own, without any need to enhance or shape it in more formal ways. This kind of inner experience and growth is something I'll be exploring more in future soul lore books.

Or, you might like to consider some additional paths for practical, applied soul work in your outer life, of which there are a potentially endless number! I'll mention just a few of them here, to give you some ideas. I'll be working on another book(s) on this broad topic of Heathen soul-craft as well, with input from Heathens with expertise in areas where I'm lacking.

The Path of Vocation

This is where you pursue Heathen soul lore, and knowledge and relationships with your own souls, as a way of enhancing your own vocation(s) in life, whether a career type of vocation, or an avocation—something you do because you love it and are dedicated to it, even though you are not hired and paid for it. As an example, perhaps you are a healer of some kind: a conventional health care practitioner, a therapist, a mentor, a counselor, or involved in alternative methods of healing. This can also include healing yourself in your own ways, and being part of healing groups such as recovery and support groups.

I believe that Heathen soul lore has an enormous amount to contribute to healing efforts, which all need to be based on a soul-level understanding of people, their wounds, their strengths, their circumstances, their hopes and fears. Introducing and guiding others along a Heathen soul lore path would be one way to do this, but many people would not be interested or comfortable with that. I am not suggesting any proselytizing here; that's not something Heathens really get into. But your own understanding of soul lore, and your own experience with it, can be applied to the work you do, without any need for drawing others into specifically Heathen beliefs and practices, unless they wish for that. You can find ways to make use of the general soul lore concepts and insights in your healing work, without making it specifically Heathen.

I've used healing as an obvious example of a vocation that can be greatly enhanced by applying soul lore to it, but I think that any vocation or avocation can be so enhanced. How about management? Any position where you are responsible for other people, and / or the work they produce, will be improved and strengthened when you understand and relate to people at a soul-deep level. People are often not treated well by supervisors and managers, and managers are themselves under a great deal of stress and pressure between the layers of people above and below them. Understanding soul lore and applying your knowledge and experience of it in the workplace can work to everyone's advantage, wherever you are in the hierarchy.

Handling stress better, enhancing job performance in any way, maintaining physical and mental health and stamina on the job, creating good relationships with your colleagues, customers, suppliers, supervisors, everyone you work with—soul lore can help with all of that. If you are working in any kind of inspirational field, including arts and crafts, technology development, performance, the benefits of a strong flow of soul-energy are clear.

Paths of Relationship with others

A great many of us think that the most important part of life is parenting. The applications of soul lore to give your child the best possible upbringing are numerous and vital. Grandparents, other relatives and close family friends, teachers, caregivers, mentors, counselors, coaches, group leaders like scouts—all who deal with children can benefit those children through their own understanding of Heathen soul lore, and applying that understanding toward supporting the healthy development of babies, children and teenagers. Again, there is no need to impose Heathen beliefs on anyone who is not interested; this is simply a matter of applying your own insights and experience with Heathen soul lore toward the promotion of children's wellbeing and growth.

The same potential for enrichment applies to all our relationships: marriage, partnership (intimate partnerships, business or community enterprise partnerships, etc.), friendships, work and neighborhood relationships. All of our relationships can be greatly enhanced by our own knowledge and practice of soul lore. Not to mention the advantages of a soul lore perspective when holding any position of responsibility or influence within Heathen groups and communities: clergy, leadership, volunteer service, etc.

The Path of Healing

There are so many ways to apply Heathen soul lore to healing, whether it is healing ourself, supporting our nearest and dearest on their healing paths, or working as a healer in many different professional contexts. Healing needs to happen on so many levels: spiritual, emotional, mental, behavioral, physical, social levels. Not only humans need healing: ecosystems, landscapes, water bodies need healing. Animals, domestic and wild, need healing. Spiritual beings like landwights need healing. Larger human groups need group healing. Even concepts, cultural memes and practices, social systems themselves, need healing.

There is work for each of us here, and our own insights and experiences with Heathen soul lore will stand us in good stead, as we pursue whichever healing paths may call to us. I believe that our healing efforts will be crowned with greater success, greater depth and rootedness, when we approach them with an experiential knowledge of Heathen soul lore, along with all of the other knowledge, experience and compassion we can bring to bear.

The Path of Creativity

Understanding and practicing Heathen soul lore can greatly inspire and expand all the creative expressions of our lives. This includes not only artistic, inventive, and other such expressions of creativity, but creativity in other areas such as problem-solving, and enhancing our relationships with humans, nature, wights, Deities.

Problems are part of life; they constantly crop up in our relationships, our work, our home life, social life, etc. Drawing on the creative powers of our various souls to find truly inspired solutions to these problems is one of the important ways that we, and all our souls, grow and mature in this life. In other words, the path of creativity means not just 'getting by', squeaking through the challenges of our life. It means applying inspiration so we can use whatever problem we face as a springboard, to make a quantum leap into something a whole lot better than 'just getting by.' It means using the good old saying, "Necessity is the mother of invention" to inspire us to invent a better way to address that necessity, not just struggle to repeat old, worn-out ways of trying to get around the problem.

Creativity can apply to all aspects of our life. It can enrich our relationships and lead them in new directions. It can bring beauty, insight and interest to our life and other people's, and inspire them in turn. It can inspire our children to develop their own inspiration, to grow and expand their own souls. Knowing and growing our own souls opens paths of creativity out into all directions of life. Following any path of creativity draws the energy of Ahma, rising from the very wellsprings of creation, here into the world of Midgard to enrich us all.

Heathen Esoteric Paths

Heathen soul lore is itself an esoteric path, and it can vigorously branch out into all of the different activities and knowledge-pursuits that can be included under 'esotericism.' This includes spirituality, mysticism, and religious practices; all the many branches of magical practice; 'natural philosophy'; all the arts of energy-working; working with wights and other non-physical entities; spaecraft and other forms of divination; helping the dying and the dead on their paths, contacting and working with ancestral spirits; esoteric work with the inner powers of nature; and many more endeavors. Esoteric work is a huge, complex and promising branch of human experience, where we can greatly benefit by bringing Heathen soul knowledge and experience into our practices and our development of esoteric knowledge.

I won't go on with more examples of soul-paths here, because there are as many examples of soul lore application, as there are people who potentially may want to apply them! If you are drawn to apply soul lore further in your life, I hope that future soul lore books, which will be focused on some of these areas, will be of use to you. But more important is to develop your own insights, skills and applications, that result from your own progress in living Heathen soul lore and using it in the activities of your life. If you can then produce blogs, podcasts, articles, books, and so forth, about what you've learned, that would be of great benefit to the rest of us! My hope is to see the applications of Heathen soul lore expand outward in many directions and ways in this world, and bring betterment to us all.

The Challenge of the Heathen Soul-Path

Life is full of challenges, and we need to be able to count on all our souls—their strength, wisdom, resilience—to cope with whatever life sends our way, and pursue our own expanding vision of life's meaning. Now as we come to a close, I want to repeat some things I wrote earlier, in the chapters on the Aldr and the Mod souls.

The Heathen understanding that life is an *ordeal*—an ongoing challenge laid down for us by ørlög and by the nature of life in Midgard—offers courage, guidance, and moral support to us on our strenuous but worthy paths of life. There is no such thing as a permanent stopping place on this path. There is only growth and striving, only the struggle to walk toward an ever-evolving vision of...something...that shines at the farthest horizon of Being. Walking this path *is* our life; this is what life really is—not the achievement of some static, idealized state, or piles of possessions and status symbols, but the striving itself toward our own ever-evolving vision. And think about it:

this path does not end when we die; the path goes on, and our souls go on with it, whether they are embodied in this life, or disembodied in other realms of existence.

We don't walk this path alone. Though we each need to follow our own vision, we have much in common with others who walk these paths of life as well, and with those who have gone before us, and those who will come after. When we are aware of our own souls and the souls of others, these commonalities become more apparent, and more important than surface differences of opinion, appearance, lifestyles, circumstances, culture, etc. I am not saying that we are all 'the same' as everyone else, whatever that means, and I am not downplaying our differences and our individual distinctions, which are important and real. I'm saying that we have meaningful things in common, and that it is worthwhile to seek a deeper comprehension of our shared humanity through a profound understanding of the souls that create who each of us really is, here in Midgard.

May the Holy Ones bless this path,
this sacred ordeal of human life,
for each one of us,
and for humanity as a whole, together.

Are these figures a group of our own souls?
Are they humans in solidarity with each other: the Feorhcynn?
Are they our Gods in modern garb,
gathered to bless us with their friendly powers?
....You decide....

Acknowledgements

I'd like first to thank the soul lore study participants for generously allowing me to quote some of their responses to the exercises in this book: Sara Axtell, Cat Heath, Leif Höglund, Laurie Sottilaro, Dale Wood, as well as anonymous study participants. All of them helped to stimulate my own ideas and understanding. Their material has enriched the perspectives of this book, beyond what one person's perspective could possibly be. I am truly grateful for their participation and their contributions to my own understanding.

My thanks and appreciation to Heathen artist Dale Wood for the lovely cover painting on this book, his painting in Chapter 14 that provides the basis for a Saiwalo-Dwimor exercise, and the handsome twig-raven between Chapters 14 and 15.

My love and thanks to my dear husband, Rosten Dean Rose, for creating the graphic forms of the bindrunes I designed, and for his essential help formatting the book cover files. My life, my writing, my souls, would not be what they are, without his steady and loving support in all ways. I also thank the many members of my extended family who offer their interest and encouragement of my work, no matter what faiths or philosophies they ascribe to.

I'm grateful to several people who have promoted my first book, *Heathen Soul Lore Foundations*, on their blogs and podcasts, including John Michael Greer on *Ecosophia*, John Hyatt's *Gifts of the Wyrd* podcast, and Raven Wulfgar's

Acknowledgements

tarot sites. If there are others who have done so, of whom I'm not aware, my grateful thanks to you, as well!

I want to express my appreciation to all the photographers and artists who generously share their work on Wikimedia Commons and allow others to make use of it. Both this book and my previous soul lore book are much enriched by their artistry.

Last, but certainly not least, my thanks and appreciation to all the members of my Heathen communities. It is a privilege to belong to such groups of fine, frithful, friendly and insightful individuals, steeped in knowledge, talent, and enthusiasm for Heathenry!

Word-Hoard / Glossary

Æweweard, Éwart: Anglo-Saxon and Old High German terms, respectively, for a Heathen priest. The meaning is 'warder of the troth / covenant / law'.

Æsir: A tribe of Heathen Gods. Prominent members are Odin, Thor, Frigg, Tyr.

Ahma: The Gothic term for 'spirit', including the breath of life. I also use this word to indicate the cosmic field of spiritual proto-being that I envision arises from the meeting of Fire and Ice within Ginnungagap.

Aldr: One of the Heathen souls, which governs our lifespan and the timing of events in our life, and channels spiritual nourishment for us. Its meaning is closely related to 'old' and 'age, age of time.'

Alf (sing.), Alfar (pl.): This term can refer to a divine tribe of beings closely associated with the Æsir Gods, and is also used to designate the spirits of deceased male ancestors. I believe that these spirits are specifically the Hugr souls of the ancestors, pursuing their afterlife.

Asgard: The divine realm of the Æsir Gods, which includes many individual God-Halls within it.

Ask & Embla: The mythical first human couple, formed from trees or logs by Odin, Hœnir and Loðurr, or by Odin and his brothers Vili and Ve.

Asmoði: An ecstatic or heightened state of spiritual and physical arousal, characterized by rage, driving determination, and great power. This is a state that some of the Gods enter into when needed, especially Thor, as is shown by the first part of the word, As, referring to an Æsir-God.

Athom: An Old Saxon word for the spirit and the breath of life.

Auðumla: In Norse mythology, a primal being in the form of a cow, whose name means 'the hornless cow of wealth / prosperity.' She appeared in Ginnungagap at the beginning of things, licked the shape of Buri, the first God, out of the enclosing ice, and fed Buri and Ymir with her milk. In my thought, she is a shape-shifting Mother-Goddess, and transformed herself into the realm of Hel. I believe she was the mother of Borr, the progenitor of the Æsir.

Bestla: The mother of Odin, Vili and Ve, and the sister of Mimir. I believe Bestla and Mimir were the unnamed pair who were generated under the arm of the primal Giant, Ymir. Thus, she, her brother Mimir, and her consort Borr were the first generation of offspring from the primal powers.

Bindrune or Bind-rune: A bind-rune is made of several runes bound together into an artistic shape that is meant to provide meditative insights, or to form the basis for a rune-magical spell.

Borr: The son of Buri and consort of Bestla. As the father of Odin, Vili and Ve, he is the progenitor of the Æsir Gods.

Buri: In Norse lore, a primal being, progenitor of the Gods, who was formed within the ice of Ginnungagap. He was licked free of the ice and fed by the Ur-Mother in the form of a cow, Auðumla.

Daemon, Daimon: A Greek word with complex meanings; here it is used to designate a soul or spirit which can exist and take action independently of its living physical body.

Dis (sing.), Disir (pl.): Literal meaning is a lady or a noblewoman; sometimes a demi-goddess or a Goddess. Most commonly used in modern Heathenry to indicate the spirits of one's deceased female ancestors. I believe that these spirits are specifically their Hugr souls.

Doppelgänger: The double or etheric twin of a person, a term used in reference to occult phenomena.

Draugr: A reanimated corpse; as used in Norse languages, it can also refer to an afterlife Ghost. In my thought, the corpse is reanimated by the Hama soul.

Dwarves: Otherworldly beings who appear in many forms and roles in all the branches of Germanic folklore. Considered to be very wise and full of craft, but can be deceptive and are famed for bearing grudges. In Norse lore,

Dwarves formed within the sacrificed body of the primal Giant Ymir; according to one account, they began as 'maggots' within Ymir's flesh, absorbing his-her energy and substance. In my view, Dwarves are masters of mod-energy, which they 'suck' or absorb from the natural and otherworldly environments, and sometimes from other beings as well, causing fatigue and illness. Dwarves absorb mod-energy, transform it, and use it to power their craft.

Dwimor: A phantom or apparition. I use this term specifically to designate the phantom of a living person which is created by the Saiwalo soul, and which serves as a matrix for holding together the energies of all the person's souls during life in Midgard.

Elivagar: A sea, encircling river, or multiple rivers that flow out of the great wellspring Hvergelmir in Norse mythology. In my thought, Elivagar is a braided system of 'rivers' of energy which arise from the cosmic wellspring Hvergelmir, and surround, separate and nourish the various Worlds upon the World-Tree.

Ferah: One of the Heathen souls, which confers life, life-force, sensation, thought, feeling, behavior, piety, wisdom.

Fjǫrgyn, Fjǫrgynn: An ancient Goddess and God, about whom little is known, except that Fjǫrgyn is one of the names of Thor's Mother, the Earth Goddess, and Fjǫrgynn is the father of Frigg. Presumably they are brother and sister, and perhaps spouses as well. Their names are cognate with the Proto-Indo-European Thunder-God, *Perkwunos.

Frigg: The great Goddess of Asgard: mother, wisewoman, wife of Odin, mother of Baldr, leader of a group of helping-Goddesses, diplomat and frith-weaver / peace-weaver. Her name means 'beloved.'

Frith is an old word from the Germanic languages that refers to a state of peaceful interaction, a low-strife condition. It also refers, in a broader sense, to the entire social fabric that is created by the maintenance of good relationships among individuals and groups within a society.

Ghost: As I use this term, Ghost is one of our human souls, our 'spirit'. It is formed from primal, unshaped, transcendent Ahma-Spirit by being enwrapped in a soul-skin which gives it shape, coherence, personal characteristics, and personal consciousness.

Ginnungagap: In Old Norse lore, Ginnungagap is a place of primal chaos or nothingness. At either end are the primal powers of Fire and Ice, and in the temperate center is where the World Tree takes root. The ancient Giant Ymir was formed from the frozen rime at the icier end of Ginnungagap. The ancient divine Cow, Auðumla (whom I regard as the Ur-Mother) also arose from Ginnungagap, as did the progenitor of the Gods, Buri.

Hama: The literal meaning is 'a covering'. In Norse folklore, the Hama manifests as a magical being, an occult shape with paranormal powers, which can fare forth from a person in spirit form, and is also associated with the womb, the caul, and the processes of gestation. In my soul lore theory, Hama shapes and ensouls our physical body, the Lich, and provides it with many abilities such as speech, behavior and action. I believe that Hama is formed from the three gifts that Loðurr / Odin's brother first gave to Ask and Embla: *La, Læti,* and *Litr.*

Hamingja: In Norse folklore, Hamingja is both a form of luck, and a spirit who bears and gives that luck to the person with whom it is associated. As with Hama, Hamingja is considered to reside in the womb / caul / afterbirth. It accompanies the child it was born with throughout life, as long as nothing dire occurs to destroy its luck or its connection to the person.

Hel: Hel, with its linguistic variations, is the term in all the Germanic languages for the place where souls go after death. It was not considered a place of punishment, but simply the residence of the dead. In Norse lore, Hel is also the name of a daughter of Loki, a Goddess of the dead and ruler of Hel. The word Hel is derived from Proto-Indo-European *kel-, meaning 'to cover, conceal.' Hel is the Hidden Land. The German Goddess Frau Holle derives her name from the same root, and is considered to be a guide and protector both during life and after death.

Hiwscip, Hiwship: An Anglo-Saxon word referring to a household or group of people living together. I use it to refer to the household of soul-beings which makes up our personal 'soular-system.'

Hlin: A Goddess and companion of Frigg, whose name means 'protectress' or 'refuge.' Quite possibly she is an aspect or emanation of Frigg's own protective powers. Germanic Goddesses were considered protectors of warriors in battle, as well as of all men, women, and children.

Holle, Frau Holle: A German Goddess much involved in all matters of daily Midgard life, especially those traditionally relating to women and children, and to food, agriculture and home. Her care for all humans extends before and after Midgard life, as well as during it. Her name is cognate with 'Hel', and Holle's domains of action include not only Midgard and Midgard's sky, but Underworld as well. Other roots of her name include words for 'benevolent, kind, gracious'. Holle draws the souls of newborn babies from her sacred pond, as they are born into Midgard, and cares for souls in the afterlife. She is especially revered by the modern Heathen sect called *Urglaawe*.

Hugr: A powerful soul focused on Midgard activities, using faculties of thought and emotion to navigate the complexities of human social life. In my thought, Hugr is the soul which periodically reincarnates, and which continues its involvement with Midgard life even after death by becoming an ancestral spirit, an Alf or a Dis, or a guiding spirit, or if ill-natured, becoming an afflicting wight.

Hvergelmir: In Norse mythology, a well or wellspring located in the cold, Niflheim side of Ginnungagap, under a root of the World-Tree, from which the Elivagar river(s) flows. In my thought, Hvergelmir is centered in Ginnungagap and is the source of the energy flows that form the cosmos.

Jotnar, Giants: Considered to be descended from the hermaphroditic proto-Giant, Ymir. Norse Giants are grouped into several tribes, including Thursar, Jotnar, Rises, Frost-Giants, Berg- or Mountain Giants, Trolls, etc. Giants such as the Anglo-Saxon Eoten and German Riesen play a role in the folklore of other Germanic lands as well. In the Norse pantheon, many of the Æsir Gods are of Jotun descent through their mothers, including Odin, Thor, Vidar, Magni and Modi, and Heimdal.

Jotunmoði: An ecstatic state of rage and driving power, characteristic of the Jotnar when they become angry. Sometimes Thor is described as entering this state, as well.

La, Lö: Life-force that expresses itself through blood and the warmth it gives to the body, and through the health and beauty of hair and skin. Given to Ask and Embla by Loðurr, or by one of Odin's brothers, Vili or Ve (Vili, in my view).

Læti: Another gift given to Ask and Embla by Loðurr, consisting of speech, the ability to move and take action, and to engage in the characteristic behaviors of human beings.

Landwights: Land-spirits, beings who inhabit spiritual planes of Earth / Midgard, and involve themselves with the features and processes of landscapes and ecosystems. They range in size / power from smaller beings inhabiting trees, rocks, small spaces, up to mighty warders of large areas and phenomena such as mountains, lakes, seas, and storms. At the latter end, they merge into the domains of the Jotnar and Deities.

Lich-Hama, Lich: Lich is the physical body; Lich-Hama or Lichama is the living body ensouled by its Hama.

Litr, Wlite: A gift of Loðurr / Odin's brother, consisting of our physical shape and appearance, enlivened by the energies of our souls shining through that appearance. *Litr* is the Norse term, *Wlite* is Anglo-Saxon.

Magni: A son of Thor and the giantess Jarnsaxa, embodiment of might and main. He survives Ragnarök and is one of the leading Deities of the new world that comes after.

Matronae: A multitude of Goddesses, demi-Goddesses, ancestral warding spirits of tribes and clans, and land- and river-warding spirits, who flourished during the time of the Roman empire. Both Germanic and Celtic Matronae are recognized, as well as some whose provenance are not clear. Many stone altars and thanks-offerings to them have been found, especially in the region of what is now Germany, but extending all over Europe and Britain in the wake of the Roman Empire and their troops. These matronly beings are honored by modern Heathens, as well.

Mægen, megin, main: Power, force, energy that is inherent in living beings, magical objects, and otherworldly beings.

Midgard: The World of Earth and all it encompasses. It means 'middle yard, enclosure', a word and meaning that existed in all the Germanic languages, often in the form of 'middle earth' meanings. This term implies an assumption that there are 'upper' and 'lower' worlds, as well as perhaps surrounding worlds. According to Norse lore, Midgard was formed from Ymir's sacrificed body by Odin, Vili and Ve.

Mimir and his Well: Mimir is an ancient, wise Giant, the uncle and teacher of Odin. He was beheaded while a hostage with the Vanir Gods, but Odin preserved his head, placed it in or near Mimir's Well of memory and inspiration, and continues to receive wise rede from it. Mimir's Well is considered a place of great wisdom and mystery. Odin pledged his eye to this well in exchange for runic knowledge, and the well also is said to contain Heimdal's horn and his hearing or his ear. My idea is that Mimir's Head / Well is 'World-Mind' or the Noösphere, the realm where Thought occurs.

Mod: One of the Heathen souls, which has a powerful influence on our character and actions in Midgard, and is reflected in our moods. Mod's strengths include Will, energy, intelligence, determination, and courage.

Mod-power: I envision this as a form of energy similar to mægen / megin, except that it is shaped by the mood and character of the being who is accessing and expressing it.

Moði: A son of Thor and the giantess Jarnsaxa, embodiment and channel of mod-power. He survives Ragnarök and is one of the leading Deities of the new world that comes after.

Word-Hoard

Niflheim: In Norse lore, the cold, icy end of the primal space called Ginnungagap. The word means 'mist-world'. In my thought, the term Niflheim describes the mist of spiritual proto-being, the field of Ahma, that continually arises from Ginnungagap, generated by the primal polarities of Ice and Fire. This mist is the basis for all subsequent shapings of worlds and beings.

Norns: Three womanly beings, possibly Giants though their origins are unclear. In Norse lore they are named Urðr, Verðandi, and Skuld, representing 'What-Is', 'What Is Becoming', and 'Debt, or What Should Be.' They live beside the Well of Wyrd / destiny, called Urðarbrunnr, and nourish the World-Tree with mud and water from the Well. They speak ørlög or fate for humans, and the council or doom-stead of the Gods takes place near their Well; presumably they participate in these councils. There are also lesser norns, who appear as fairy godmothers and similar beings involved with people's fates. In Anglo-Saxon, these beings are called the Wyrdæ.

Odin, Oðinn, Woden: One of the chief Gods of the Aesir. In Norse lore, he is the son of Borr, brother of Vili and Ve, husband of Frigg, father of Thor, Baldr, Viðar, Vali and others. Odin involves himself heavily in Midgard affairs, more often in pursuit of his own purposes than of ours, but we can often attune our purposes with his.

Oðrœrir / Odrerir and other spellings: This word means 'wode-stirrer', or the stimulator of ecstatic states. It is a name for the sacred mead of inspiration, and is sometimes also used as the name for the magical kettle within which the mead was brewed.

Ǫnd: Old Norse word meaning both 'spirit' and 'breath'.

Ordeal: An "or-deal" in a Heathen philosophical sense means *'the primal roots of a given ordeal-circumstance: the ørlög, the weaving of wyrd, which has been dealt out for one to face here and now, in this place, in this time.'* An 'ordeal' has the connotation of a struggle, a challenge, a personal testing, and it is that, but it is more. It is fateful, it is a weaving of wyrd, a drawing-together of the strands of our life into a nexus-point of deep significance. Much of our past has gone into reaching this nexus-point of the ordeal, and much will lead forth from its outcome, that will shape our time to come. (In other words, an ordeal is a really big deal!)

In my understanding of Heathen philosophy, life itself is an ordeal in this sense: a complex, patterned knot or nexus of strands of ørlög, arising from the past, gathered together in the present, and shaping the future to come. The ordeal of life is a challenge and a struggle, indeed, but more than that, it shapes the whole pattern of our Being, and shapes the meaning that our life holds.

Our purpose in life is not to avoid or escape true Heathen ordeals, but to rise to the challenge they offer: the challenge not only to meet the ordeal successfully, but to use that challenge to emerge from the ordeal with greater soul-qualities than we had when we went into it. This is the 'path of the hero' in Germanic culture.

Ørlög, Orlay: This word means the 'ur-layers, primal layers', and is related to the words for 'law.' These layers are laid by the Norns, shaped from the deeds and events of humankind and Midgard, as well as the other Worlds and beings. In turn, ørlög influences the lives and life-spans of living humans. Ørlög is the Old Norse term, Orlæg or Orlay is Anglo-Saxon.

Proto-Germanic: A language which has been reconstructed by modern scholars; the prehistoric ancestor of Germanic languages such as Anglo-Saxon, Old Saxon, Old Norse, Frisian, Old High German, Frankish, etc. Gothic is the closest historical language to Proto-Germanic.

Proto-Indo-European, PIE: The prehistoric, reconstructed root of all Indo-European languages, ancient and modern.

Ragnarök: 'The destiny or fate of the Gods,' a great battle between the Gods and the Jotnar or Giants, with the dead from different realms participating on different sides. Some modern Heathens regard Ragnarök as having already happened, in the form of the forcible conversions from Heathenism / Paganism to Christianity during the early Middle Ages. Others regard it as an event yet to come, and some see Ragnarök as a cyclical, recurrent event, having already happened in the past, and still to come again in the future.

Saiwalo, Sawl, Seola, etc: The root of our word 'soul'. In Heathen belief, this is the afterlife soul or the 'shade', which naturally goes to Hel as the realm of the dead.

Sefa, Sebo: In old Germanic texts, a soul or soul-part especially attuned to emotions and relationships. The word probably relates to other words for 'sib' or 'relative', and to words for 'self.' In my thought, Sefa is a soul which arises from the interactions of all our other souls. It contains our perception of 'self' and 'self in relation to others.' I call it 'the soul who cares,' in all senses of the word 'care'.

Seiðr, Seidh: In Nordic cultures, a practice similar to witchcraft, with a strong focus on oracular work and faring in spirit-forms. In modern Heathen use, it often refers to oracular trance practices.

Sif, Sibbe, Sippe: A Goddess, in Norse mythology the wife of Thor and mother of Ullr and Thruðr. Her name is related to the words for 'kinship, relationship' in all the Germanic languages, and she supports and protects this important domain of life. Some also consider her to be the Goddess of grain, with a belief that thunder and lightning are necessary to cause the grain to ripen, reflecting the relations between Sif and Thor. I envision her as the 'frith-sib of the folk', a peace-weaver who graciously shares her home and blessings with living folk and with the many human Ghosts who reside with her, Thor and their family in the afterlife.

Sjöfn: A Goddess and companion of Frigg; a promoter and protector of love, marriage and relationships generally.

Soular-system: An expression I invented to designate the group of soul-entities who collectively create a living person here in Midgard.

Spaecraft, spaework: As used here, and in modern Heathen terminology, these words refer to a practice of oracular trance work, often performed in a group setting, other times performed individually, to explore questions and issues of interest to the querents.

Syn: The Goddess Syn wards the doors of the hall, and closes them against those who must not enter. She is called on at the Thingsteads (assemblies) when one wishes to refute an accusation, and is considered the Goddess of Denial. (*Gylfaginning* p. 30, Edda). I view her as the "Just Say No" Goddess, the one who helps us protect our healthy and necessary boundaries against intrusion.

Thor, Thunor, Donar, Donner: A well-loved and much-trusted God among ancient and modern Heathens, wielding the power of thunder and lightning. His great Hammer is used to defend the Deities and Midgard against destructive forces, and is also used for hallowing and blessing. Thor is Sif's husband, and is the father of Magni, Modi and Thruðr. His hall Bilskirnir ('ray of light lightning-strike') lies within his realm, Thruðheim ('strength-home, strength-world'), and is the afterlife residence of many human Ghosts whose patron he was during life.

Thorlings: A term I invented, based on the Germanic suffix *"ling, lingas"* that implies 'belonging to or descended from' the name the suffix is attached to. Thus, Thorlings are those who are descended from Thor: Magni, Moði and Thruðr.

Thruðr: Daughter of Thor and the Goddess Sif. Her name means 'Strength'. Presumably she, like her brothers Magni and Modi, survives Ragnarök and becomes one of the leaders of the new world. Her father's godly domain bears her name: Thruðheim or 'strength-home, strength-world.'

Valhöl, Valhalla: 'Hall of the slain', Odin's hall where spirits of slain heroes—Einherjar—reside.

Werold: A word meaning 'man-age', used in Anglo-Saxon, Old Saxon and Old High German, and referring to the totality of a person's life-span and life-experience. In Old Norse, the word is Veraldr.

Wode: One of the gifts given by Hœnir / Odin's brother when two trees were transformed into the humans Ask and Embla. Wode refers to an ecstatic state of heightened spiritual—and sometimes physical—energy, which can take forms ranging from inspired eloquence and prophecy, artistic and intellectual genius, warrior focus and strength, to berserker rage, or outright madness. I see the gift of wode as a divine spark or a bridge, that enables humans to reach divine consciousness and communication with the Deities. If the person is not fit nor prepared for this, if their motives are skewed, or if they approach the Deities in inappropriate, offensive ways, the resulting flow of wode may backfire into negative forms such as outright madness.

World-Tree, Yggdrasil: The cosmic Tree, the structure of Space and all that exists within space. It has roots in the three great Wells of power in Norse myth: Hvergelmir, Mimir's Well, and Urðr's Well, and the Nine Worlds are supported by its branches and roots.

Word-Hoard

Worlds, Nine Worlds: Norse mythology envisions nine worlds as the home-bases for different kinds of beings: Asgard for the Æsir, Vanaheim for the Vanir, Alfheim for the Alfar or elves, Midgard for humans, Svartalfheim for the Dwarves, Hel for the dead, Jotunheim for the Giants, and the Worlds of the primal energies: the World of ice and cold, Niflheim, and the World of Fire, Muspelheim.

Wyrd, and Well of: An Anglo-Saxon word derived from 'to become, to happen, to come to pass'; basically, 'to come into being.' This is the name of a being or a power that brings about destiny and fate in Anglo-Saxon lore, in particular, the circumstances of one's death. Wyrd is cognate with Norse Norn-name Urðr, and Wyrd's Well is the same as Urðarbrunnr: the Well of Fate (approximately). 'Fate, Destiny' and 'Wyrd' are not exactly the same, but overlap a good deal in meaning.

Ymir: A Giant, said to be hermaphroditic, who came into being within Ginnungagap at the beginning of the cosmos. Jotnar / Giants are descended from him-her, and I believe that the unnamed pair who were generated from beneath Ymir's arm were Mimir and Bestla, the uncle and mother of Odin, Vili and Ve. Ymir was sacrificed by Odin, Vili and Ve, and his-her body formed the foundations of Midgard and some of the other Worlds.

Yggdrasil: The 'steed of Ygg'. 'Ygg' means the 'terrible one', and is a byname of Odin. His 'steed' here is the World-Tree upon which he hung for nine days and nights to win the Runes.

Word-Hoard

Art and Photograph Credits

Artist's names are included with their paintings in the text. Other required attributions are listed here, by chapter.

Cover: Dale Wood.

Dedication:
Squirrel digging: Son of Groucho from Scotland, CC BY 2.0 <https://creativecommons.org/licenses/by/2.0>, via Wikimedia Commons

Introduction:
Bridge: By Óðinn, CC BY-SA 2.5 CA <https://creativecommons.org/licenses/by-sa/2.5/ca/deed.en>, via Wikimedia Commons

Chapter 1:
Matterhorn sunset: Sam Ferrara samferrara, CC0, via Wikimedia Commons, (Unsplash) 2016.

Chapter 2:
Diver with Whaleshark: Feefiona123, CC BY-SA 4.0 <https://creativecommons.org/licenses/by-sa/4.0>, via Wikimedia Commons

Pottery making: Jared Sluyter jaredsluyter, CC0, via Wikimedia Commons

The sea: Felipe Skroski, CC BY 2.0 <https://creativecommons.org/licenses/by/2.0>, via Wikimedia Commons

Credits

Chapter 3:
People on roots of tree: Michael Ocampo (a.k.a. MicahPiosDad), CC BY 2.0 <https://creativecommons.org/licenses/by/2.0>, via Wikimedia Commons

Exposed roots: Avebury - Tree Roots by Chris Talbot, CC BY-SA 2.0 <https://creativecommons.org/licenses/by-sa/2.0>, via Wikimedia Commons

Between Chapters 3 and 4:
Ahma-swirls (Jupiter): NASA/JPL-Caltech/SwRI/MSSS, Public domain, via Wikimedia Commons

Chapter 4:
Jupiter and Earth: Lunar and Planetary Institute from Houston, TX, USA, CC BY 2.0 <https://creativecommons.org/licenses/by/2.0>, via Wikimedia Commons

Viking woman with drop spindle: Peter van der Sluijs, CC BY-SA 3.0 <https://creativecommons.org/licenses/by-sa/3.0>, via Wikimedia Commons

Between Chapters 4 and 5:
Sparking campfire: Mark limb, CC BY-SA 4.0 <https://creativecommons.org/licenses/by-sa/4.0>, via Wikimedia Commons

Chapter 6:
Cocoon: User:Vmenkov, CC BY-SA 3.0 <https://creativecommons.org/licenses/by-sa/3.0>, via Wikimedia Commons

Chapter 9:
Gallehus horn: Nationalmuseet, CC0, via Wikimedia Commons

Credits

Nordendorf fibula: Bullenwächter, CC BY-SA 3.0 <https://creativecommons.org/licenses/by-sa/3.0>, via Wikimedia Commons

Chapter 12:
Doorways: Derek Harper / Door, No 10 Cathedral Close, Exeter

Between Chapters 12 and 13:
Handshake: Aidan Jones, CC BY-SA 2.0 <https://creativecommons.org/licenses/by-sa/2.0>, via Wikimedia Commons

Chapter 14:
Sailboat and sun: Arnas Goldberg, CC BY 3.0 <https://creativecommons.org/licenses/by/3.0>, via Wikimedia Commons

Chapter 17:
Rock climbing: BLM Nevada, CC BY 2.0 <https://creativecommons.org/licenses/by/2.0>, via Wikimedia Commons

Credits

A note about the book *Goddess Holle,* listed on the next page: At this time of writing, this book is produced only in Europe, in print form, and is expensive to ship elsewhere. If you are drawn to Frau Holle strongly enough for the expense to be worth it, this is a thorough and excellent 400-page resource about her and her many interests and domains of action, including copious folklore, folktales, herb-lore, and illustrations. (The illustrations are not of the best quality, but nevertheless add value to the book.) The author discusses other German Goddesses as well, though the main focus is on Frau Holle. The book is available in a good English translation as well as in German.

Book-Hoard / Bibliography

Baer, Jeremy. *Hammer, Oak and Lightning: A Thor Devotional.* Philadelphia, PA: The Troth, 2019.

Becker, Gertraud. *Geist und Seele im Altsächsischen und im Althochdeutschen: Der Sinnbereich des Seelischen und die Wörter gest-geist und seola-sela in den Denkmälern bis zum 11.Jahrhundert.* Heidelberg, Germany: Carl Winter Universitätsverlag, 1964.

Chickering, Howell D., Jr. *Beowulf.* New York: Doubleday, 1977.

Durkan, Maire. *Circle of Frith: A Devotional to Frigg and her Handmaidens.* Philadelphia, PA: The Troth, 2021.

Goos, Gunivortus. *Goddess Holle, 3rd revised and supplemented edition.* Norderstedt, Germany: Books on Demand, 2019.

Greer, John Michael. *A Magical Education: Talks on Magic and Occultism.* London UK: AEON Books, 2019.

~~~. *The Druid Magic Handbook.* San Francisco CA: Weiser Books, 2007.

Griffiths, Bill. *The Battle of Maldon.* Middlesex, England: Anglo-Saxon Books, 1991.

Grimm, Jacob. *Teutonic Mythology*, transl. James Steven Stalleybrass. London, UK: George Bell and Sons, 1882.

Heath, Cat. *Elves, Witches & Gods: Spinning Old Heathen Magic in the Modern Day.* Woodbury, MN: Llewellyn, 2021.

Jonsson, Finnur. *De Gamle Eddadigte.* Köbenhaven, Denmark: G.E.C. Gads Forlag, 1932.

Larrington, Carolyne, transl. *The Poetic Edda.* New York, NY: Oxford University Press, 2014.

Lockett, Leslie. *Anglo-Saxon Psychologies in the Vernacular and Latin Traditions.* Toronto: University of Toronto Press, 2011.

McCarthy, Josephine. *Magical Healing.* Berkeley, CA: Golem Media, 2014.

~~~. *Magical Knowledge, Book I: Foundations / The Lone Practitioner.* Oxford, England: Mandrake, 2012.

Meyer, Elisabeth Marie. *Die Bedeutungsentwicklung von Germanischen *moda-.* Halle, Germany: Buchdruckerei des Waisenhauses, 1926

Paxson, Diana L. *Odin: Ecstasy, Runes & Norse Magic.* Newburyport, MA: Weiser Books, 2017.

~~~. *Taking Up the Runes: A Complete Guide to Using Runes in Spells, Rituals, Divination, and Magic.* York Beach, ME: Weiser Books, 2021.

~~~. *The Essential Guide to Possession, Depossession, and Divine Relationships.* San Francisco, CA: Weiser Books, 2015.

~~~. *The Way of the Oracle: Recovering the Practices of the Past to Find the Answers of Today.* San Francisco, CA: Weiser Books, 2012.

~~~. *Trance-Portation: Learning to Navigate the Inner World.* San Francisco, CA: Weiser Books, 2008.

Rose, Winifred Hodge. https://heathensoullore.net/
~ "A Short Blog on Orlog and Wyrd"
~ "All in a Day's Work: Frigg's Power of Creating Order"
~ "Disir, Hama and Hugr as Healing Partners."
~ "Earth, Water, Wind and Fire: Elemental Modes for Relating to the Deities"
~ "Images of Orlay"
~ "In Thanks to Frigg, the Silent Knower"
~ "Landwights and Human Ecology"
~ "Threads of Wyrd and Scyld: A Ninefold Rite of Life Renewal"
~ "Webs of Luck and Wyrd: Interplays and Impacts on Events."

Book-Hoard

Rune Poems: https://en.wikisource.org/wiki/Rune_poems

Schreiwer, Robert, and Ammerili Eckhart. *A Dictionary of Urglaawe Terminology.* www.urglaawe.org. 2012.

Sturlason, Snorri. *Edda.* Translated and edited by Anthony Faulke. Rutland VT: Charles E. Tuttle Co. 1987.

Verny, Thomas R., MD. *The Embodied Mind: Understanding the Mysteries of Cellular Memory, Consciousness, and our Bodies.* New York: Pegasus Books, 2021.

Waggoner, Ben. *A Pocket Guide to Runes.* Philadelphia: The Troth, 2019.

~~~. *Hávamál: A New Translation.* Philadelphia: Troth Publications, 2017.

~~~. *Our Troth, 3rd Edition, Volume 1: Heathen History.* Philadelphia: The Troth, 2020.

~~~. *Our Troth, 3rd Edition, Volume 2: Heathen Gods.* Philadelphia: The Troth, 2021.

Book-Hoard

About the Author

Winifred Hodge Rose is an Elder of the Troth, an inclusive, international Heathen organization. She has followed a Heathen path for the past thirty years, serving as a scholar, writer, leader, teacher, priestess, and oracular spaewife in many Heathen venues.

Winifred grew up as the daughter of a US diplomat stationed in various countries during the 1950s and 1960s, and later lived for years in Greece and Germany. These experiences enabled her to learn foreign languages through immersion, and to develop the ability to observe and adapt to different cultures and world-views. This has stood her in good stead in her efforts to understand, as well as possible, ancient Heathen world-views and adapt them for modern Heathen use.

Winifred published her first Heathen book, *Heathen Soul Lore Foundations: Ancient and Modern Germanic Pagan Concepts of the Souls*, in 2021. The present book is the second in her Heathen Soul Lore Series. Her website, with many articles, poems and songs, ceremonies, fiction and more, can be found at *HeathenSoulLore.net*.

She is retired from her career as a research scientist working on methods for watershed and natural resources management on military installations in the US and Germany. Winifred has two grown children and three growing grandsons, and lives with her blacksmith husband in the Illinois countryside.

A Word about Wordfruma Press

Fruma means "origin, beginning" in Anglo-Saxon, and *ordfruma* means the fount or the source. The Anglo-Saxon word Os means "a God of the Esa or Æsir tribe", and the Rune Poem for the rune Os goes as follows:

Os is 'ordfruma' of every speech,
The support of wisdom and the benefit of the wise,
And for every earl, prosperity and hope.
(my translation)

The Esa-God referred to here is Woden or Odin, the fount and origin of speech, eloquence and wisdom. Since my work relies in large part on understanding the roots and sources of words, I have made a play on words here, changing *ordfruma* to *wordfruma*: the origin of words. The ultimate origin of words flows from godly inspiration, a divine gift that underlies the formation and emergence of our entire species, *homo sapiens sapiens*. Wordfruma Press thus honors the gift of speech, and the origins of the gift: all of the Holy Ones.

The trademark logo pictured here, conceptualized by myself and created by Forest Hawkins, shows the rune Ansuz, an analog of Os, rising up from a wellspring. Ansuz takes shape as a fountain that represents the power of speech and wisdom. The shape of the logo also represents the Well and the Tree, with dew from the Tree dropping into the Well. Wordfruma Press publishes scholarly and inspirational Heathen works.

com/pod-product-compliance

477